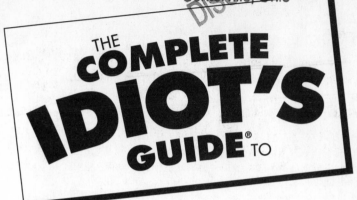

THE COMPLETE IDIOT'S GUIDE® TO

Managing Your Moods

by John D. Preston, Psy.D., ABPP

ALPHA

A member of Penguin Group (USA) Inc.

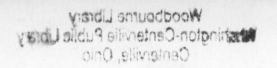
To Jan Groesz

ALPHA BOOKS

Published by the Penguin Group

Penguin Group (USA) Inc., 375 Hudson Street, New York, New York 10014, U.S.A.

Penguin Group (Canada), 10 Alcorn Avenue, Toronto, Ontario, Canada M4V 3B2 (a division of Pearson Penguin Canada Inc.)

Penguin Books Ltd, 80 Strand, London WC2R 0RL, England

Penguin Ireland, 25 St Stephen's Green, Dublin 2, Ireland (a division of Penguin Books Ltd)

Penguin Group (Australia), 250 Camberwell Road, Camberwell, Victoria 3124, Australia (a division of Pearson Australia Group Pty Ltd)

Penguin Books India Pvt Ltd, 11 Community Centre, Panchsheel Park, New Delhi—110 017, India

Penguin Group (NZ), cnr Airborne and Rosedale Roads, Albany, Auckland 1310, New Zealand (a division of Pearson New Zealand Ltd)

Penguin Books (South Africa) (Pty) Ltd, 24 Sturdee Avenue, Rosebank, Johannesburg 2196, South Africa

Penguin Books Ltd, Registered Offices: 80 Strand, London WC2R 0RL, England

Copyright © 2006 by John D. Preston, Psy.D., ABPP

International Standard Book Number: 1-59257-513-7
Library of Congress Catalog Card Number: 2006927519

08 07 06   8 7 6 5 4 3 2 1

Interpretation of the printing code: The rightmost number of the first series of numbers is the year of the book's printing; the rightmost number of the second series of numbers is the number of the book's printing. For example, a printing code of 06-1 shows that the first printing occurred in 2006.

Printed in the United States of America

Note: This publication contains the opinions and ideas of its author. It is intended to provide helpful and informative material on the subject matter covered. It is sold with the understanding that the author and publisher are not engaged in rendering professional services in the book. If the reader requires personal assistance or advice, a competent professional should be consulted.

Publisher: Marie Butler-Knight
Editorial Director: Mike Sanders
Managing Editor: Billy Fields
Acquiring Editor: Tom Stevens
Development Editor: Nancy D. Lewis
Production Editor: Kayla Dugger
Copy Editor: Jan Zoya

Cartoonist: Shannon Wheeler
Book Designers: Kurt Owens/Trina Wurst
Cover Designer: Kurt Owens
Indexer: Heather McNeill
Layout: Chad Dressler
Proofreader: Mary Hunt

Contents at a Glance

Contents

Foreword

Human beings are endowed with a vast range of moods and emotional experiences. While much of our emotional life is positive and rewarding, eventually all of us will encounter stress and strain that will result in significant emotional turmoil and distress. What's more, as extensive as our emotions are, there is an even greater array of self-help books and psychological therapies that can baffle even the most sophisticated consumer in the mental health marketplace.

This might help explain why, while almost half of the population will experience a psychiatric disorder over the course of their lifetime, and practically everyone else will have times of significant emotional pain and suffering, relatively few people ever seek professional help for their mood problems.

This, in turn, might explain the tremendous popularity and proliferation of self-help books. They're a private and generally nonthreatening way for people to get a handle on their emotional distress.

When people are suffering from mood difficulties, however, the last thing they have the motivation or concentration for is to struggle through a dense, voluminous book loaded with complicated jargon and detailed information. This is why *The Complete Idiot's Guide to Managing Your Moods* is such a fantastic and desperately needed addition to the library of self-help books. Like all of the *Idiot's Guides*, it delivers the undiluted crux, the essential take-home points of the material. Yet, amazingly, despite boiling it down to the key ideas, *The Complete Idiot's Guide to Managing Your Moods* remains comprehensive, thorough, down-to-earth, extremely reader friendly, practical, and immediately usable. Moreover, and very important, it destigmatizes and normalizes the many mood problems we humans inevitably experience.

Best of all, this is not a book that will have readers merely embark on a psychoarcheological dig into their unconscious, or excavate insights from their childhood. Nor will it simply provide facts and information. Rather, *The Complete Idiot's Guide to Managing Your Moods* is more like having a personal therapist and life coach that emphasizes the here-and-now and teaches you vital skills while motivating you to take control of your moods by learning and applying a wonderful assortment of strategies and techniques that are firmly grounded in some of the most current scientific knowledge.

But it doesn't stop there! In addition, *The Complete Idiot's Guide to Managing Your Moods* provides an important spiritual component often overlooked by most scientifically grounded books. It also offers crucial information on medical factors that can masquerade as mood problems, psychiatric drugs, and on herbal and over-the-counter products.

As is the case with all *Idiot's Guides*, the bottom line is simple. *The Complete Idiot's Guide to Managing Your Moods* is a fantastic addition to self-help literature. I intend to enthusiastically recommend it to almost all of my patients and colleagues alike.

Clifford N. Lazarus, Ph.D.

Clifford N. Lazarus, Ph.D., is the Co-Founder and Clinical Director of The Lazarus Institute in Skillman, New Jersey (www.thelazarusinstitute.com), a facility dedicated to providing a full range of scientifically verified, evidence-based psychological services. An internationally respected lecturer, he earned his doctorate in clinical psychology at Rutgers University in 1989 and is the author or co-author of more than 20 publications. His two popular books, *Don't Believe It for a Minute* and *The 60 Second Shrink*, have been translated into over a dozen languages.

Introduction

Human beings are remarkable in their ability to face so many difficult times in life. The human psyche, like a shock absorber, is adept at helping people go through and bounce back from so many life challenges. Most people are amazingly resilient.

Life can be rewarding and filled with positive experiences: loving friendships, beautiful sunsets, exciting adventures, and new life. Yet, let's face it, life can also be exceedingly difficult. Sooner or later, all of us will encounter a very rough road. All humans must, at some time, face painful losses and disappointments, and sometimes, great tragedy. It is the rare individual who can skate through life and not be bumped and bruised by painful life experiences. Author Jane Wagner states, "Reality is the leading cause of stress among those who are in touch with it."

Millions of people suffer from serious psychological disorders such as depression, panic disorder, or bipolar illness. According to the American Psychiatric Association, in their diagnostic manual (DSM-IV: Diagnostic and Statistical Manual of Mental Disorders) a mental or emotional disorder is defined by the presence of particular symptoms. However, central to the definition of a *disorder* is "impaired functioning." Here, emotional symptoms or suffering is severe enough to noticeably interfere with one's ability to adequately carry out the normal tasks of living (for example, the ability to work; to succeed in school to raise children; or to maintain healthy, intimate relationships).

Approximately 40 percent of people experience a psychiatric disorder at some point over the course of their lifetime. One reason this statistic may be so surprising is that most people experiencing a psychological disorder don't tell others about it … they keep it private. Almost everyone I know has either experienced a psychiatric disorder or has a loved one who has. Especially common are depression (affecting 17 percent of people over the lifespan) and anxiety disorders (affecting 25 percent of people).

For practically everyone else, there are also at least some times of great struggle and emotional suffering. Countless millions of us may never have a formal psychiatric disorder, but do encounter times when life is incredibly hard. And for many of us, the intensity of emotional suffering (sadness, despair, hopelessness, disappointment, frustration, fear …) goes off the chart, yet we keep going to work, keep raising our kids. We struggle and manage to cope, yet personally grit our teeth and suffer inwardly. Some people are remarkably resilient and do bounce back after living through a difficult time, while others may experience emotional troubles for a lifetime.

Even the founder of psychoanalysis, Sigmund Freud, lived through incredibly difficult times. In one of his last works, *Civilization and Its Discontents*, he stated, "Life as we find it is too hard for us; it entails too much pain and too many disappointments."

Curiosity with a Purpose

Have you ever noticed how large the "self-help" section is in a bookstore? People in our culture are very interested in psychology in general. Lots of times this is born of curiosity about what makes people tick. We all know people who are especially sensitive or have peculiar habits, and we want to be able to figure them out. This is especially so if they are creating problems in our life. However, probably more likely, most of us buy self-help books because we are having a difficult time. That may be the reason you bought this book. Lots of times emotions can be very confusing, and perhaps it's hard to really get a handle on why you feel a certain way or how come you are especially sensitive to certain experiences.

The first thing we'll look at in this book is the human mind and the nature of emotions. I want you to become an expert in figuring out the complicated nature of your own human emotions and moods—why you react the way you do and what your emotional "buttons" are. Understanding this is not just academic or for interest's sake, but rather, this knowledge will give you some important keys to help you more successfully manage your emotions and moods.

The noted astronomer and professor Carl Sagan has said, "Those creatures who find everyday experience a muddled jumble of events with no predictability, no regularity, are in grave peril. The universe belongs to those who, at least to some degree, have figured it out."

What follows is a sort of road map for navigating through life, especially when life gets hard. We'll take a look at some fascinating new research from psychology that will help you more fully understand your unique emotional style and help you take action to more successfully manage troublesome or painful emotions and moods.

Coping, Healing, and Growing

In the journey of life, all of us must figure out ways to cope with painful life events. *Coping* is about adaptation and survival. Coping occurs on two fronts: the first one is outwardly observable, taking action, e.g. resolving a conflict with your husband or wife, looking for a new job, taking a stand and voicing your opinion about something that matters deeply to you, or deciding to openly cry and grieve the loss of a loved one by sharing your feelings with a trusted friend.

The other side of coping, on the second front, is referred to by psychologists as *intra-psychic:* the internal and more private realm of thoughts and feelings. This may involve thinking things through so that you can devise a sound action plan to change something in your life; inwardly trying to distract yourself from noticing some form of inner suffering, such as grief; trying to anticipate the future; giving yourself words of encouragement, for example, silently thinking to yourself, "Just keep doing my best … This is a very hard time in my life and I gotta just keep focused and maintain perspective" or "Hang in there … I think I can see light at the end of the tunnel."

Emotional healing involves a large number of things people do to regain emotional stability or to once again feel in control in the aftermath of some very disturbing life events, such as going through a divorce or the loss of a job.

Psychological growth usually involves some amount of coping and healing, but it goes beyond this: it is transformational. In some ways it changes who you are. This includes experiences and internal psychological processes that ultimately open new awareness to certain truths. For example, Rick's dawning awareness that, despite a lifetime of being a nonemotional tough guy, he does have a tender heart and can allow himself to be vulnerable while sitting at the bedside of his dying mother. Or Sally, who in midlife becomes increasingly clear that her general approach to life, one marked by passivity and submission, is not what she wants for her life. She begins to discover ways to find her own voice, and for the first time, to really speak out, express her opinions, and take a stand.

The Journey of Life

As early pioneers prepared to journey west, they certainly could not predict the numerous events and potential dangers that would come around each bend in the road. But those who made the journey successfully first learned something about survival. They developed some general coping strategies that might have come in handy as they encountered any number of difficult experiences. They also learned as much as they could about the territory ahead, speaking to others who had made the journey. We, too, are going to learn as much as we can about the human mind, mood, and emotions, and how to develop effective coping strategies. The circumstances of each individual human life are unique and we can't anticipate every challenge that will come our way; there are no pat answers to complicated emotional struggles. But we are going to learn something about the general landscape of human emotions and a lot about how to cope and to survive.

This book focuses on three things: understanding yourself, being compassionate and decent toward yourself, and then taking action. No sugar-coated platitudes or quick fixes here, but a lot of practical strategies for living through hard times … strategies based on solid psychological research.

How This Book Is Organized

Part 1, "Understanding the Human Mind, Emotions, and Moods," sets the stage for understanding human emotions. We'll see how our cultural values often make it difficult for people to experience and express normal feelings. We'll take a close look at why people view the world and react in very different ways, including how to understand your own "emotional buttons." Also included are ways to determine if your emotions are healthy or unhealthy and ways to determine if you might benefit from professional psychological treatment.

Part 2, "Taking Action: First Things First," looks at many factors that commonly ignite strong emotions and negative moods. A first place to start is to make sure that you do not have an undiagnosed medical condition; some medical illnesses can cause stress symptoms … these can last for years and never be suspected as arising from an underlying medical problem (especially hormonal disorders). Likewise, a number of prescription drugs and so-called "recreational drugs" can cause stress symptoms or depression. You've got to check these things out first before taking any other steps to get professional treatment or using self-help approaches. Quality sleep is a critical factor in maintaining good emotional control. We'll look at high-yield strategies for improving the quality of your sleep. Finally, we will explore a number of strategies for directly calming the mind and the body.

Part 3, "Psychological Self-Help Strategies," first considers how many people who are under significant stress inadvertently try coping in ways that backfire and actually end up making things more difficult. Then we will launch into a number of simple and effective approaches for reducing distress and combating shame, guilt, and low self-esteem. The chapters in this part will help you find balance in your life, take action to address problematic interpersonal relationships, and, finally, utilize the role of spirituality as a valuable resource for many during times of crisis.

Part 4, "Areas of Particular Concern," looks at very common human experiences such as grief, anger management, and living through very traumatic life events. We'll explore essential ingredients in successful coping and emotional healing in the wake of very challenging life events. We'll also take a look at ways to help children cope with major life stresses.

Part 5, "Professional Help in Dealing With Mood Problems," will include a brief and user-friendly guide to psychotherapy: what it is, how it works, and what to realistically expect in terms of outcome. We'll also talk briefly about common psychiatric disorders and the use of psychiatric medications.

Extras

Throughout this book you will find many tidbits of information including little-known facts, self-help tips, and quick definitions for psychology buzzwords. Look for these sidebars throughout the book.

def•i•ni•tion

Here you will find the definitions for useful psychological terms.

Think About It

Specific tips for coping with difficult or stressful events.

Possible Meltdown

Things to be concerned about with regard to your mental health and safety.

Bet You Didn't Know

These are interesting tidbits that relate to the topic in the chapter.

Acknowledgments

I would like to gratefully acknowledge the following people for their help and support in completing this project: my literary agent Marilyn Allen, acquisitions editor Tom Stevens, and publisher Marie Butler-Knight, for their wise guidance and support …. Many thanks to the superb editing advice from Nancy Lewis, Jan Zoya, Megan Douglass, and Dr. Michal Duveneck. As always, thanks to Michelle Housh for her help in the manuscript preparation.

And most of all to my wife Bonnie, who helps to save my sanity every day of my life.

On a Personal Note

Songwriters Whitfield and Holland poetically sing out a truth, "Into each heart some tears must fall."

I have been a practicing psychologist for 30 years, a professor of psychology and the author of a number of psychology books. But please, do not think for one moment that this professional background has been able to insulate me from the pain of life. I have had tragedies in my life and I am far from figuring it all out. We are all in a similar boat … there are smooth waters and treacherous rapids. And we all have feet of clay.

Noted author and public speaker John W. Gardner offers these words of wisdom, "We can draw on deep springs of the human spirit, to see our suffering in the framework of all human suffering, to accept gifts with thanks, and endure life's indignities with dignity." We can also take action to reduce emotional suffering, and that's what this book is all about.

I sincerely believe and hope that this book can offer encouragement, comfort, and practical coping strategies.

Publisher's Note

This publication is designed to provide accurate and authoritative information in regard to the subject matter covered. It is sold with the understanding that the publisher is not engaged in rendering psychological, financial, legal, or other professional services. If expert assistance or counseling is needed, the services of a competent professional should be sought.

Trademarks

All terms mentioned in this book that are known to be or are suspected of being trademarks or service marks have been appropriately capitalized. Alpha Books and Penguin Group (USA) Inc. cannot attest to the accuracy of this information. Use of a term in this book should not be regarded as affecting the validity of any trademark or service mark.

Part 1

Understanding Human Emotions and Moods

The starting point for our discussion of managing moods is understanding the nature of the human mind, emotions, and moods. Often during very stressful times, people can be overwhelmed, confused, or perplexed regarding what is happening to them. In this first part of the book, you will become aware of your unique emotional self. You'll see what your particular emotional "buttons" are, and we'll focus on developing an attitude of compassion for yourself, especially when going through difficult times.

The chapters in Part 1 set the stage for understanding the moods and emotions that will be necessary before planning coping strategies.

1

How We View Emotions

In This Chapter

◆ Society's misunderstanding about emotions

◆ Peoples' reactions to expressing normal human emotions

◆ What drives normal human emotions underground

Who are our heroes? Charles Lindberg, John Glenn, General George Patton, Mohammed Ali, Amelia Earhart, John Kennedy, Arnold Schwarzenegger ... for me as a boy it was John Wayne. Branded into my memory is a movie scene when John Wayne is told of the murder of Billy, his life-long friend and the town sheriff. The "Duke" momentarily looks shaken, and then says, "He was a good man," drinks a shot of whiskey and exclaims, "Enough grievin' ... let's organize a posse." What is admirable about this? What characterizes the prized public image of so many of our heroes? Often embodied in these personas is an emotional toughness ... a determined self-reliance, and the ability to put feelings aside and move ahead against all odds.

I've often wondered whether any of these people were plagued by fears, self-doubt, apprehension, guilt, embarrassment, or shame. Did they ever feel timid, shy, or humiliated? How did normal human emotions figure into the outcomes of the stories we know so well? Were such emotions simply absent or perhaps just ignored or tucked away? It's hard to know.

In 1972 Senator Thomas Eagelton, the democratic vice presidential candidate, revealed that he had been treated for depression. In the aftermath of this disclosure, the public saw this as a major political liability, and he was dropped from the ticket like a hot potato.

Edmund Muskie had been the Democratic front-runner in the 1972 presidential elections. However, his popularity ratings took a nosedive after he was seen on television shedding tears during an emotional political rally. It was not a good year for the Democrats.

But let's take a closer look. Abraham Lincoln, arguably our greatest president, will long be honored for enormous contributions to humanity. During his service to the country, few people knew that he suffered from serious bouts of depression and harbored persistent, agonizing grief over the death of his son. His personal diaries revealed the intensity of his sensitivity and the depth of his emotional anguish. Consider this excerpt from Lincoln's diary: "I am now the most miserable man living. If what I feel were equally distributed over the whole human family, there would be not one cheerful face on Earth."

Obviously Lincoln had strong feelings and suffered a lot. But, he didn't go public with it and he's a hero. I guess that was the politically correct thing to do, even in the 1800s. So maybe being able to hide emotions is key.

Cultural heroes, whether actual historical figures or characters portrayed in popular movies and myths, transmit societal ideas that inspire and encourage desirable behaviors such as courage, sturdiness, and fortitude. Yet such stories rarely acknowledge many important elements of human experience such as tenderness, sensitivity, neediness, compassion, humble acceptance of one's limits, loss, grief, anguish, embarrassment, humility, exhaustion, loneliness, empathy, and other softer human emotions. Not only are these human experiences neglected in mythic tales, but also they are often diminished and devalued. A common social message is that if you want to be seen as successful, desirable, mature, healthy, and psychologically fit, you should either not experience emotional sensitivity, or at the very least you should keep it to yourself and deal with it.

In this opening chapter, we'll take a close look at how cultural values in our country strongly influence how people feel about having normal human emotions. As we'll see, some prevailing ideas about how people "ought to be," may be very misguided and actually in the long-run, interfere with adaptive emotional coping.

In the Beginning

How do people get exposed to these cultural values? When do we start learning about how we "ought to feel" …? Earlier than you may think.

Clichés and admonitions quickly become a part of every child's lexicon. Some have a positive, pro-social spin, such as "Honesty is the best policy" or "Do unto others as you would have them do unto you." But in many subtle (or not-so-subtle) ways these lexicons scold and condemn. Adults say these things to kids, and sooner or later the words get encoded in the child's mind. Thereafter, even when completely alone, a person may notice that he is telling himself the same scolding statements. These have then become a type of internal self-talk. Psychologists refer to these as *injunctions*. See if any of these sounds familiar:

- Pull yourself by your bootstraps

- Don't take it so personally

- Buck up

- Don't cry over spilled milk

- Get over it

- Be a man

- Don't be a crybaby

- Grow up!

- Don't be a sissy

- Snap out of it

- Put it behind you … get on with your life

- Don't be a complainer

- You are making a mountain out of a molehill

- Don't be so sensitive

- You are just too emotional

- Don't make such a big deal out of it

- You are just trying to get attention

def•i•ni•tion

Injunctions are rules for behaving that initially are spoken to children, but with time become a part of the child's own internal self-talk. Injunctions do not encourage or support. They scold and criticize.

- Don't get your hopes up

- Don't rock the boat

- Don't be childish

- Get a grip

- Just deal with it

- Why can't you be more like your _____ (brother, sister, etc.)

All too often such statements stir inner feelings of guilt, inadequacy, and shame rather than inspire hope or positive coping.

Let's add to the list some words of advice that at first glance sound optimistic and encouraging:

- Time heals all wounds

- This, too, shall pass

- Every cloud has a silver lining

- Look on the bright side

Of course these phrases are often shared with sincerity and good-hearted intentions; and they may provide comfort to some. However, in the midst of a serious life crisis, many people detect a less positive underlying message: "Look on the bright side … and if you can't, then there is something wrong with you."

So What's This All About? True Grit?

Somewhere along the road of cultural evolution our society came to value some traits, and to devalue others. What has emerged is a "grit your teeth, ignore your feelings, and get on with your life" mentality. And, part and parcel of this is the view that strong feelings or emotional sensitivity are signs of weakness, immaturity, and inadequacy. The big question is, does this pervasive cultural tradition actually *help* people? Do such attitudes contribute to people having fuller, more satisfying and healthier lives? Some of the research suggests not.

Some might point to recent cultural phenomena that could be signaling a change. How about the "Men's Movement," in which guys hug each other more frequently and athletes appear to be more okay about shedding tears? Well, maybe. But has this actually trickled down into a meaningful level that really matters when life gets hard and people inwardly experience strong emotions? I would suggest that it has not, and that a dominant attitude in twenty-first-century America continues to be what might be called "emotion phobia."

It certainly may be in vogue to say, "I feel your pain" or "get in touch with your feelings." And it's probably true that more men do cry during movies these days. But, as they say, when the rubber meets the road, when people are face to face with real-life emotional heartache, how okay is it really to be "emotional?" And often if it is okay to be emotional, is it really okay to keep being emotional tomorrow, or next week, or next month? Aren't we supposed to get over it and get on with our lives?

Emotions Can Be Scary, Overwhelming, or Unnerving

Intensely painful emotions can overwhelm or scare people. This is understandable. They are hard to face personally and it's also dammed hard for a lot of us to witness suffering in others (especially in those we know and love). So what do people do when faced with intense emotions? Here are some examples:

- Pretend like it doesn't exist, or if it does, minimize it (Oh, it's not big deal … other people have it worse … I'll get over it).

- If emotions leak out, label them as signs of weakness, inadequacy, or mental illness.

- Quickly medicate away painful feelings with alcohol or prescription drugs.

- Encourage people to get over it quickly.

- Praise those who are "strong" (e.g., "He is such a rock!" said about someone who appears to show little emotion at times of crisis or tragedy).

- Allow shame to drive emotions underground. (Hidden from view, pesky emotions may not bother others, but they often fester.)

- Inwardly experience loss, sadness, etc., and then begin to feel guilt, shame, and embarrassment about having such emotions.

We all encounter some form of this pressure to be and to feel a certain way. Here is the truth: whether emotions are expressed outwardly or held in check by gritting your teeth, human beings do have feelings! As we'll see, some of these emotions are healthy, adaptive, and completely normal (let's call these primary emotions: sadness, anger, grief, fear). Others are the by-products of pressures to conform and to please others (secondary emotions such as shame, guilt, embarrassment).

Primary and Secondary Emotions

Let's take a brief glimpse into six human lives …

Carolyn (age 37): "I lost my dad last fall, it's been nine months since he died. We were very close and, God, I miss him so much. Two or three times a week I think about him, and I break down crying. My husband thinks I'm just too sensitive and says I need to be strong and just let go and get on with my life. I guess he's right … what's wrong with me?"

Jill (age 27): "I was absolutely convinced that I had the best marriage in the world. Our future looked bright, and everyone said that we were the perfect couple … and there's nothing terribly wrong, but … I just feel sad and empty all the time. Jerry is so busy all the time with his work. And when I try and talk with him or try to give him a hug, he looks at me, and he has this expression on his face like he's irritated and impatient with me. I don't want to complain and whine about this. Other people have problems that are a lot worse than mine. I don't know why but I just feel terrible all the time. Ever since I was a child I've always just been too sensitive."

Mac (age 31): "I'm the man … I'm the father … I've always been self-reliant and sturdy … I know I need to be strong. And I am in a lot of ways. But I also know that I am slowly losing my mind. My daughter, Hannah, is wasting away before my eyes. Every day the cancer is taking her away. She's suffering so much … and sometimes I think she's stronger than me. Moments before I walk into her hospital room, I literally feel like I am going to throw up … I feel shaky, and on the verge of breaking down. Sometimes I just want to run away. What the hell is wrong with me?! I feel like a god-damned coward. I know that I love her with all my heart, and yet I feel this incredible urge to avoid seeing her. I feel so ashamed of myself. God, what a nightmare!"

Ethel (age 73): "My husband, Ray, died two years ago. He was my whole life. And I miss him so much. I feel like my heart has been ripped out and broken beyond repair. And, I think that if I hear one more person say, 'Oh, I understand' or 'Well, he had a good life and you have your good memories' or 'You just need to let go,' I think I'll just scream! Nobody knows how lonely I feel!"

David (age 15): "I hate myself! I brought my report card home with three As and two Bs, and my dad said, 'David, you've got so much potential … couldn't you just apply yourself more!' And when I got upset, he said, 'What the hell is wrong with you?! You are so damned sensitive to criticism. You are acting like some grade-school kid. Grow up!'"

Donna (age 24): "Something is terribly wrong with me. I was molested when I was a young girl. It happened over a period of two months one summer, and never again. That was 17 years ago. But I still get terrified when a man starts to get interested in me. My best friend, Sally, says I just need to forget about it. I must be seriously screwed up."

These life events are different, but each of these people share three things in common. At this moment, life is very hard and they inwardly experience very strong emotions about things that matter to them deeply. Secondly, each is encountering the reactions of others: society in general, or friends and relatives, many of whom love them and are concerned. But in each instance, messages bleed though either in direct or subtle ways. Others are not able to be fully accepting of the person's emotions. When this occurs for Carolyn, Jill, David, or the others, their suffering now becomes complicated. Beyond their core, heart-felt (primary) emotions of sadness, loneliness, and fear are secondary emotions: feelings of guilt, shame, embarrassment, anger turned toward one's self, or humiliation. Finally, in addition to the felt sense of criticism or misunderstanding coming from others, each has started to experience some degree of self-doubt. Rather than viewing his or her suffering as an understandable response to painful life events, each is plagued by worries, "What's wrong with me? I'm too sensitive. I'm seriously screwed up. I must be going crazy."

Like it or not, most of us either are currently having a very rough time, or will at some time in the future. Emotional hurt cannot be completely avoided on our journeys through life. Feeling ashamed about having normal human emotions is one of the most common ways that people intensify emotional suffering.

The Least You Need to Know

- Lots of clichés and platitudes may sound supportive, but often carry an underlying message of criticism.

- There are powerful social expectations that people must keep a stiff upper lip and just "get over it" when they have encountered very difficult emotional events in their lives.

- Many people have been misunderstood and needlessly hurt by expressing normal human emotions.

- Many times it is shame or embarrassment about having feelings that ends up causing more emotional distress than the underlying, normal human emotion.

2

Emotions: Friends or Foes

In This Chapter

- ◆ Emotions can offer us important information worth paying attention to

- ◆ Emotions operate as an internal self-guidance system

- ◆ Expressing some painful emotions may help facilitate effective coping and emotional healing

- ◆ How bad feelings build up into a bad mood

- ◆ How to know if your emotions are healthy or not

Contentment, excitement, happiness, apprehension, despair, shame, rage … the range of human emotions is huge and complex. Clearly it's emotions that give life meaning, fuel inspiration, and bring people together. Emotions can also stoke the fires of worry and send us into dark places … sometimes driving us to our knees.

In this chapter, we'll look at the essential aspects of emotion: how they can aid adaptation, contribute to aliveness, and help to promote emotional healing and growth.

Why Emotions?

Mr. Spock on the original *Star Trek* TV series was a serious guy. As a Vulcan, he presumably was free from the experience of emotions—a pure intellect. He lived long and prospered, but probably didn't have much fun.

Emotions are not just about feeling. They can serve very useful purposes, and, in fact, may at times save our lives.

Emotions: A Sixth Sense

To navigate safely through the world, people are highly dependent on accurate information about their environment—delivered to the brain by the sense organs. Let's take the senses of smell and taste as an example. If you bite into a rotten apple, it would serve you well to quickly notice that it's rotten and spit it out. The unpleasant taste (which actually is always a combination of taste and smell) immediately alerts you that it's not edible.

In a fraction of a second, morsels of the apple excite taste buds and nerves in the nose, which send nerve impulses to the brain. Here the brain interprets the incoming information. Sensations are evaluated in complex ways, and it is here that the brain interprets the information. It recognizes the smell and taste, and it also makes a judgment, "This tastes terrible." This leads to a reaction—spitting the apple out of your mouth. You may have just saved yourself from getting food poisoning. These senses tell us something about the world in that moment.

Think About It

Emotions can operate like radar or sonar, providing valuable information about our environment and our interpersonal world. It pays to pay attention to this data.

In a very similar fashion, most human emotions also provide us with information that can guide our behavior—in helpful and adaptive ways. For example, Ann attends a party where there are a number of guests she does not know. A man she has never met before approaches her, and after they talk for a few minutes, she begins to feel a vague sense of uneasiness about him. Paying attention to her emotions, she excuses herself and moves across the room to visit with a woman friend she knows from her work.

Ann wasn't engaging in mind reading, per se, but she was picking up on certain bits of information about the man. Her perceptions led her to believe that there was something about him that left her feeling uneasy. It was this inner emotion that prompted her departure. She may not have been able to articulate just exactly what she was picking up on, but all the same, her emotions and her intuition told her to say good-bye and seek out someone else to talk with. Ann's uneasiness is not an emotional problem … it is valuable information.

Thus, one purpose our emotions play is to help take in information about the world, interpret what is going on, and then influence action. Next time you step into a street then suddenly notice a bus heading right toward you, and the momentary startle and fear prompt you into getting quickly out of the way, you will have experienced a very common example of how emotions guide behavior and ultimately can help you stay alive. Emotions play a critical role in helping people to evaluate safety versus danger: what to approach, and what to avoid. It is important to pay attention to and take seriously emotions and gut feelings.

Emotions as an Internal Self-Guidance System

Whether it is something as small as deciding what movie to watch on television, or a much more important life decision such as choosing a career or who to marry, emotions serve as a sort of internal self-guidance system. Gathering information by speaking with friends about and pondering situations always evokes inner thoughts and feelings. These feelings, such as excitement, boredom, fear, apprehension, and enthusiasm, lead to conclusions such as "Go forward," "Stop and be careful," or "This ain't for me."

Some people are in touch with their emotions, and this can help tremendously, especially in making major life decisions.

However, many people (for various reasons) are not fully aware of how they truly feel. Such people may only come to a gradual awareness that they hate their job, or are not truly in love with their spouse. Being cut off from awareness of inner emotions is an all-too-human condition that can be hazardous to one's emotional well-being. A blind person is in potential danger crossing a busy street. An emotionally blind person is also in great peril when making major life decisions.

Think About It

Emotional blindness is a common malady in Western culture. In our culture, most people are raised to value thinking, and often emotions are seen as a nuisance or worse. Yet those who pay attention to their emotions often are in a much better position to cope with a myriad of difficult life events.

Emotions Are Ways of Making Contact with Others

Psychologist Sheldon Kopp has said, "In sharing, we seek relief from our loneliness, reassurance about our worth, and release from our guilt."

The outward expression of feelings can be a powerful way to make and maintain a connection with other people. A prime example is the crying of a hungry infant. His tears give a clear message: "I need help," and those who love him come to the rescue. In a similar fashion, outward displays of emotion continue throughout a lifetime to convey human needs to others, and can elicit support or bring people together in times of need. For example, when a husband comes home and clearly looks worried, his wife notices his distress and begins to speak to him and to provide understanding and support for what may have been a very difficult day.

Emotions Convey Personal Values

The expression of emotions almost always is a way of conveying personal values. The reasons for feeling strongly about something relate directly to the way you perceive events and what matters to you on a very personal level. An example might be feelings of sorrow when watching a news report about the suffering of innocent people who have lost their homes and loved ones in a tragic earthquake. Even more personal might be in situations of domestic violence, where a woman is outraged at how she could be so devalued and so abused by someone who presumably loves her. This violates one of her deeply held personal values.

As Dr. Martin Luther King Jr. said, "Our lives begin to end the day we become silent about things that matter."

Some Distressing Emotions Can Actually Reduce Negative Moods

It may seem paradoxical, but often expressing unpleasant emotions ultimately results in less intense suffering. An example is when people cry. Often a crying spell can result in relief. Noted neuroscientist, William Frey has studied the biology of crying and has demonstrated that the shedding of emotional tears actually reduces stress hormone levels.

Although for many people, crying is accompanied by inner feelings of shame or self-criticism (e.g., "What's wrong with me? I feel like a crybaby"), 75 percent of those who give themselves permission to have a "good cry" report that just a few minutes of crying results in (on average) a 40 percent decrease in feelings of anger, anxiety, frustration, sadness, or other intensely felt emotions.

Honest emotional expression often leads
to a sense of relief, even if in the moment
it feels unpleasant. If the emotion is shared
with another person (depending on how
open and accepting they are) it can also
feel good just to know that you have been heard
and understood. Feeling validated for having
emotions, in itself, can often be healing. Henry
David Thoreau said it so well, "It takes two to
speak the truth … one to speak and another to hear."

Think About It

As the poet W. B. Yeats so
eloquently wrote, "When such
as I cast out remorse … so
great a sweetness flows into the
breast."

A Multitude of Human Emotions

Psychologists generally agree that, universally, people experience seven basic emotions: happiness, sadness, anger, fear, disgust, surprise, and shame. Culture and individual personal experiences during one's lifetime certainly have an impact on whether or not people outwardly express emotions. But all human beings, at one time or another, inwardly feel these seven common emotions.

All of these basic emotions may be also described in terms of their intensity, such as …

- fear → terror or panic
- anger → rage
- happiness → feeling euphoric or ecstatic
- sad → miserable, depressed or despondent

Many more complex emotions also exist: envy, guilt, hatred, pity, impatience, boredom, loneliness, and so on.

From a Feeling to a Mood

People talk about emotions in a number of ways. Often they are experienced as a momentary sensation, such as the sudden fright you feel at the movies when something in the film jumps out of the dark. Ten seconds later that emotional reaction disappears as new things unfold on the screen. Life is full of these momentary reactions, like ripples in a pond when a stone is thrown into the water … noticeable, but soon gone.

However, some emotional reactions appear to be more enduring. Such is often the case when people are going through major life changes, for example, when someone falls in love or when a loved one dies. Here emotions are experienced as more enduring and often pervasive. The man who is grieving the loss of his wife, for example, may feel sadness permeating most of his waking life.

A widely held theory is that more pervasive feelings (often referred to as moods) are made up of recurring series of emotional moments—like one stone after another thrown in a pond in which one ripple builds on another, and at some point it feels continuous. Let's look at an example.

Craig just got laid off from his job. In a general way he feels down, discouraged, and negative. His day starts off with a plan to go out and look for a new job. But, one of the first things to happen that day is that he accidentally spills his cup of coffee. He feels irritated. Five minutes later he nicks himself shaving. Another irritant. When he goes out to get on his way to search for work, he has trouble starting his car. Craig thinks to himself, "I can't believe it … everything in my life is going wrong!" He now could appropriately be seen as being in a bad mood. One frustration piling upon another. His general view of his life at this point in time is negative, only to be punctuated this morning by a series of irritating events.

Momentary events have provoked inner thoughts for Craig. The fact that he is out of work has likely resulted in an underlying emotion state; he feels negative and down. In human beings these undercurrents of emotion have their greatest impact on people by selectively influencing perception. For example, Craig's general state of feeling down biases how he views on-going events. Let's say that his day holds prospects for a new job; he had just gotten a good job lead from a friend and he will go to apply for the position that morning. This might leave many people feeling at least somewhat hopeful. However, owing to his overall negative mood, when he spills his coffee or cuts himself shaving, he is much more prone to interpret these events in ways that turn up the volume on his already negative and pessimistic mood.

It is the accumulation of negative perceptions and conclusions that change his "Maybe I will get that new job" perspective into "Everything in my life is going wrong." Here frustrating events are interpreted with a particular spin … tuning out the positive and accentuating the negative. Thus what may otherwise be an annoying experience, (spilling coffee) operates like a spark on dry timber, and a more pervasive negative mood is ignited. As he gets more and more caught up in the negative mood, Craig finds it hard to maintain a focus on what otherwise might be something positive and hopeful, such as the job lead.

Negative moods bias perception: bad things are noticed or amplified and potentially positive events are either ignored or downplayed.

Three months later, Craig got the new job and has now been working there for the past nine weeks. And he loves it. One morning, it's déjà vu … he spills his coffee, nicks himself shaving, and has trouble starting his car. Yet this morning his reaction to these events is only mild irritation. Nothing like that morning three months ago. The frustrating events are exactly the same, but they are now interpreted in an entirely different context. This morning Craig thinks, "Oh well, it's no big deal." His perceptions are now more balanced. He sure doesn't like spilled coffee or a razor cut, but it's now seen from a different perspective.

In the midst of trying times, most people, to some degree, lose perspective, and this results in more distress. In later chapters, we will look at a number of powerful and simple techniques for regaining a realistic perspective during very emotional times.

Judging Versus Understanding

It is common for people to judge others' behavior and emotional reactions. Let's say Karen is standing in a long line at the post office. When it is finally her turn to be served, the postal clerk clearly looks impatient, irritable, and annoyed. Karen walks away thinking, "What a jerk!" Would her reaction have been the same if she knew that the clerk's wife just told him last night that she wanted a divorce? Of course it wouldn't. She would see things from a very different perspective. We are not mind readers and are rarely privy to much information about the lives of people we encounter each day. People are very prone to making a lot of conclusions every day based on little accurate information.

People are equally, if not more, inclined to be quite judgmental toward themselves. So many times in therapy sessions, I've heard just such harsh self-criticism, "What the hell is wrong with me?" "I'm just too sensitive," "I feel like a complete loser," "I hate myself."

A very important and central feature to successful coping and emotional healing has to do with your ability to develop a compassionate inner voice, an inner attitude of kindness and internal support. Harsh self-criticism is the root of an enormous amount of unnecessary human suffering. What is clear is that when people come to really understand the true nature of their emotions, to have an accurate appreciation for why certain life events hurt so much, this understanding can become the foundation of an attitude of self-compassion. A frequent turning point that I have witnessed in my clients during therapy is when, instead of remarking, "God, I'm just so screwed up," they see more clearly the origins of their emotional pain. And, I'll hear a very different kind of comment such as, "No wonder I feel so bad … just look at what I've gone through."

Oftentimes in the course of psychotherapy many people don't so much get cured, but they do experience a transformation. Their view of themselves shifts from pathologizing their emotions (concluding they are screwed up or mentally ill) to recognizing their emotional reactions as entirely understandable.

Necessary and Unnecessary Emotional Pain

In Chapter 1, we spoke about primary and secondary emotions. Another helpful way to understand different kinds of emotional pain is to consider the following two types of suffering: necessary pain and unnecessary pain.

Think About It _____

Some forms of emotional suffering are simply unavoidable. It's like cutting your finger; no matter who you are, you are going to bleed. Some human experiences are the same way; lose a loved one and there is grief. Grief may be outwardly expressed or kept on a very private level, but it is grief all the same. It's the nature of the human heart to have certain emotional reactions.

Necessary emotional pain is basic, common, honest human anguish that virtually all people would feel when they encounter a tough life event, like the loss of a child, being fired, going through a divorce, or encountering serious financial problems. If you get burned, it hurts. You have little choice but to feel the pain. Certain life events just hurt.

In addition, there is general agreement among psychologists that at least some types of painful or distressing emotions need to be both felt and expressed to facilitate healing following very difficult life events. In this respect some suffering is also deemed necessary. No one likes to bleed, but when you cut yourself it is inevitable. Furthermore, bleeding, in itself, is a part of healing. It cleans bacteria out of the wound and clots to form a scab.

Unnecessary pain is suffering that goes beyond the core emotional response. It is exaggerated, intensified, and prolonged suffering that, generally, is due to extremely self-critical thinking. In the wake of a seriously distressing personal event, many people launch into a ruthless attack on the self, either with actual statements spoken aloud to others or with private inner thoughts and beliefs. Examples of this include, "I'm so screwed up," "Nothing I do is right," "What the hell is wrong with me?" or "I'm being silly and childish to feel so upset about this."

An almost constant inner barrage of self-condemning thoughts represents one of the most common sources of human emotional suffering. While facing the truth of necessary pain is probably essential to successful coping and emotional healing, unnecessary pain only intensifies and prolongs suffering.

Distracting yourself, denying inner feelings, or numbing yourself with drugs or alcohol can temporarily avoid necessary pain. But those who manage best during stressful times are those who can acknowledge this legitimate pain and take the difficult path of what psychotherapists call *working through*. As the poet Robert Frost said, "The best way out is through."

def•i•ni•tion

Working through describes the process of carefully thinking about things, feeling emotions, and finding personal meaning in particularly difficult life events. Over a period of time as people go through this process, generally two things result: some of the intensity of painful emotions diminishes, and people come to a greater understanding about what has happened and how it has affected them.

Emotional coping and healing can take place as you confront the truth of difficult experiences and inner feelings and walk through these times (not "go around" or "get over," but work through) by expressing emotions, struggling to find meaning in your suffering, and by confiding in others. This pathway is what psychiatrist M. Scott Peck refers to as "the road less traveled" … many people understandably do not choose this path, because it involves squarely facing painful feelings. Avoiding painful feelings is not a crime or a sin; it's natural. But it can also be a major stumbling block to effective coping.

One way to distinguish between necessary and unnecessary pain is to ask some basic questions:

1. Even though this emotional pain hurts a lot, is it understandable?

2. Does it make sense to me that I'm feeling this way given the fact that I'm going through a very stressful time in my life?

3. Does this pain lead me to take corrective action? Does expressing the pain result in any sense of relief/release?

4. Does this pain bring me closer to loved ones?

Of course, these can be difficult questions to answer with certainty, since a good deal of necessary pain initially hurts so much that it's hard to imagine that it can serve any helpful purpose. But it is very important to learn how to recognize necessary pain, and find ways to face it and accept it, while also being able to spot unnecessary pain. Unnecessary suffering is an extraordinarily common source of emotional distress; the kind of distress that you can learn how to control. Later chapters will offer a number of action strategies for turning down the volume on unnecessary emotional pain.

Are My Emotions Normal and Healthy?

How can you tell if certain emotions or moods are normal and healthy or if they are somehow maladaptive? At times this is hard to judge. In part this is due to how you define "normal." In the aftermath of the loss of a loved one, most people experience very painful feelings of sadness and anguish. In a recent study (San Diego Widowhood Project) 88 percent of those having just lost a spouse stated that they felt worse than they ever had at any other time in their lives. If you could somehow measure the intensity of emotional suffering, such sadness would go off the chart for most of these people. However, it would also be correct to say that such emotional pain is normal. It is normal in two respects.

First it is *normative*, meaning that it happens to most human beings. Second, it is clear that a central feature in emotional healing following tragic losses is at least, to some degree, to feel and express the emotions of grief. Here it is normal because it helps to foster healing. It is in no way pathological. In fact, gritting your teeth (refusal to mourn) increases the likelihood of what psychologists call complicated bereavement. Complicated bereavement often leads to greater risks for developing depression, psychosomatic symptoms (e.g. insomnia, tension headaches), and substance abuse.

def•i•ni•tion

The term **normative** simply reflects whether or not something is common, i.e. it does it happen to most everyone. It doesn't necessarily imply good or bad. Death is normative. Enjoying a vacation is normative.

This question of healthy versus unhealthy is also strongly influenced by your individual cultural values and reactions from friends and loved ones in your life.

Take an Emotional Inventory

An additional step to take in evaluating your mood or emotions is to take inventory of the following, any one of which may signal that your painful emotions go beyond "necessary pain" and that you may benefit from professional help from a psychotherapist.

1. Do I find that my suffering sometimes seems intolerable?

2. Has my mood resulted in noticeable difficulties in carrying out the tasks of everyday life (e.g. being unable to work or effectively raise my children)?

3. Have I seriously thought about suicide or wished that I would die?

4. Do my feelings often result in my making bad decisions, e.g. rushing into problematic relationships, risk-taking behavior, drinking too much or using illegal drugs, doing things that might be unhealthy (such as working too much, or excessive sexual promiscuity … especially unprotected sex)?

5. Have I noticed that my mood is bothering other people, for example, are people worried about me, or irritated with me, or avoiding me? Some people going through hard times can become quite irritable and this might get them in trouble at work. Grieving individuals may find that people are avoiding them (possibly because they don't know what to say), and the result can be a felt sense of isolation.

6. Have I experienced any of the following symptoms (which may be stress related)?

    Severe sleep disturbance

    Intense waves of anxiety or panic

    Overwhelming fatigue

    Marked increase in weight or significant weight loss

    No motivation or enthusiasm

    Stress-related psychosomatic illnesses such as high blood pressure or recurring tension headaches

7. Do I see a pattern or cycle of reoccurring involvements, life situations, or crisis that perpetuates my emotions, symptoms, or sufferings?

If you find that you are answering "yes" to several of these questions, it is important to consider professional help. The final part of this book provides a guide to professional psychotherapy and also medication treatments for some types of emotional problems.

The Least You Need to Know

♦ Paying attention to your emotions can help you to know what really matters to you and can also help guide you to make decisions that make sense in your life.

♦ Expressing some types of very unpleasant emotions can help to foster effective coping and emotional healing.

♦ It is important to determine if what you are feeling is an expression of healthy emotions, and to be on the lookout for sources of "unnecessary pain."

♦ Taking an emotional inventory may help you decide if you want to pursue psychotherapy.

Understanding the Human Mind, the Brain, and Emotions

In This Chapter

◆ Developing effective action strategies for coping

◆ Understanding people's different emotional responses to identical life events

◆ Things that can influence inherent emotional sensitivity "set points"

◆ The perception of controllability of stressors matters a lot

When it comes to finding ways to effectively deal with difficult emotional struggles, there are no simple answers, no quick fixes, and no magic. People are not simple minded. All human emotions and moods are certainly influenced by stresses you encounter in your life, but, ultimately, how you feel and react will almost always be unique. Confronted by identical, difficult life circumstances, no two people will respond in the exact same way. And the nature of this very unique and highly individual response is determined by a number of crucial factors. This is one reason that many pop-psychology, simplistic suggestions about how to handle "stress" are too general and may offer little real help to those who are going through truly difficult times.

We will devote a lot of chapters to specific coping strategies, but before doing so, it is essential for you to become knowledgeable about the nature of the human mind and also how the brain influences emotions. In this chapter, we'll begin to look at some of this complexity … how the human mind works and how this relates to your own unique emotional self.

It may be tempting to skip these early chapters and move directly to the later chapters that deal specifically with managing your mood. But I want to strongly encourage you to read the chapters in Part 1. Understanding the nature of emotions and how the human mind and brain work is the first step in preparing yourself to take action.

It's as Easy as 1, 2, 3 (Well, Maybe Not All That Easy)

Let's take a first glance at how the human mind and brain play a role in producing emotions (in this book we will refer to these parts of the brain as the emotional brain). Research in the neurosciences during the past decade have given us important information that relates directly to understanding how emotions work and what we can do to manage moods more effectively.

Example One: All people have particular parts of their brains that are devoted to creating emotions. Most of the time these emotions and emotional behavior are directly tied to physical and psychological survival. For example, fear ignites a fight-or-flight response. Loneliness propels people into interaction with others.

Example Two: With rare exceptions, emotions do not just spontaneously erupt. They are reactions to external stressful events, such as getting fired from a job or taking an exam in school, or being stuck in traffic. Psychologists refer to these events as "stressors." Emotions are also a response to inner thoughts or needs. For instance, thinking, "I am worried that my teenage son may be using drugs," or an inner longing to find someone to love can certainly stir emotions. Stressors, thoughts, and needs can light the fuse for emotional reactions (stress responses).

Example Three: Just how you perceive and interpret events matters a lot. Let's illustrate this point by way of three examples: the first is touching a hot stove with your finger; the second is being confronted with physical danger to your life when a man wanting to steal your purse or wallet approaches with a knife; the third is the social fear of public speaking.

What happens between the input of stressors and output of stress responses has to do with appraisal: the mind's capacity to rapidly perceive and interpret what is happening, moment to moment. Just how situations are perceived is profoundly influenced by a host of factors that work together and determine one's degree of emotional sensitivity and what I'll refer to as your own unique emotional style (more information on this in the section "Beyond Stimulus-Response: Your Emotional Control").

Think About It _____

In large scaled polls, Americans most commonly report that their number-one fear is giving a talk in front of an audience (public speaking). To put this in perspective, a fear of death is ranked as fear number seven.

Let's take a look at our three examples. In example 1, touching a hot stove, every human being will feel and react in the exact same way. You experience pain and the feeling automatically evokes a reaction: you pull your finger away from the stove. This is simple stimulus-response. In example 2, being assaulted by a man with a knife, most of us will also have the same reaction: fear and the impulse to run away. But in this situation there may be differences. The ex-Navy Seal with expert training in self-defense probably will react differently, as would the undercover cop who has a firearm. Their prior life experiences and their ability to feel more in control of the situation matter a lot. They are assessing the stressor in a different way than most of us would.

In example 3, with getting up in front of an audience to give a talk, it gets even more complicated. What goes through a person's mind five minutes before getting up in front of a group of people to give a talk depends on a multitude of factors. Thoughts, memories, past experiences, how well you have prepared your talk, anticipation of what will happen, your perception of the facial expressions of the people sitting in the audience, self-confidence, and so forth, now matter a lot in how you look at this situation. Many life events push your own unique emotional buttons. When you consider many similar emotionally complex situations—

Think About It _____

Beyond danger to one's life and limb, many other experiences can be seen as a form of danger: fear of humiliation, shame, rejection, embarrassment, abandonment, powerlessness, loss of control, failure, criticism, vulnerability. Do any of these ring a bell? If you are like me, some of them sure do. Welcome to the human race!

asking someone out on a date, going on a job interview, hearing about the death of a loved one, finding out that your spouse has had an affair—people's emotional reactions are all over the map. In these situations, individual differences are paramount. Let's take a look at what is happening in the brain.

Here's a metaphor. Smoke detectors are set a particular level of sensitivity at the factory. They need to be sensitive enough to detect smoke if your house catches on fire. But the threshold of sensitivity should not be too low. A smoke detector should not sound an alarm when it perceives minute traces of smoke from a blown-out candle. Likewise, those parts of the human brain that are designed to be alert to potential danger in the environment, in a sense, also have certain sensitivity thresholds. It's important to rapidly notice real dangers, but would be overwhelming if every tiny sight or sound set off an alarm. These biological set points (or thresholds for perceiving danger or distress) are different for every individual, and are the topic of the next section.

Sensitivity Set Points

Some people are born with their sensitivity set point at a lower level. They are just naturally more sensitive. Initial sensitivity set points are not completely set in concrete, but they do tend to be rather enduring over one's lifetime. As we'll see, your initial sensitivity threshold is strongly influenced by genetics and early brain development.

This more enduring sensitivity set point can also be changed (for better or for worse), at least for a while, by a host of factors throughout life. Want to test this out? Try not sleeping for 2 nights in a row, or drinking 8 cups of coffee, or working 80 hours a week (well, actually don't really do this). But the point is that these kinds of things do turn the volume up on emotional sensitivity. They change brain functioning and can increase the likelihood of feeling overwhelmed.

In addition, as we shall see, there are many things you can do or experience that can, in positive ways, enhance your ability to feel less distress and to deal more effectively with stress.

How the Brain Turns on Emotions

If anyone experiences a completely unexpected, very loud bang, they will automatically respond. Sensitive people, tough-guys, little kids, it doesn't matter. Again, this sort of thing is simple stimulus-response. The brain immediately reacts and alerts the body. You feel the impact of this response in a nanosecond. This reaction is referred to as the fight-or-flight response.

The whole body is activated. The heart rate increases, blood pressure goes up, stress hormones are dumped into the bloodstream (thyroid hormones, adrenaline), and more glucose is dumped into the blood stream, all of which immediately prepare the body for fight (defend yourself) or flight (run for cover).

An automatic biological reaction to the perception of danger in the environment is characterized by some or all of the following symptoms.

Changes in physical sensations …

- Increased heart rate, palpitations
- Trembling
- Sweating
- Nausea or queasiness
- Dizziness
- Light-headedness
- Feelings of shortness of breath
- Tingling or numbness (usually in the fingers or toes)

Changes in perception or thinking …

- Becoming hyper-alert
- Worries that you are going to die, go crazy, or lose control
- Sometimes having confused thinking or a lack of mental clarity

Changes in emotions …

- Fear
- Panic
- Apprehension
- Sometimes feeling irritation or anger

Changes in behavior …

- Run or dive for cover

◆ Defend yourself

◆ Temporarily freeze

An unexpected loud bang, for example, will invariably cause the same reaction in every single person (except those who are completely deaf). This is not about being sensitive, or about being emotionally weak, or emotionally mature, it's just being a normal human being wired for this kind of instinctual response. Once these stress hormones get launched, just try and stop them. Good luck!

Beyond Stimulus-Response: Your Emotional Control

In more complex emotional situations, something often happens between stimulus and response. This is a crucial element that strongly influences your emotional style. It is referred to as *behavioral inhibition*.

def•i•ni•tion

Behavioral inhibition is the capacity of the mind and the brain to hold back outward emotional reactions when inwardly strong emotions are being activated. This is commonly referred to as "emotional control."

Let's say two people, Gail and Cindy, are watching a tear-jerking movie. Let's also assume that both are equally emotionally sensitive. At a particular poignant moment in the film, Gail cries and Cindy does not. They both feel a similar strong inner emotion of sadness. For Gail, her emotions find outward expression; she becomes tearful. This may be due to the fact that she feels okay about showing her tears; she is not embarrassed or ashamed. But Cindy keeps her feelings bottled up inside. She feels them, but does not express them. For any number of reasons, she does not feel comfortable about letting them show outwardly. She inhibits the outward expression of emotions (behavioral inhibition).

This matter of behavioral inhibition, or, in plain English, emotional control, is strongly influenced by two factors:

◆ The first factor is a person's attitude regarding emotional expression. For Gail, "It's normal … it's fine to show feelings." For Cindy, "I feel too embarrassed about being outwardly emotional." Each has grown up exposed to any number of reactions from others when "being emotional" and they have each gradually developed their own specific attitudes about outwardly expressing inner feelings.

◆ The second factor is what psychologists refer to as *ego* strength. The concept of ego strength is a bit complicated and we'll be coming back to it in later chapters.

But here I want to focus on one central feature of ego strength: the ability of the human mind to control emotions. It is also very important to emphasize that another sign of ego strength is the ability of a person to let her guard down and be emotionally open when she is in the presence of trusted family or friends ... a part of her strength is this ability to face and express emotions.

def•i•ni•tion

The term **ego** has been used in a number of ways. In popular lingo it often refers to self-confidence, cockiness, or arrogance.

The ego, in psychological literature, often is synonymous with the concept of "self." Having a well-developed ego might mean having a solid sense of self. In this book we will mainly talk about the ego as that part of the human personality that is devoted to coping and survival. People who demonstrate ego strength are more emotionally sturdy, and when they face big-time stressors, they handle things relatively well. Like the old Timex commercial said, "It can take a lickin' and keep on tickin'" ... people with strong egos can face difficult times and keep on tickin'.

So here are the possibilities; let's illustrate by adding a third person viewing the movie. Assume that all three women are equally sensitive inwardly (identical levels of emotional sensitivity), but they differ in a couple of major ways: their inner attitudes about outward expression of emotions and ego strength. Gail and Cindy have sturdy egos; our new moviegoer, Laura, does not.

	Outward Emotional Expression	Her Inner Thoughts	Reactions to How Each Respond to the Movie
Gail	Cries	It's okay to cry	Okay
Cindy	Does not cry	I feel embarrassed crying	Probably okay crying
Laura	Cries	I feel embarrassed crying, but I can't help it ... what's wrong with me?!	Embarrassed, possibly feeling vulnerable or out of control.

Laura tries to maintain control, but cannot.

Many things influence one's level of ego strength. Shortly we'll see how genetics, brain development, and early life experiences can either contribute to strong egos, or conversely result in less-than-optimal ego strength. Beyond this, a host of life experiences can negatively impact ego strength for you, for me, for anyone. Some of these factors include not getting enough sleep, alcohol or other substance abuse, exposure to very traumatic events, or prolonged and severe stress.

Am I Out of Control? Powerlessness Versus Control

An additional way that the brain and the mind also play a role in creating emotions has to do with a particular kind of appraisal that automatically goes on all the time (sometimes consciously, but often unconsciously). People continuously scan the environment looking at life in general and at specific events as they unfold moment to moment, taking stock of two issues:

1. What are the specific risks, dangers, and challenges I am facing?

2. In this moment, how confident am I that I can handle this situation?

Based on prior experiences handling various tasks and challenges and being well aware of my skills, resources, and talents, will I be effective in coping with the current stressful situation (for example, a problem in an important relationship)?

The answer to this question matters a lot. This has to do with a very important type of appraisal: the evaluation of *controllability*. Any even mildly stressful situation can provoke some at least minor stress symptoms (e.g. increased heart rate or muscle tension). But if a situation is judged to be uncontrollable or a person begins to have strong doubts about his ability to effectively cope, the brain and the body are much more likely to respond in significantly intense ways.

A conclusion "I am not in control" or "I doubt myself" can happen in one of four different ways.

> **Kevin:** "I am in control." When Kevin is faced with stressful events, he knows, based on past experiences, that he can handle it. "It's no big deal … I know how to deal with this sort of thing." The magnitude of his emotional stress is minimal.

> **Brenda:** "I am not in control." Brenda has well-developed coping skills. She knows full well that during most challenging situations in her life she has managed well. We could say that her baseline level of self-confidence is good. However, at this particular point in time, she is encountering an extraordinarily large number of very emotionally difficult events (most of us have had times like this). Despite her long-standing sense of positive self-confidence, in the face of recent events, she is beginning to feel overwhelmed and questions her ability to effectively cope.

> **Tony:** "I am not in control." Tony generally sees himself as a competent guy. For most of his adult life he's handled tough situations well. Yet, recently, there has

been a shift. It's not that life is especially more demanding, but what has changed for him is a loss of self-confidence.

Bet You Didn't Know

Two things commonly can cause changes in a person's assessment of her ability to cope. The first has to do with recent events. Lots of us who ordinarily feel confident can have that confidence shaken if we have recently experienced some failures or have been significantly criticized by others. The second very common cause for what can be very significant erosion in self-confidence is depression. Some of the chemical changes that often occur in the brain during depression can play an important role in one's ability to accurately evaluate self-efficacy (we'll talk a lot more about this in Chapter 26, which addresses depression).

Kayla: "I am really not in control." For any number of reasons, Kayla's life has been much harder and she goes through almost every day riddled with self-doubts. She does not have a good track record of effectively coping with emotionally difficult experiences. She enters each day with a measure of dread, hoping that things will be okay but worried that she will have a tough time making it through the day. In a chronic and rather pervasive way, Kayla doubts herself and feels a general lack of control over her life.

How we perceive controllability and our degree of self-confidence may be one of the most crucial aspects of coping. Many of the chapters that follow will suggest strategies that will give you a greater sense of control when moving through difficult times.

The Least You Need to Know

♦ The way you perceive and interpret stressful events matters a lot. An especially important perception is whether or not you feel in control and confident to handle the particular challenges facing you.

♦ Everyone starts off life with an internal set point (or threshold) for emotional sensitivity. These set points for sensitivity become a part of the fabric of everyone's personality, however they can be influenced by a number of factors (such as whether or not you are getting good quality sleep, or are using too much alcohol).

◆ Emotional control and ego strength play an important role in determining how you will respond to emotional situations.

◆ Remember that most emotional reactions and moods are highly individual and usually complex.

Chapter 4

Why Some People Are More Sensitive: Understanding Your Emotional Self

In This Chapter

- ◆ Your existing set point for emotional sensitivity
- ◆ What emotional sensitivity is and how this is influenced by temperament
- ◆ How maternal stress hormones can damage a fetus's nervous system
- ◆ Helping an infant to develop a stress-resistant brain
- ◆ Decision-making as related to temperament and your inner level of emotional sensitivity

What factors contribute to emotional set points, ego strength, and attitudes about expressing feelings? It's important to look at and really understand several crucial points of a complex puzzle … those factors that determine or influence emotional reactions and moods. This understanding will be the foundation for many of our later discussions of effective coping strategies.

In this chapter, we'll cover how genetics, brain development, and the early forma-tion of character truly set the stage for determining how all of us see and react to the world. Then, throughout life as we run into challenges or very difficult times, here and now factors also play a crucial role in determining how we'll each react.

Everyone Is Unique

At first glance, all human brains look pretty much the same. All are comprised of similar brain structures and all have about 100 billion nerve cells. But when it comes to the functioning of the brain, especially how it regulates emotions, we now begin to see that a very large number of factors can result in some brains that are highly stress resistant, while others are not.

Genetics and Temperament

For all of us it literally starts at the moment of conception as our genetic blueprint begins to direct the growth of the nervous system. A significant amount of how we react emotionally is influenced by this genetically determined *temperament*.

def•i•ni•tion

Temperament refers to those rather enduring personality char-acteristics that are influenced by genetic factors. For example, the inborn tendency to become eas-ily overwhelmed or in some indi-viduals, the need to constantly seek out excitement and novelty.

Studies have demonstrated that some basic traits seen in infants (such as a tendency to be shy, sensitive, or overly anxious) can be very stable over a long period of time, perhaps a lifetime. For people born with this more sensitive temperament, the tendency to approach most situations in an overly cautious and fearful way may have absolutely nothing to do with one's particular life experiences. Many of these kids have good, loving parents and have not in any way been traumatized. Rather, what comes into the world, as a part of their "original equipment," is this sensi-tive nervous system.

When people with a sensitive temperament have the good fortune to be born into a loving family, they may develop in psychologically healthy ways. Yet they may always be prone to feeling somewhat uneasy, especially in novel situations or when exposed to environments that are intensely stimulating. People with this temperament, for example, might find it a better fit to live in the country rather than in the busyness and commotion of a large city.

Problems, however, can occur when people with a sensitive temperament are born into a stressful environment. They may come into the world with good parents, but parents who are under enormous stress. Or such children may be born into highly chaotic, toxic, or abusive families. Here, inherent sensitivity collides with an adverse emotional environment, and these children may be overwhelmed or traumatized.

Many people with a sensitive temperament conclude that "There is something terribly wrong with me … I am neurotic or in some other way, psychologically maladjusted." Often when sensitive people can come to see and appreciate the reality of their own temperament (without being harsh or judging toward themselves), they can then better seek out relationships, jobs, or living conditions that offer a better fit. So many times as a therapist I have known clients who initially believe that they are mentally ill or otherwise emotionally damaged, only to eventually discover and accept that they are simply by nature sensitive or anxious.

Think About It

Often the notion of emotional sensitivity is cast in a negative light: "You are just too sensitive!" According to psychologist Elaine Aron, fundamental sensitivity is about being open, being more acutely aware of things, noticing subtleties and nuances. This more exquisite receptivity to the world may also include increased sensitivity to cold, to noise, to fatigue, or to chaos. This can set the stage for emotional difficulties (e.g. becoming more easily hurt or overwhelmed). However, sensitivity is an important element in many valued human attributes such as empathy, intuition, and creativity.

Julie, one such woman, after years of struggling emotionally and feeling inadequate, ultimately came to appreciate that she was, by nature, sensitive. She found out her own truth that she was not especially gregarious and thus living in a big city was not her cup of tea. She moved to a smaller town and began to give herself permission to live life on her own terms (e.g. not attending what had previously been obligatory parties, and allowing herself to have more solitude and long walks in the countryside). Her life began to feel not only more comfortable, but it began to also feel more "real" … she was being true to her own nature. Julie didn't get "cured" of anything, she just got clear about who she is and developed a lifestyle that honored it. There was a goodness-of-fit between her temperament and her new lifestyle.

Often what looks like psychiatric illness is just a poor fit between one's particular temperament and his or her lifestyle. The symptoms of distress are the mind's way of saying, "There is something wrong with the way I am living my life." Rather than pathology, this is emotional health. The symptoms are messengers telling you to look carefully at how you are choosing to live your life.

Other Types of Temperament

In addition to the sensitive temperament, several additional characteristics have also been found to be related to one's genetic temperament, including the following:

◆ Distractibility. Difficulties maintaining focus when there are distractions. Such people do best if they work and live in quiet and noncluttered environments.

◆ Regularity. Some people inherently have a greater need to maintain regularity in their lives including patterns of eating, social interaction, exercise, and sleeping.

◆ The need for stimulation. While sensitive people may be easily overwhelmed, others are more prone to feeling bored unless life is constantly exciting. The high-stimulation temperament is seen in people who like a lot of activity and intensity. They may work a lot, stay very busy, party hardy, and sometimes get into risk-taking behaviors, while trying to avoid situations where it is quiet and subdued.

◆ Adaptability. People differ in their inherent ability to readily adapt to challenges, novelty, and transitions. For some, these life experiences are simply more difficult. Here, pacing yourself, giving yourself permission to take time to process experiences, and understanding that you may need to be more self-protective can be very helpful in coping with life.

◆ Extraversion or introversion. Extraverted people are more comfortable being engaged in the world. They often are gregarious and may have difficulties being alone or isolated from interaction with other people. Extraverts are also often action oriented. When problems arise they are likely to jump in (maybe somewhat impulsively) and try to fix things or in other ways take concrete actions to solve the challenges facing them. In contrast, introverted people prefer more alone time. They do value and seek out attachments with others, but tend to have just a few close friends. They may also problem-solve by first really sitting with thoughts and reflecting before taking action.

For a more in-depth discussion, see the books by noted psychologists Jerome Kagan and Elaine Aron in Appendix E.

Life in the Womb

Other factors occurring long before birth can also play a powerful role in the development of the nervous system and ultimately one's emotional style. While good nutrition and, in general, a mother's good health can facilitate appropriate brain development in utero, a number of adverse events may harm the developing nervous system.

Fetal Alcohol and Other Drug Exposure

One very common example that has now been well documented is fetal alcohol exposure (as well as fetal exposure to other drugs of abuse). In children exposed to such substances, it is common to see that from early in life, they have trouble handling emotions. Often these children will become easily overwhelmed, have difficulties paying attention and concentrating, and are prone to significant emotional upset (especially irritability). Fortunately, this problem has received wide media attention, which has resulted in increased caution exercised by pregnant women regarding substance use. However, clearly fetal exposure to alcohol and other toxins continues to be an enormous problem.

Exposure to Maternal Stress Hormones

During extremely severe and prolonged stress or when people experience severe depression, the body hyper-secretes the stress hormone cortisol. Very high levels of cortisol have been shown to cause particular types of damage to the brains of both children and adults. If a woman has very high levels of cortisol during pregnancy, it is possible that this can damage the developing brain of the fetus. Such infants are born with smaller head circumferences and smaller brains. The particular damage to the nervous system caused by hyper-cortisol does not affect the whole brain. Rather it targets specific brain structures that play an important role in regulating emotions. Thus, again we see the potential for a prenatal factor that may influence one's tendency for increased risk of being emotionally more sensitive.

For all human beings, even mild stress will activate the release of the stress hormone cortisol. This hormone is made in the adrenal glands and released into the bloodstream. Most of the time this hormone is not harmful to the body; quite the contrary. When stressors ignite a fight-or-flight reaction, cortisol helps by making more glucose available in circulation (if you have to run away or defend yourself, your muscles will need an immediate energy supply). Cortisol also contributes to increasing the heart rate. Finally, once danger has passed, cortisol operates in the brain to help shut off the stress response. Thus, most of the time, this hormone is important for ensuring survival.

However, there are three conditions that can cause the adrenal gland to release huge amounts of cortisol into the bloodstream. This condition is called hypercortisolemia and can be seen in (1) very severe, prolonged stress; (2) severe depression; and (3) Cushing's disease, which is a disease of the adrenal glands. The levels of cortisol can be so high that they become toxic to the body. As mentioned earlier concerning a fetus, hyper-cortisol can potentially damage particular parts of the brain, especially the hippocampus, amygdala, and cerebellum. These brain regions all play a role in facilitating emotional control. Thus damage results in people becoming more emotional and less capable in dealing with stress.

Nutritional and Other Prenatal Factors

It has also long been known that a host of other adverse events happening to a mother during pregnancy may interfere with normal brain development in a fetus: poor nutrition, dehydration, excessive exposure to radiation, severe illness (e.g. viral infection), and so forth.

Think About It

In 1944 and 1945 the Nazis occupied Holland. As food supplies began to dwindle, the Nazis seized food for their troops and Dutch people began to starve. Many thousands of people starved to death. Fetuses that were exposed to this severe state of poor maternal nutrition, when followed years later, had a significantly higher rate of medical problems (e.g. diabetes and heart disease) and higher rates of psychiatric disorders.

For people who have been exposed to toxins or high levels of stress hormones in utero, it is especially important to develop a strong sense of compassion for yourself. Like those with a sensitive temperament, some of the emotional struggles in a very real way are simply not your fault. They are a reflection of your sensitized nervous system. I have known many people, once again, who spend a good deal of their lives castigating themselves for their emotional sensitivity … and harsh self-criticism never helps. Often a significant turning point for such people comes when they can squarely face this reality and without shame admit, "I am a sensitive (or, an emotional) person." The struggle against this awareness is, in itself, a source of considerable distress.

"What the hell is wrong with me?" or "I shouldn't be so damned emotional!" This kind of self-judging always has the effect of amplifying other negative moods such as sadness, frustration, shame, or self-hatred.

Beyond finding ways to be accepting of yourself, there are also some very specific strategies that we'll address later in this book that can significantly help sensitive people hurt less and cope more effectively (especially in Part 2). Many of these techniques directly influence the brain in healthy ways that result in greater stress resistance.

Building a Stress-Resistant Brain

As noted previously, particular aspects of the nervous system are heavily involved in the regulation of emotions. The very wiring of these brain structures, although influenced by genetics, has a lot to do with the amount of stimulation an infant receives (especially rocking and holding), and the quality of love and nurturing experienced, especially during the first six months of life. Severe neglect during the first six months of life can result in permanent changes in the nervous system that lead to excessive emotional sensitivity and problems with behavioral inhibition. On the other hand, love, comfort, and the simple experience of being held as an infant can help to lay down the neurological hardware that affords some people remarkable stress resistance.

Rock-a-Bye Baby

Throughout the world, on average, mothers hold their infants about four hours a day. However, in the United States, Canada, and a number of Western European countries the amount of time mothers hold their babies is only about two hours a day. In an amazing study conducted by Dr. Ron Barr and colleagues in Canada, a group of new mothers entered a research project in which they kept records of the amount of time they held their babies each day. These mothers were randomly assigned to two groups. The first group was given no special instructions, but to just do what comes naturally and record the amount of time they spent holding their infants (turns out it was about two hours a day, as predicted). The other group was instructed to hold their babies for at least four hours a day. By six weeks of age, those

> **Bet You Didn't Know**
>
> Numerous recent animal studies have demonstrated that marked neglect (experimental animals provided with warmth and food, but not being held) show actual structural differences in brain development. Tragically this has also been noted in children raised in certain Eastern European orphanages that provide little human contact for these infants.

babies who had been held four hours a day showed, on average, 43 percent less crying than those held only two hours a day.

Studies with newborn mammals have also shown convincingly that receiving more holding and rocking (in monkeys) or licking and grooming (in kittens, puppies, and rodents) also result in animals who are noticeably more stress resistant throughout the rest of their lives.

This Is Not Just About Bad Parents

Clearly some children are neglected because of dysfunctional parents, for example, having parents who do not love their children or who abuse them, or parents who are into significant alcohol or other substance abuse. Many children, however, may not receive adequate early nurturing for a host of other reasons:

- ◆ A good, loving mother experiences a very severe post-partum depression. She finds it extraordinarily difficult to be with her child in the way she longs to be.

- ◆ Either the mother or the infant experience very serious medical problems during the first few months of life, possibly requiring prolonged hospitalization.

- ◆ In families experiencing enormous stresses, otherwise loving parents may be overwhelmed. Such may be the case in families living in poverty.

- ◆ Orphans from some Eastern European orphanages experienced severe neglect during the first six months of life. Loving and caring parents later adopt these very unfortunate infants. Despite being rescued from these orphanages and given a chance to have a better life, often the damage is done. The early and pervasive neglect has left a permanent mark on brain development. The love they receive from their new parents of course helps, but regardless, they go into their lives with an impaired ability to handle stress. Such children are also especially later prone to developing depression.

Such brain changes, either those leading to a more stress-resistant brain or a hyper-sensitive brain, now have been set in place. These are the most crucial factors establishing your baseline emotional set point. To a large degree, this is permanent.

This is not character or personality; it is neurobiology. Please do understand that positive experiences later in life can make a difference. Sometimes a big difference! And in later chapters we'll also carefully consider a number of specific coping strategies that can make a noticeable difference, as well, in helping sensitive people cope more effectively. However, I must once again strongly encourage those who, owing to adverse inter-uterine experiences or neglect, have a sensitive temperament, to adopt a particular perspective: acknowledge that a good deal of your tendency for sensitivity, anxiety, or depression is literally not your fault. This is not about making excuses; it's about facing a hard reality with compassion. It's also not about *passive resignation*. The starting point is acceptance and kindness toward yourself, and then the next step is to take action (we'll map out specific action strategies beginning in Part 2 of this book). As the humorist Will Rogers said, "Even if you are on the right track, if you just sit there you'll get run over." Self-acceptance followed by action; that's the key.

def•i•ni•tion

Passive resignation is adopting a belief that there is absolutely nothing that I can do to cope, to fight back, or to help myself. It is understandable that some life experiences may lead to this kind of helplessness and hopelessness. However, such resignation never helps. In fact, what noted psychologist, Martin Seligman has found, is that "helplessness" can greatly increase the risks of severe depression and a host of stress-related illnesses.

The Least You Need to Know

- One's basic set point for emotional sensitivity is established very early in life.

- Genetically influenced temperament plays a significant role in establishing an individual's emotional set point.

- Holding, rocking, and other forms of nurturing infants can have a very positive effect, influencing the development of more stress-resistant brains.

- Many people who experience significant stress are not neurotic or mentally ill, but, rather, have not found a good fit between their temperament and their lifestyle choices.

5

Perceiving Stress: It's Always in the Eye of the Beholder

In This Chapter

- ◆ How the human mind and brain perceive reality
- ◆ Reactions to situations depend heavily on your perceptions
- ◆ Logical thinking versus intuitive thinking and hunches
- ◆ How certain parts of the brain constantly engage in rapid fear appraisal

Sigmund Freud, the founder of psychoanalysis, said that emotions are "over-determined." What he meant by this is that hardly ever do people react in a simplistic stimulus-response fashion. As an example, the exact same life event can occur to two people and yet each may have completely different reactions.

Each human brain takes in about 20 million bits of data per second. Your sense organs constantly scan the environment and send this massive amount of information to various parts of the brain. How all of this data is organized, perceived, and processed matters a lot! In this chapter, we take a look at the brain and discuss the role it plays in perceiving reality.

The Brain's Job Description

When it comes to survival, the brain carries out three main functions:

1. It regulates bodily functioning (e.g. temperature, heart rate, breathing, and levels of glucose in the blood stream).

2. It constantly scans the environment, looking out for potential risks or challenges.

3. If danger or other challenges are encountered, it is the brain that launches adaptive responses to the world in order to reduce harm and assure survival.

The human brain is designed to rapidly process information in complex ways. And this is accomplished by the interaction of three rather separate information-processing systems in the brain. To understand how you react to particular life circumstances, it is important to know something about these three ways of perceiving events.

Are You Thinking in Your "Right" Mind?

The human brain is divided into two hemispheres (right and left) with the most highly developed aspects of the brain in the cortex, that thin layer of nerve cells covering the outside of each hemisphere. For the vast majority of people, the left hemisphere is engaged in a specific type of information processing, one that is well suited for perceiving and producing spoken language. This is also where logical thinking takes place.

In contrast, the right hemisphere is quite adept at picking up on the nuances of emotion in others. It is the part of the nervous system that readily detects subtle changes in others' facial expressions, body language, and vocal tone. It is also the site for thinking that involves hunches and intuitions.

Taken together, the left and right hemispheres engage in what has been called parallel information processing. Let's see how this works.

We have two couples in our example, Jill/Bob and Cindy/David. Let's assume that Bob says, "You know I love you" and these words are perceived by Jill in her left hemisphere. Further, let's say that Bob's facial expression and tone of voice (being perceived by Jill's right hemisphere) clearly convey the same message. When he says he loves her, he really means it! He looks how he feels and feels how he looks. The perceptions and conclusions arrived at from each hemisphere are in harmony.

In contrast, David says the exact same words, and they, too, are processed by Cindy's left hemisphere. However, the truth is that David has fallen out of love with Cindy; in his heart of hearts he feels distant and uninvolved with her. However, out of obligation or guilt, he says, "You know I love you." But Cindy's right hemisphere picks up on something else. His eyes, his facial expression, and his vocal tone strongly suggest that his words are not sincere.

Given this second example, two things can (and do) commonly occur. Either Cindy notices the discrepancy, which raises doubts about David's true feelings. Or, (and this often happens) she so strongly wants to believe in his love that she pays more attention to the words. Out of hopefulness and a measure of denial, she tries to convince herself that things are fine in the relationship. Generally, when such disharmony exists (when interpretations made by the right and left hemispheres don't agree) many people will simply experience a vague sense of uneasiness. They may find the specifics of this dis-ease hard to really put their finger on.

> **Think About It**
>
> Predominate cultural values and child-rearing practices in our Western culture have trained most of us to put more stock in logical thinking rather than intuition. It has programmed many of us to ignore the valuable information being perceived and processed by the right hemisphere.

Rapid Threat Appraisal

The threat appraisal center of the brain is a tiny structure in the temporal lobes called the amygdala. Pioneering work by the noted neuroscientist Joseph Le Doux had led to an understanding about how the amygdala works. Incoming sensory information travels along two separate pathways. One goes to the cortex (where such data can be carefully analyzed by the cortex in the right and left hemispheres); the other goes to the amygdala.

Remember the set point metaphor we considered in the previous chapter? Well, if you go looking for that smoke detector in the brain, the amygdala is the prime candidate. A part of how sensitive people are to noticing emotionally distressing things in their environment depends a lot on just how sensitive their amygdala is (and this sensitivity level is often set before birth: more about this in the next chapter). Both the cortex and the amygdala are privy to the same information, but they process it separately and in uniquely different ways. In some respects, the amygdala is like a separate brain. It takes in information, makes decisions, and ignites action.

The amygdala is the brain structure that is responsible for learning about danger in the environment and is the rapid threat detector. Here is how this works. A man walks in the forest and suddenly sees what appears to be a large, coiled-up snake in the path. As a young child (like most of us) he learned that some snakes are poisonous, and the general size and shape of snakes was branded into his memory bank in the amygdala. The amygdala is an expert at what psychologists call pattern recognition. That is, the moment it registers this visual image (a round, long, coiled-up object) this is analyzed and it matches the general configuration of a snake. The amygdala then ignites a sudden response, stress hormones are released, and the man immediately jumps back. This is completely independent of what is happening upstairs in the cortex.

The cortex also rapidly takes in this information, but it does something the amygdala cannot do. It can *reality test*. This is a psychological term that implies the ability to take a second and more careful look at situations. The amygdala says, "In general it looks like a snake … therefore it is a snake." The cortex may arrive at the same conclusion, but let's consider in this example that it is not a snake but, rather, it is a coiled-up piece of rope. The general configuration could be a snake, but not necessarily. On further inspection (all of this taking a fraction of a second) the cortex, owing to its superior information-processing capabilities, refines its observation: "It's not a snake; it's a rope."

def•i•ni•tion

Reality testing is a psychological term that refers to the ability of the brain and mind to carefully consider and reconsider perceptions. Rather than jumping to abrupt conclusions, reality testing involves a more careful and thoughtful consideration of information coming into the brain.

In this case there is a difference of opinion between the cortex and the amygdala. Both take in data and both can independently set in motion a fight-or-flight response. Under the conditions described, in another fraction of a second the cortex, however, wins the disagreement, accurately sees reality, and, as it were, overrides the amygdala … the man calms down and goes on his way.

False Alarms and Jumping to Conclusions

Often problems develop when the amygdala predominates. Let's say that as a young boy, Steven was treated in a very harsh way by his father. Sometimes without warning, his father would strike him. The memories of this (stored in the amygdala, likely in the form of a general visual pattern of a tall man quickly approaching him) continue to play a role in Steven's life. Often when in a store or other public place, if a tall man walks near him, he automatically flinches. His cortex says, "There is no danger … it's just a man shopping," and Steven certainly knows that this man is not his father and he is not a little kid any more. Yet he can't help it. The persistent memory buried in the amygdala keeps evoking such "false alarms." Steven may wonder why in the world he reacts the way he does.

Let's take another example and see how this amygdala-level perception can operate at a completely unconscious level. When Pam was age 7 she was molested several times by a man who lived in her neighborhood. She was threatened that if she told anyone about it, he would kill her. She was terrified. Thankfully the abuse was soon discovered and the man sent to prison. She was never again in danger.

Pam, like all humans, took in this terrible experience, including some general physical features of the sexual predator. It got registered in memory banks in the amygdala. Let's say he was a somewhat overweight man with a black mustache.

Thirty years pass, and Pam is doing well. She may have distant memories of the molestation, but only on rare occasions does it cross her mind; it is no longer a part of her life. One day she attends a continuing-education conference required by her place of work. It just so happens that the speaker is a man who (in a general way) looks a bit like the perpetrator (overweight and black mustache).

He comes across as a friendly person and good speaker. Yet for reasons that Pam cannot comprehend, she begins to feel increasingly anxious. Her heart rate increases, her palms sweat, and she has a vague sense of danger. With her conscious mind (her cortex) she scans her environment and concludes that there is absolutely no danger. All of the people look calm and cordial. Consciously she is completely unaware of the similarities between the speaker and her abuser of long ago. But her amygdala is sounding the alarm and she certainly cannot ignore the escalating anxiety that she is experiencing. At some point she excuses herself and leaves the seminar. Ten minutes later she sits in her car, more calm, yet completely perplexed, thinking, "What in the world is wrong with me?!"

Successful coping with life events is aided by people becoming very consciously aware of their particular learned fear responses. Take a close look at your life and come to know what kinds of situations are likely to activate your threat detector. When the alarm sounds and you notice anxiety or distress, it's of course always important to take it seriously. You might be responding to actual here-and-now danger. Scan the environment. But also pause for a moment and take stock of the situation. Give your cortex a few moments to reality test and keep in mind your tendency to have your own unique false alarms.

The Unconscious Mind

Most of the time the perceptions occurring at the level of the amygdala are completely outside of awareness (i.e. the perceptions are unconscious). In our Pam example, like anyone else, she will try to figure out what has just happened. She wonders if she has some kind of medical problem … maybe its PMS … maybe, she thinks, "I'm going crazy."

Memories stored in the amygdala do not go away. And, for many people, occasionally they continue to have a strong influence. Sometimes people can (upon careful reflection or with the help of psychotherapy) learn what they are responding to. This happened for Pam. She was in psychotherapy, and after carefully looking at her life she eventually put the pieces together. She no w knows that it is in her makeup to respond to people who have certain physical characteristics. There is a rhyme and reason to this. This is not craziness; it's just an understandable "false alarm." Thus when on occasion this kind of thing happens again, she does scan the environment to first make sure there is no identifiable danger, and if the coast is clear, she compassionately tells herself, "I know what's going on here … I'll be okay."

Hiding the Hurt

Let's consider two more all-too-common variations on this theme: Robert and Sarah.

When Robert was young, like all children, he had times when he was injured—skinned knees and the like—and, like all kids, he had times of sadness or emotional hurt. His father always responded to Robert's tears with anger and shaming. He thought his son was acting like a crybaby, and would scold him. During Robert's childhood, he gradually found ways to emotionally grit his teeth. When hurt or sad feelings began to percolate up inside of him, without him even noticing it, he began to automatically push such feelings down, completely out of his awareness. The shaming just hurt too much.

Now as an adult Robert has a problem. Like all of us, he has experienced many times of emotional hurt. Yet each time as he begins to internally feel sadness, or other forms of emotional vulnerability, these inner feelings are perceived unconsciously (at the level of the amygdala). Rather than feel or express sadness, Robert, in what seems a very automatic way, reacts by pulling away from others.

In his conscious mind, he knows that his friends and his wife are decent and understanding people. There is absolutely no evidence that this is not the case. Yet his unconscious mind is in control, and false alarms are driving him to habitually hide his hurt feelings. He doesn't share his emotional pain. He is not consciously choosing to do this; it's now just automatic. Another negative consequence for this style of reacting is that it has left some of his friends perceiving him as aloof and somewhat emotionally cold. That's not Robert's intention, but that's what they think.

Sarah was very close to her father. Yet when she was 8 years old, her dad died of cancer. This was terribly traumatic for her, and her grief was completely understandable. To this day, at the age of 23, she often continues to feel his loss when she remembers those painful childhood memories. This, too, makes sense to her.

But what does not make sense is that every time she has started to feel close to others, including a boy in high school and again a young man while in college, she eventually would feel increasingly uneasy, especially if she started to fall in love with them. This anxiety somehow oddly led her to pull away, and in both instances she broke up with the boyfriends. She now feels lonely and perplexed at why she broke off what looked like good relationships with two very decent people.

The Point

As we've said, emotions almost always are reactions to particular stressors. Sometimes feelings make perfect sense because we can use our conscious mind to notice what's going on … to figure out what we are reacting to. In those instances, it's a "no brainer"—emotions make sense. However, since the human mind has this capacity to interpret events on three levels, often emotional reactions do not make sense … they seem inexplicable or sometimes "crazy."

It is important to get as clear as you can about what you might be reacting to in the environment, especially during those times when feelings do not make sense. Often the key to understanding this comes from carefully looking at your prior experiences … experiences that may be continuing to influence how you react to the world.

The Least You Need to Know

- ◆ Emotional reactions are based largely on your perception of troublesome, dangerous, or challenging events taking place in your environment.

- ◆ The amygdala is responsible for lightening-fast threat appraisal and can launch a fight-or-flight response in a fraction of a second.

- ◆ Unconscious perceptions can be very accurate, but they are also prone to "false alarms."

◆ The key to optimal emotional survival is to take in information from the world on multiple levels; it's your best shot at truly understanding what is going on, and to try and figure out why you are reacting to what is happening.

◆ Most of the time, puzzling emotions begin to make sense when you understand their origins.

Chapter 6

Understanding Your "Emotional Buttons"

In This Chapter

- Early life experiences that result in emotional sensitivity
- How pushing emotional buttons can account for especially strong emotional reactions
- Early life experiences that leave indelible influences
- Core self-concepts and their impact on life events

To a degree, all of us have what you might call generic emotional reactions. The best example of this may be a startle reaction and an abrupt fight-or-flight response if a car almost crashes into us on the freeway. Basically everyone reacts the same way.

Beyond such generic reactions, however, are the totally individualized areas of emotional sensitivity, such as an exquisite sensitivity to criticism or to rejection. Of course no one likes criticism or rejection, but some people take these experiences harder than others do. We all have our own Achilles' heel. We all have our own buttons that get pushed. A lot of this, it turns out, is very strongly influenced by individual character ... each person's personality that has at least initially been shaped by early life experiences.

Psychologist, Theodore Millon says, "Significant experiences of early life may never recur again, but their effects remain and leave their mark … they operate insidiously to transform new experiences in line with the past."

In this chapter, we'll take a close look at your unique personality and explore how early life experiences contribute to particular areas of emotional sensitivity; your emotional buttons.

Early Experiences: Prelude to Personality

Almost all of us have been strongly affected by the day-in, day-out emotional atmosphere that existed in our early families. Recall your own childhood. The family is a child's entire world. At times, sudden, brief, highly distressing events do affect the developing personality of the child. However, by and large, it is the repeated contacts with a child's parents that begin to give shape to her view of the world.

Tom is an infant. Like all young children, his first experiences with people are severely limited in scope. Aside from occasional brief visits by neighbors and grandparents, his world of human interactions is exclusively that of his family. These early encounters with his parents will influence this boy tremendously as he starts to form his first impressions of the world.

If most of the time Tom notices periods of hunger or other discomfort, quickly followed by relief—holding, soothing, feeding by his mother or father—then it is very likely that he will begin to lay down some extremely powerful beliefs and expectations about the world. Maybe the beliefs will be, "There is comfort in this world … I can count on this," "There is reason to be hopeful that others can help me," "I can trust that any pain I feel won't last forever," or "My needs matter."

At this early stage of development, such beliefs are not really thoughts or words in Keith's mind, but are more an inner sense about the world etched into deep levels of his psyche. It's a bit like when you're thirsty and take a drink, you don't really think about it, but you just know that you can count on the fact that the water will quench your thirst. This belief has always been your experience throughout life. This belief also leads to an expectation: "If I'm thirsty, I know what to do. I fully expect water to quench my thirst." Emotional expectations also operate on a similar automatic and unconscious level.

Who Do You Trust?

The earliest human beliefs and expectations center around what famed psychoanalyst and author Eric Erickson calls "basic trust"—trusting that others can be counted on to provide nurturing, soothing, and protection. It is this trust that leads to the capacity to form attachments. Very severe adverse conditions—betrayal of trust—during the first year of life can result in the laying down of powerful negative beliefs.

If Keith were profoundly rejected, neglected, or abused during infancy, he might grow into adulthood without the inner ability to form attachments with others. Such children believe that the world is harsh and that people do not provide comfort. These beliefs color their perceptions of life. Everywhere they look, they see rejection, abuse, and harshness. They could never count on love or nurturing as infants, and even if they have the good fortune to encounter a loving person later in life, the early, severe deprivation has left its mark.

Pervasive, severe emotional trauma or neglect early in life may, in a sense, set these beliefs in psychic concrete. Such people often go into the world profoundly detached and want absolutely nothing to do with closeness, intimacy, or the human race. Others who have been so terribly hurt early in life may become self-centered narcissists and psychopaths who can never genuinely give to others, but, rather, can only hurt and use others to meet their own needs.

Most very early life experiences, especially those occurring in the first three years of life, are hard if not impossible to remember. Yet they leave their marks. Child developmental specialist Margaret Mahler calls these early experiences "unrememberable but unforgettable."

Core Self-Concepts: Positive and Negative

These inner beliefs usually develop into the nucleus of one's self-concept. And they define "who I am," "who others are," and "what to expect from human interactions." Deeply etched negative beliefs (negative core beliefs) can be seen to emerge in two forms. The first, somewhat more malleable negative core beliefs are negative views of the world and the self that, under the right circumstances, can be altered by later positive experiences with others.

Softening of Negative Core Beliefs

Jennifer was ignored by her workaholic father and largely rejected by her mother. She came to strongly believe that, "There must be something wrong with me. I am defective and, in a very basic way, unlovable." Yet during her childhood, from about ages 5 to 10, her next-door neighbor, a kind and gentle older woman, did provide her with a considerable amount of warmth and affirmation.

Jennifer periodically continues to have times of feeling unlovable, but this belief is not rigid; it is not etched in stone. She is able to remind herself of her good qualities and can recall times when she has been in positive, meaningful relationships with others. The early experience left its mark, but later relationships have modified her beliefs so that they do not dominate her life.

The malleability of Jennifer's negative core beliefs probably has to do with having experienced only moderately severe neglect/rejection, and yet the positive effects of the relationship with her neighbor provided a buffer. In the end, her early experiences were certainly painful, but not at a magnitude considered to be traumatic.

A Technique for Modifying Negative Core Beliefs

People are also able to modify negative core beliefs by challenging them, putting them to the test of reality. Jennifer might do this by first clearly noting that one of her emotional buttons has to do with believing she is unlovable. Many if not most people are only vaguely aware of their particular core self-concepts. Carefully thinking about this and writing down your thoughts can help you become more consciously aware of these inner beliefs (and later in this chapter there will be an exercise to help you figure this out).

The next step is for Jennifer to think, "Is this statement 100 percent true, 100 percent of the time?" When asking this question she will likely be able to think of some specific examples where this belief is not accurate.

It helps a lot to write down the specific examples that come to mind (you'll see throughout this book that many coping strategies include writing things down). It has been shown that the process of writing down thoughts, feelings, and observations can, in powerful ways, help people become more conscious and aware of inner and outer realities. Most people will be able to find examples that can dispute their negative core concepts. After Jennifer does this, she may find it helpful to keep what she has written as a reminder, should later experiences touch on these inner painful beliefs and feelings.

Joel had been dating Lucy for a year, and had fallen in love with her. However, for reasons that he never fully understood, Lucy rather abruptly broke off the relationship. It hit him hard. In the weeks following this experience, Joel would often think, "I'm just not good enough for anyone to want to love me." This event hit his "I'm not good enough" button. However, he tried the strategy of challenging his beliefs and writing things down. Here is what he wrote:

Lucy did leave me and I feel a lot of sadness about this.

I know that I have often been told that I am smart and have a very good sense of humor.

I know that I am loyal to people I care about.

I know that I have a good heart.

These are characteristics that many people would really like in a person.

My sadness over the break-up is completely understandable, but the belief that "I am not good enough" just simply is not true.

Unshakable Negative Core Beliefs

A second version of negative core beliefs can arise in conditions of very severe emotional harshness. This version is characterized by rigidity and unshakable negative beliefs. Bill grew up in a home environment of pervasive harshness, brutality, and ruthless criticism. Daily his father told Bill he was worthless, a loser, and a "piece of shit." Bill's incredibly passive mother would shrink into the shadows and seem to disappear at these times, offering him no protection from his tyrannical father.

Bill is now a man in his mid-40s. He is single, lonely, and chronically depressed. He interprets his inner belief, "There is something wrong with me. I am defective and, in a very basic way, unlovable," as an absolute fact; it is a deeply held conviction. He has never thought even for a moment that the belief was untrue. Very severe early emotional trauma and toxic family environments often result in such rigid and unshakable negative beliefs.

It is important to note that Bill rarely thinks back about his father or his childhood. He is not feeling or re-experiencing any kind of direct pain from childhood memories or wounds. But the powerful beliefs, laid down years ago, wreak havoc in his daily life. Negative core beliefs influence here-and-now perceptions and expectations. Let's take a look at how this process continues to happen in Bill's life.

Think About It

The most potent way that negative core beliefs have an impact on human lives is by significantly influencing and biasing here-and-now perceptions of the world. It's not just about the past; it's generally not about remembering bad things that happened long ago; it's about re-experiencing negativity everywhere, every day.

Bill's firm conviction that he is unlovable influences his perceptions of the world. He is quick to notice any events that confirm or even come close to confirming his beliefs. At a recent social event that took place at his office just after business hours, he entered the room full of fellow employees. For the first two minutes he was there, no one spontaneously came up to greet him. He looked around the room, but no one met his eyes. He very quickly concluded, "They don't give a damn whether I'm here or not."

This perception, this conclusion, was very likely to have been exactly what he anticipated. At that moment, he abruptly left the party, went home, and felt lousy. He has had similar experience many times before. And many more times he has been so convinced that he would be rejected or unwanted that he didn't even attend social functions.

The Impact of Rigid Negative Beliefs

Bill's inner belief has taken its toll in three ways. First, current perceptions (and conclusions) are greatly influenced by the beliefs. Possibly there are times that his perceptions are accurate, but very likely his quick conclusions may not be completely accurate or realistic.

Second, like many whose core beliefs about life are essentially negative, Bill is always ready to see rejection in social contacts and, as a result, is likely to jump to unwanted or distorted conclusions.

And third, powerful expectations have often led to choices (e.g. he doesn't go to parties) that keep him further cut off from interpersonal contact. Also, a person who rarely attends gatherings and never initiates social interaction is likely to be seen as disinterested: a loner, a snob, or a grump. Often, others are likely to start treating that person in the very manner anticipated: with rejection. Is time healing this childhood wound? Of course not.

Can Rigid Core Beliefs Ever Be Changed?

Deeply ingrained, rigid, and severe maladaptive beliefs can be extremely resistant to change or alteration by later positive life circumstances. In most cases, recovery and emotional healing will require involvement in psychotherapy.

People who suffer these long-lasting and profound psychic wounds almost never felt a real sense of trust or safety with other human beings. Because psychotherapy involves a deep and confiding relationship with another person, the whole idea of seeking out treatment can be understandably terrifying for these people. Many never consider it as an option. Choosing to enter psychotherapy represents an act of tremendous courage. Fortunately, if the person finds the right therapist, treatment can be helpful, although the road to recovery is long and rocky. Successful treatment is what psychologist Steven Johnson has termed "a hard-work miracle."

People with less-negative core beliefs can often eventually modify these beliefs as they begin to encounter new experiences: by experiencing successes in their lives or by developing positive and loving relationships with others.

We All Have at Least Some Negative Core Beliefs

In healthy, growth-promoting families, children are felt to naturally develop positive and realistic inner beliefs. However, it is probably true that most of us encountered at least mildly negative experiences at least some of the time while growing up.

The experience of the majority of people lies somewhere between the extremes of optimal positive experience and severe early trauma. When this is the case, as mentioned before, negative core beliefs and self-concepts are not likely to be as pervasive or rigid. Such people may not feel inadequate continuously, but from time to time, this inner belief is triggered or reactivated by life events. It's as if the core belief lies dormant and is periodically awakened by certain stressful events.

Let's Get Personal

I'd like to give you a personal example. In growing up I was fortunate enough to have a loving family. However, my father really pushed me, especially in school. Lots of times my best just wasn't good enough. One of my core negative beliefs has been, "I'm basically capable, but down deep inside I doubt myself and I am afraid people will see me as inadequate and be critical of me."

I have been doing public speaking for more than 25 years. I so keenly remember many times, especially in the first years of giving talks, having this experience. I'd be speaking and I would notice someone in the audience looking sleepy and yawning.

Here is the truth: there are lots of reasons people might yawn in this kind of setting … they stayed up late last night, they didn't sleep well last night, they are taking medication that has a side effect of sedation, and, just maybe, they are bored to tears and they hate the talk I am giving. All of these are realistic and possible explanations for the yawn. But owing to my inner negative core belief, guess what conclusion immediately would pop into my mind? You know.

"They are bored ... my talk is no good ... I feel inadequate." Furthermore, in that moment I felt convinced that my conclusion was absolutely the truth. What I was doing was kind of like trying to be a mind-reader, and my conclusions would always result in two outcomes. First, it made me feel worse in the moment (embarrassed, anxious, and self-doubting). Second, every time I had this experience, it would work to confirm my negative belief.

This is how these early beliefs have their greatest impact on human lives. It's not about remembering what my dad said to me; it's about the belief influencing my here-and-now conclusions.

With some positive experiences in speaking and a round or two of psychotherapy, I finally got to the place that when I see a yawn in the audience I will think, "Maybe they didn't sleep well last night ... maybe they are taking a sedating medication, and maybe they don't like my talk." I'm not trying to fool myself into discounting the possibility that the person is bored or that my talk isn't so great. You can't please all the people all of the time. But my perceptions and conclusions in more recent years are usually more balanced. I also get it that I can't read minds.

Turning Down the Volume on Negative Core Beliefs

Thankfully for many of us, negative core beliefs can be modified by positive experiences throughout daily life, or can be changed in powerful ways by the experience of psychotherapy. However, most of the time, they do not go completely away. I carry within me, somewhere down deep inside, this lack of confidence in myself, and from time to time life events touch upon it.

All sorts of negative core beliefs may result from early experiences in your family. Psychologist Jeffrey Young has given us a brilliant analysis of the areas of life in which negative beliefs develop (see the section "Common Core Beliefs" that follows). It's likely, if you are like most people, you'll probably notice one or two primary negative core beliefs that are dominant undercurrents in your emotional life.

Take a close look at those times in your life when you felt the most upset, hurt, frustrated, or disappointed. Is there a common theme, a particular nerve that gets touched on? The more you know about your own particular areas of vulnerability, the better. This can help you plan ahead and possibly avoid certain relationships, interactions, or situations that are high risk for pushing those buttons. Conversely, it will also help you take steps to modify your negative core beliefs (something we'll look at in Chapter 13).

Common Core Beliefs*

Core Beliefs and Important Aspects of Emotional Life	Healthy and Positive Beliefs	Mild to Moderately Negative Beliefs	Significantly Negative and Rigid Beliefs
Dependency	I am able to take care of myself and stand on my own two feet.	I often feel unable to function on my own.	I am totally unable to function on my own.
Subjugation	I may care about others' needs, but my own needs are important, too.	I often feel that others' needs must come first.	Others' needs always must come before my own.
Vulnerability to Harm	By and large my world is generally a safe place.	I need to be cautious because often the world is unsafe.	The world is an extremely dangerous place.
Mistrust	Most people I am close to can be trusted in and counted on.	I must be on guard with others.	Others will always hurt, abuse, use, or take advantage of me.
Abandonment/ Fears of Loss	My relationships are stable and enduring. I can allow intimacy.	I often worry about losing people who are close to me.	Ultimately I will lose those whom I love. I will be rejected.

continued

Core Beliefs and Important Aspects of Emotional Life	Healthy and Positive Beliefs	Mild to Moderately Negative Beliefs	Significantly Negative and Rigid Beliefs
Emotional Deprivation	There is hope that I will be able to find love in the world.	I often feel a lack of love and support.	My needs for love and support will never be met.
Defectiveness/ Unlovability	I am basically an okay person. I have worth. I am lovable.	I often worry that if others really know me, they wouldn't like me.	I am profoundly defective and unlovable.
Incompetency	I have confidence in my ability to deal with the demands of life.	I often doubt that I am capable and competent.	I am completely incompetent and destined to fail.
Shame/Guilt	I may make mistakes, but I am basically a good, decent person.	I often feel ashamed or bad about myself.	I am morally bad, shameful, and deserving of criticism and punishment.

Adapted from J. Young (1999)

Making Sense of Strong Emotional Reactions

It's a common experience for people to encounter stressful life situations and to respond with very strong emotions. At first glance, such emotions may appear to be inappropriately intense. Upon close inspection, however, we may find that a particular life event or interaction with another person has evoked such a strong reaction largely because it has activated our own unique, underlying negative core belief. It's hit a nerve … pushed our emotional buttons.

In attempting to understand yourself more fully, it will be helpful to take inventory of your inner core beliefs and then ask the question, "Is there anything about the stresses in my life right now that touches on this emotional chord in me?"

Try this exercise. First take a look at the questions below and think about your memories of how you were treated in general in your family, day in and day out, when you were young. Here are some suggestions to get you thinking about this.

1. Did people in my family notice when I felt bad (sad, scared, etc.)? Or was I ignored?

2. Was I comforted with warmth, support, and affection when I got hurt or emotionally upset?

3. Were my feelings taken seriously and understood? Or did I experience excessive criticism, harshness, shame, or humiliation when I felt upset, sad, hurt, scared, etc.?

4. Did I feel included in my family?

5. Did I feel valued and cherished?

6. Did my parents believe in me? For instance, did they have confidence in my ability to learn, to make friends, to succeed …?

7. When I accomplished something positive, did I receive praise? Or was I ignored or criticized?

8. Did I feel that I could count on my parents to be reliable, for example, being confident that if I needed them, they'd be there for me? Or were things always unpredictable and erratic?

9. Did I feel safe?

10. Did I generally feel hopeful? For example, if bad things happened (in general) did I believe that with time, things would be okay? Was I reassured by my parents?

11. Did I feel a lot of competitiveness from my parents or siblings?

12. Was I used or abused (sexually, physically, or emotionally)?

13. Did my parents ever call me names such as "stupid, loser, worthless" or make comments such as, "You are too sensitive!" or "You are too emotional."

Of course there are many other questions to ponder, so, please, take a few minutes to do so. Then, write down the first few thoughts that come to your mind. Take a careful look at what you have written and then consider something else. If there were negative or difficult experiences early in your life, have you also encountered anything like this in other relationships (friendships, intimate relationships, etc.)? It is not at all unusual that similar patterns of interaction occur in later relationships.

Finally, ask yourself: have these early experiences ever colored what I anticipate, what I worry about, or what I often perceive? How do these early influences affect my life now? And, are any of my current life experiences touching on these sensitive nerves?

I once saw a cartoon, in which a psychotherapy patient was on the psychoanalyst's couch, and said, "My mother sure knows how to push my buttons!" The analyst said, "Well, of course she does … she is the one who installed them."

The Least You Need to Know

- ◆ Character is profoundly influenced by day-in and day-out interactions with family members early in life.

- ◆ Core self-beliefs can continue to have a life-long impact on people, primarily by significantly influencing how you perceive and interpret experiences.

- ◆ Early life experiences may be impossible to remember, but they still have a huge impact on people throughout life.

- ◆ An important way to understand your own moods and emotional reactions is to become very clear about your own core self-concepts.

Chapter 7

When Emotions Overwhelm

In This Chapter

- Controlling and over-controlling your emotions
- Facing and tolerating overwhelming feelings
- Ego weakness and a loss of emotional control
- Psychiatric disorders that can complicate coping and emotional healing

We have taken a look at a number of aspects of moods and emotions and have considered how many human feelings can be necessary and positive. It is very important to now consider those emotional reactions that simply hurt too much and can be overwhelming. In this chapter, we'll also see that sometimes what "feels" overwhelming initially, can, in fact be faced. Finally, we will consider those emotional responses and psychological disorders that are caused by changes in brain chemistry.

Degrees of Emotional Control

Psychiatrist Mardi Horowitz and his colleagues have developed a simple and useful model for understanding emotional experiences. People can respond to significant life experiences in one of three ways:

◆ Emotional control (keeping emotions at arm's length)

◆ Getting defensive (over-control)

◆ Dyscontrol (emotional meltdown)

Emotional Control: Keeping Emotions at Arm's Length

States of emotional control represent those times when people are in fact encountering significant stress in their lives. However, when in emotional control, emotions are held at arm's length. People may certainly know that inwardly they have very painful or distressing emotions. However, in this moment they do not directly feel it. Emotional control is an essential aspect of coping.

Let's say that Jim's daughter has leukemia, her prognosis is guarded, and Jim oftentimes feels consumed with grief and worry. However, when at work as a high school teacher, he always manages to stay focused on his work. His inner anguish stays contained during the workday. Fortunately, he has a very good marriage, and often, when in the privacy of his home, he lets down his guard, and openly cries as he speaks with his wife about their daughter. He is able to control his emotions at work and also has the emotional strength to be open with his feelings when with his wife, and sometimes also with his best friend, Mike.

People maintain such control in a number of ways. Some keep distracted with work or by watching sports on TV. Some anesthetize themselves with alcohol or tranquilizers.

Lots of people consciously try to fight off feelings, often attempting this by engaging in a sort of internal self-talk. Here are some examples:

◆ "I have to just be strong."

◆ "Don't get so emotional; pull yourself together."

◆ "I can't let my feelings out … it will upset my kids."

◆ "Other people have it worse off than I do … don't overreact."

Sometimes those efforts to avoid feeling painful emotions work. Sometimes they don't.

Getting Defensive: Over-Control

Many people in very automatic and unconscious ways simply don't feel their inner emotions. Here *defense mechanisms* play a role. Defense mechanisms are psychological functions that block out or mute emotions. By definition, defense mechanisms are automatic (they are not willfully or consciously chosen). An example is when someone experiences a tragedy, such as the sudden loss of a loved one. Some people will appear to go into shock ... they feel numb. They absolutely know that this event is terrible and yet feel nothing. They may be very perplexed by their lack of emotion. Here, defenses have repressed emotions.

Emotional control is a natural and normal way that most people react to painful life circumstances. It is not inherently good or bad. In many circumstances, as we saw with Jim, his ability to keep control over emotions at work helped him cope. However, a problem can arise, one that is extraordinarily common: emotional control can become pervasive.

def•i•ni•tion

> **Defense mechanisms** are automatic and unconscious ways that the mind blocks awareness of inner, painful, or frightening emotions.

Here, people do not have access to inner feelings. In a sense, they are constantly emotionally gritting their teeth. Excessive over-control almost always leads to problems. Common outcomes include a significantly increased risk for developing severe depression, anxiety disorders, and psychosomatic illnesses (e.g. high blood pressure).

Dyscontrol: An Emotional Meltdown

Dyscontrol is not just feeling strong emotions. It is a state of mind where feelings are so intense that they lead to a disorganization of the self. In the midst of dyscontrol, people may become very confused, may experience psychotic symptoms (such as hallucinations), and completely lose the ability for critical thinking. This massive emotional meltdown can lead to desperate actions such as very severe substance abuse, suicide, rage and violence toward others, or self-harm (such as burning or cutting oneself). Psychologists call this *decompensation*. In popular lingo, dyscontrol is a full-blown "nervous breakdown."

Decompensation is a term used to describe a marked breakdown in emotional controls.

It must be emphasized that true dyscontrol is relatively rare. It most often occurs in people who have psychotic illnesses, such as schizophrenia or severe mania, or in people who have very weak ego strength. In psychiatry, people who have chronic ego weakness are often said to suffer from borderline personality disorder. Dyscontrol can sometimes be seen at least transiently in emotionally sturdy individuals who have been exposed to catastrophic traumas.

Think About It

The following are symptoms of borderline personality disorder:

- Extreme emotional sensitivity and reactivity.

- History of very problematic, volatile interpersonal relationships.

- Intense fears of real or imagined abandonment.

- May self-inflict injuries (e.g. cut or burn) when under stress. Often this injury actually produces a sense of relief.

- Under stress may develop chaotic or unrealistic thinking. Very prone to losing perspective.

- High risk for depression and alcohol or other types of substance abuse.

Zone of Emotional Tolerance

When people move from over-control into the zone of emotional tolerance, they then begin to feel their emotions. But a very important difference between this state of mind and dyscontrol is one of tolerance. In this zone of emotional tolerance, feelings may be incredibly intense, yet the person does not become psychotic or experience severe fragmentation of the self. As we saw in Chapter 3, this is a sign of ego strength.

Many people try to hang on to emotional control to an excessive degree. This may be something they consciously intend to do, or it may be occurring completely at an automatic and unconscious level.

It is not that they cannot tolerate strong feelings; the truth is that ultimately they can. But generally the tendency to maintain excessive emotional control is either because people are afraid of being overwhelmed (e.g. "If I start crying, I won't be able to stop") and they are afraid of the intensity of their feelings, or they anticipate extreme vulnerability, shame, or embarrassment should they open up to their feelings, especially in front of others.

One very common experience people have in the course of psychotherapy is eventually opening up to the truth of inner emotions … experiencing and expressing strong feelings, yet truly understanding that it does not kill or overwhelm them. Likewise, a frequent experience is initially feeling shame about certain feelings, only to, at some point, have the shame begin to evaporate. Most times this is accompanied by a sense of relief and a new view of oneself where the emotions are now seen as very difficult or painful, but understandable.

The lessening of defenses and openness to inner emotions is at the heart of emotional healing and growth. But this is not for everyone, and can, in fact, be very risky for people with weak ego strength. Also, even for very emotionally sturdy people, it's generally not a good idea to dive into the deep end of the pool. Sometimes emotions just hurt too much.

Think About It _____

The lessening of defenses and openness to emotions is at the heart of emotional healing for most people. But for those with weak ego strength, it can be risky.

Thus the pathway to noticing and expressing inner feelings oftentimes needs to be taken with gradual and cautious steps. Moving too quickly can feel overwhelming.

Emotional Thermostats

Another metaphor is this: the thermostat in your home is set at a particular temperature. This is pretty much the temperature that you want to maintain to feel comfortable. When changes in the weather make it either cooler or warmer in your house, the thermostat automatically monitors this change, and it either turns on the heater or the air conditioner. There is input, perception, and output (a response). If the thermostat and your heating and air conditioning system work, then you are able to create a living condition where there is comfort control.

Likewise, all human brains automatically do the same thing. The goal is to stay safe and to maintain a particular emotional comfort zone.

Sometimes there is a neurological equivalent of a thermostat malfunction. Often this is due to a genetic predisposition for or vulnerability to particular psychological conditions such as depression or anxiety disorders. And as we have seen, temperament and early life experiences (such as severe neglect) can also contribute to increased risk.

These vulnerability factors do not invariably cause the disorder; they simply increase the risk of developing the disorder (for example, children born to a parent who has a history of suffering from severe depression only have a 25 percent risk of developing depression themselves; thus the majority of offspring do not get depressed).

Those with a genetic risk (who may have parents that have suffered from psychiatric disorders) may not initially experience the disorder themselves; however, at some point, significant life stressors might hit the person, and the disorder emerges. This is akin to a bridge that has some structural flaws, but for years has safely carried the weight of thousands of cars and trucks. However, if a hurricane blows into town, the additional stress on the bridge is more than it can handle, it may collapse during the storm or it's damaged in ways that then make it unsafe for vehicles to cross.

Neuropsychiatric Disorders

The following psychiatric disorders are at least somewhat influenced by genetic predispositions. Furthermore, each of these disorders is due to or accompanied by abnormal chemical functioning in the brain. Thus they are often referred to as *neuropsychiatric disorders*. In each disorder, the particular symptoms of course differ, but all of them represent a sort of biologically based, malfunctioning emotional thermostat.

def•i•ni•tion

Neuropsychiatric disorders are psychiatric syndromes that are presumed to be either caused by changes in brain chemistry or in which, once the disorder begins, noticeable changes in brain functioning begin to develop. Owing to the fact that they involve some degree of chemical malfunction in the brain, treatments that directly target and normalize brain biochemistry are important to consider (such as the use of antidepressant medications).

The following list contains the most common psychiatric disorders that have a biological basis and mentions the most common symptoms of each disorder. The reason for mentioning them briefly here is so you can take a glimpse at these major symptoms and see if you are experiencing any of them. If so, then you will find more information about the diagnosis and treatment of these disorders in Chapter 26.

Please note that there are some biologically based psychiatric disorders that are not addressed in this book, such as schizophrenia or other psychotic disorders, autism, attention-deficit disorder, severe substance-abuse disorders, or dementias (e.g. psychiatric conditions associated with Alzheimer's disease). Of course, these disorders are significant and a source of great emotional suffering. However, a discussion of these disorders is beyond the scope of this book.

Depression:

- Sadness, irritability, feeling hopeless

- Extreme fatigue

- Sleep disturbances: insomnia or sleeping too much

- Marked changes in appetite (increased or decreased appetite) and corresponding changes in weight

- Loss of sexual desire

- Lost of interest in normal life activities

- Suicidal ideas

> **Bet You Didn't Know**
>
> Some depressions have little to do with biological changes in the brain; however, most cases of moderate-to-severe depression do involve a significant change in brain biochemistry.

Bipolar Disorder:

- Frequent severe depressions (symptoms mentioned above)

- Mania: agitation, racing thoughts, rapid speech, decreased need for sleep (may only sleep four or five hours a night, and yet the next day be full of energy), hyperactivity and excessive energy

Panic Disorder:

- Overwhelming surges of anxiety that come on suddenly and generally last from 1 to 20 minutes

- Physical symptoms of fight or flight (see Chapter 3)

- Intense fears of dying, loss of emotional control, or fear of going crazy

Obsessive-Compulsive Disorder:

- Almost-constant worries about germs, dirt, disease

- Rituals to reduce anxiety, such as excessive hand washing. Checking behavior, for instance, repeatedly checking to see if doors in fact are locked prior to retiring for the night (e.g. checking and rechecking a dozen times)

- Excessive need for order and symmetry in the environment

Bet You Didn't Know

Post-traumatic Stress Disorder (PTSD) is not caused by a biochemical disturbance in the brain. It is a reaction that can occur in response to exposure to very intensely frightening or disturbing events. However, in cases of severe PTSD, changes in brain function can begin to occur once the disorder begins, and there are medical as well as psychological treatments for this disorder.

Post-traumatic Stress Disorder (PTSD):

◆ Very intense anxiety attacks

◆ Nightmares

◆ Disturbing and intrusive images or memories of the traumatic event

◆ A generalized sense of high emotional arousal

◆ Sometimes, states of emotional numbness: a conspicuous absence of any feelings, often accompanied by poor concentration, feeling "spacey," and an odd sensation that things don't seem real

To the extent that at least some aspects of emotional disorders are tied to abnormal brain chemistry, emotional coping becomes considerably more difficult. Also, if you are suffering from one of these disorders, it then makes sense to consider treatments that focus on normalizing brain chemistry. As we'll see in Chapter 26 and Appendix D, some of these treatments include psychiatric medications. However, there are also a number of nonpharmacological approaches, which we will also explore.

The Least You Need to Know

◆ Emotional control is essential for effective coping, but if taken to an extreme, it may lead to increased risks of developing psychiatric disorders.

◆ Many feelings that seem overwhelming are not. They may be tremendously distressing or painful, but many people discover that they can feel these emotions and not fall apart.

◆ Getting in touch with your feelings may be an essential aspect of emotional coping and healing. But it can be risky if you do not have adequate ego strength.

◆ The presence of a psychiatric disorder makes coping significantly more difficult.

◆ Many psychiatric disorders are accompanied by significant changes in brain chemistry, and, as such, medical and nonmedical treatments that normalize biochemistry and brain functioning are often very helpful.

Part 2

Taking Action: First Things First

A number of factors can trigger distressing or painful emotions and moods. Determining the cause of negative moods is critically important. Many serious emotional problems ultimately are found to be associated with an underlying medical illness, or due to medication side effects, substance abuse, or the presence of a biologically based psychiatric condition. Countless numbers of people needlessly suffer from anxiety, depression, anger-control problems, and other types of distress, often for months or years, never realizing that the problem is attributable to a change in the chemistry of the body or the brain.

This part is where we begin to address specific action strategies for emotional coping, focusing first on ways to calm the body and the mind.

Chapter 8

Biological Factors That Can Affect Negative Moods

In This Chapter

- ◆ Brain chemistry and emotional suffering

- ◆ Medical conditions that can lead to serious mood changes

- ◆ The effects of prescription and recreational drugs that can cause serious mood problems

Human beings have a very strong need to make sense of their experiences. When people feel sad, for example, most will search their minds for reasons. They will take stock of recent life events, past hurts, etc. Many times it's obvious. There are clear-cut life events that explain the feeling. But sometimes it's hard to really figure out why one is having an unpleasant mood. Sometimes it is not life events that trigger moods, but, rather, changes in brain functioning.

When medical illnesses or drugs are causing changes in brain chemistry and serious negative mood states people can suffer for months or years, unable to effectively cope. It is necessary to make sure you are not having emotional symptoms that may be attributed to such causes. That is what we'll address in this chapter.

Biological Malfunctions and Negative Moods

A number of things can happen to people that result in marked changes in the chemistry of the body that then can begin to affect the emotional brain, producing emotional symptoms. Let's take a look at Caroline, George, and Roberto.

How a Hormone Can Ruin Your Life

Caroline is a 63-year-old retired schoolteacher. In recent times, her life has become a dream come true. Her two passions are painting and gardening. And now she has time to pursue these activities. However, beginning about four months ago, something started to change. Gradually at first, she began to feel nervous. Within a few weeks the nervousness escalated to agitation, and this was accompanied by intense feelings of helplessness, hopelessness, and depression. She even had thoughts about suicide. She lost weight and developed insomnia. She searched her life for plausible explanations. At first nothing came to mind, but gradually she began to wonder if her intense suffering was somehow tied to the loss of her son, who died in a car wreck 30 years ago.

Caroline confided in her pastor and he offered her comfort and support. The two of them spoke about her tragic loss. And it was clear that she continued to carry a lot of grief inside of her regarding the loss of her son. Yet the symptoms got worse and worse. Thank goodness Caroline just happened to go in for her yearly physical exam. On routine blood work, it was discovered that she was suffering from hyperthyroid disease (where the thyroid gland secretes excessive amounts of thyroid hormone). Hyperthyroid often causes severe anxiety and depression. This was medically treated, and within a few weeks, all of the emotional symptoms went away.

She had always felt grief over the loss of her son, but as it turns out, this was not the actual cause of her recent distress. People have a great need to make sense of their experiences. This led Caroline to search for explanations, and led her to conclude that her loss was the source of her suffering … but that was a red herring. She had a medical illness that profoundly affected her emotional brain. She was treated and cured. Caroline went back to her garden, to her painting, and to her well-deserved retirement.

Many people assume that symptoms of emotional distress are always caused by adverse life events (and, of course many are) but their search for psychological explanations may lead them astray and prevent them from discovering the true cause, which may be entirely medical.

Maybe I'm Not Going Crazy After All

George is a 54-year-old mechanic who was accompanied by his wife to the mental-health clinic. He was so tense and anxious that his wife did most of the talking. "Doctor, I don't know what's wrong with my husband. He's never been this way before, but during the last six months he has become a bundle of nerves." Her description was accurate. George was incredibly tense as he sat trembling in his chair. He, too, was perplexed by his problem. He reported feeling "very nervous all the time" and was plagued by insomnia and fitful, restless sleep.

George and his wife were completely at a loss to explain his severe symptoms. He'd never experienced this before and he had not experienced any recent life changes that might account for his suffering. He and his wife just assumed that he must be going crazy.

As they talked, at some point the therapist noted that George was using a nasal spray. The third time that he used the spray the therapist inquired about its use. George had begun to use it six months ago during the hay fever season. He apparently used it too frequently and his use had continued well past allergy season. To keep his nasal passages open, he found it necessary to use the spray many times each day. The decongestant was immediately suspected as the cause of his anxiety. Chronic over-use of nasal decongestants (sprays or pills) is known to cause nervousness and anxiety symptoms. With his primary-care doctor's help, George was able to wean himself from the nasal spray successfully. Three weeks later, he was himself again. "I thought that I was going nuts. It's hard to believe that a little nasal spray can change a man so much!"

Medical Illness and Tragedy Collide

Roberto came to the therapist's office in terrible shape. Three months ago, his wife, aged 33, had been killed in a car wreck. He has three young children, and all of them have been devastated by her loss. He has become severely depressed.

Despite weeks of psychotherapy and eventual use of antidepressant medications, he has shown virtually no improvement. Week 8 of therapy, Roberto casually mentioned that he needed to get a refill for both his antidepressant and his high-blood-pressure medication. A light bulb went on in the therapist's mind. What about the high-blood-pressure medication?

The therapist had made two critical mistakes. Mistake number one was that he did not initially inquire about any prescription drugs that Roberto was using. Turns out that the high-blood-pressure medication was a beta-blocker, a drug known to sometimes cause severe depression. Mistake number two was that the therapist (and Roberto, as well) assumed that his terrible depression was solely due to the loss of his wife. It was such a devastating tragedy that this explanation made good sense.

Ultimately Roberto was switched to a different class of high-blood-pressure medications (one not associated with causing depression). Within a few weeks, his depression began to lift. He continued to experience grief, but the all-consuming depression abated.

This man had intense grief and a biological cause for his depression. The drug had altered brain chemistry and was responsible for both some of the severe depression symptoms and for his failure to respond to standard psychological or psychiatric treatment. We must keep in mind that multiple factors can contribute to the development of emotional symptoms.

Getting Yourself Checked Out

If you are suffering from any type of significant mood disorder, before you do anything else, it is important to make sure the cause is not medical or associated with medication side effects. This is very important even if it is also clear that your distress is strongly associated with difficult life events.

I'm not talking about getting a million-dollar work-up at the Mayo Clinic. But there are some very basic steps you can take to get this checked out.

If You Already Know That You Have a Diagnosed Medical Condition

Some medical illnesses or conditions can, on occasion, cause anxiety, depression, or other noticeable changes in mood. They can produce marked emotional symptoms by changing the chemistry of the body and, ultimately, the brain. Certainly people may have strong psychological reactions to having a medical illness as well; for example, with conditions that result in chronic pain, daily suffering may greatly interfere with a person's ability to live a normal life. People obviously are emotionally affected by such life-changing experiences. But what I am speaking of here is how these medical disorders may also have a direct impact on the chemistry of the brain.

Many medical conditions can cause significant mood changes. A more comprehensive list can be found in Appendix B. Listed there are the most common medical conditions that may cause emotional symptoms.

Bet You Didn't Know

Changes in estrogen levels often have an impact on mood. Seventy percent of women have noticeable, but subtle, mood changes premenstrually. However, 5 percent of women suffer from premenstrual dysphoria. Dysphoria is a term meaning unpleasant mood, and this can include irritability, anxiety, and/or depression. Premenstrual dysphoria is a marked mood change that occurs on a very regular basis in the days prior to menstruation. Symptoms can be so severe as to be incapacitating. Premenstrual dysphoria is considered to be a biologically based mood disorder and has little to do with one's personality, ego strength, or level of emotional maturity. Treatments for premenstrual dysphoria are discussed in Chapter 26.

Possible Meltdown

The normal range for TSH is 0.3 to 3.0. In the past few years, medical researchers have found that slight elevations in TSH may either cause depression or make standard treatments with antidepressants ineffective. Thus even though you may be told, "Your thyroid levels are all in the normal range," please inquire regarding the specific TSH level. Generally, TSH levels above 2.5, although thought to be in the "normal" range, may suggest a very subtle version of hypothyroidism and may be associated with depression. Further, please note that some labs still report "normal TSH ranges" that are 0.4 to 5.0. More recent research suggests that 0.3 to 3.0 is more accurate. Finally, many primary-care doctors are unaware of this connection between slight TSH elevations and depression.

An Undiagnosed Medical Condition May Be Causing Your Mood to Change

Although there are numerous medical conditions that may cause or contribute to unpleasant emotions, the most common are picked up on a routine physical exam if it also includes a complete blood count and a test of thyroid functioning. Thyroid disease may be one of the most common medical causes for significant mood problems, especially depression. There are various types of lab measurements for thyroid functioning. The most important test to run is to assess TSH levels (TSH stands for thyroid stimulating hormone).

Taking Inventory of Prescription and Over-the-Counter Medications

The following lists indicate those medications that may cause emotional symptoms. If you are taking any of these drugs, it is important to speak with your physician or pharmacist and inquire about the possibility that the meds are the culprit in causing mood symptoms.

The following medications may cause depression, low energy, or low motivation:

◆ Antianxiety drugs: tranquilizers (e.g. Valium, Librium, Xanax, Ativan, Klonopin)

◆ Antihypertensives (for high blood pressure or to prevent migraine headaches)

◆ Antiparkinsonian drugs

◆ Birth-control pills

◆ Corticosteroids and other hormones (e.g. Cortisone, Prednisone, Estrogen, Premarin, Progesterone and derivatives, Provera, Depo-Provera)

The following medications may cause nervousness, irritability, or anxiety:

◆ Appetite suppressants

◆ Asthma medications

◆ Decongestants (pills and nasal sprays)

◆ Steroids (e.g. Prednisone, Cortisone)

◆ Tranquilizers (withdrawal from tranquilizers if they have been taken on a daily basis for more than two weeks)

If you learn that a particular drug is responsible for mood changes, you have two good options. First, as with our preceding example of Roberto, he still needed to be treated for high blood pressure, but a change in classes of high-blood-pressure medications did the trick. Oftentimes you can try other medication options for treating various medical illnesses that may be less problematic in terms of affecting moods. The second option is that if you cannot be switched to another type of medication, then often treatment with antidepressants or other types of psychiatric medications may be helpful.

Finally, many drugs interact with other medications, and at times these interactions may cause mood symptoms. Such interactions are very complex. Of course, bring this up with your physician. However, as noted earlier, another person to speak with about possible drug interactions that may cause emotional symptoms is your pharmacist. Pharmacists are often more knowledgeable regarding drug interactions than are physicians. They also have access to computer databases, which may provide information regarding complex drug interactions.

Recreational Drugs and Negative Moods

Nicotine, caffeine, alcohol … do any of these have a place in your life? How about methamphetamine, cocaine, marijuana, hallucinogens, or heroin? How about prescription painkillers used to relax or "get high"? We have all seen the old fried-egg commercial: "This is your brain … and this is your brain on drugs." Substance use and abuse may be one of the most common causes for emotional suffering. All of these drugs are *psychoactive*. They all influence brain functioning. Hard drugs do this in striking ways. Cocaine and methamphetamine (although they produce a sudden pleasurable feeling) are both associated with causing very severe depression and can cause paranoia and psychosis. Opiate abuse (heroin and narcotic pain killers such as codeine, hydrocodone, and oxycodone) can result in depression and very severe addictions.

Nicotine, caffeine, and alcohol, in comparison, may seem less severe in terms of their impact on brain functioning. However, excessive use can result in enormous psychological problems ranging from significant sleep disturbances and anxiety to severe major depression.

The big problem with recreational drugs is that their immediate impact makes people feel better (relaxed, "high," or euphoric). These drugs, in this way, are quite seductive. If you feel very anxious or depressed, a few stiff drinks of alcohol may temporarily ease your distress. However, it has been proven beyond a shadow of a doubt that alcohol use always makes depression and anxiety worse, in the long run. Likewise, during times of heightened stress, many people get worn out and feel exhausted. A cup of coffee or tea may be the kind of rocket fuel that rapidly energizes a person. Yet (as we'll see in Chapter 9), even modest amounts of caffeine can ruin sleep and also result in a significant increase in blood levels of adrenaline.

These are quick-fix solutions to distress that can backfire. Often, the overuse of recreational drugs is the primary or sole cause for terrible emotional suffering. Likewise, many people take psychiatric medications or are in psychotherapy, yet experience limited improvement from their treatment if they are overusing such drugs.

Here is another big problem. People who abuse alcohol and illicit substances generally feel very ashamed or embarrassed about it. When asked by physicians or psychotherapists

def•i•ni•tion

The term **psychoactive** means that a particular drug has a noticeable effect on brain functioning. Some psychoactive drugs have a negative impact on the brain, while others have a positive effect. For example, anti-convulsant drugs affect many types of nerve cells in the brain and successfully reduce seizures in people suffering from epilepsy. Antidepressants are often very effective in reducing the symptoms of severe depression.

about substance use, as many as 90 percent of people either deny substance use or greatly minimize it. As a therapist, I learned a long time ago that if one of my clients says, "I only have one beer a day," I'll ask, "Is that one can or one keg?"

I want to be very clear about this. The use or overuse of recreational drugs that is never reported to a physician or therapist may be the number-one reason why standard psychological and psychiatric treatments do not work! In my opinion, use of recreational drugs is not a moral issue (although some people might disagree with me on this point). It's just an issue of practical concern. These drugs throw a wrench into the brain. If human beings have any real chance of overcoming severe negative moods, the reduction or elimination of recreational drugs is essential.

In later chapters, we'll explore numerous effective ways to manage your mood. However, one of the most important steps to take is to make sure your brain is functioning optimally. This means taking seriously the information we've covered in this chapter and what we'll talk about in the next two chapters. To not proactively address these critical issues can spell disaster or significantly prolong suffering.

Possible Meltdown

If you have been using moderate to heavy amounts of recreational drugs on a daily basis, it is very important to consult with your physician before discontinuing use of the drug. Abrupt discontinuation of many of these drugs may result in substantial withdrawal symptoms. Sometimes "cold turkey" withdrawal from some types of drugs, including alcohol, can literally kill you. It is important to gradually discontinue under medical supervision.

The Least You Need to Know

◆ Changes in brain chemistry frequently cause emotional symptoms. Some medical illnesses change brain chemistry and may be the primary cause of emotional suffering.

◆ Many people unknowingly have underlying medical conditions that can cause mood changes.

◆ There are simple medical tests you can take that may determine if your suffering has a physical basis. Get this checked out!

◆ Co-occurring medical illnesses, medications, or drug abuse can contribute significantly to increased suffering, and can cause a failure to respond to standard psychological and psychiatric treatments.

◆ A host of prescription, over-the-counter, and recreational drugs are responsible for causing emotional suffering.

Chapter **9**

Sleep: The Guardian of the Brain

In This Chapter

- ◆ Sleep's role in maintaining good emotional functioning
- ◆ How caffeine can ruin sleep
- ◆ Common causes for sleep disturbances

Each night during sleep, in very complex ways, the brain performs maintenance on itself. A multitude of chemical reactions occur during sleep that keeps the brain operational and able to manage emotions more successfully. In this chapter, we will learn about sleep and how to maximize quality sleep.

Sleep: Necessary but Fragile

In studies of sleep deprivation, even modest amounts of deprivation, for example, two nights without sleep, result in the following:

- ◆ Fatigue (of course).
- ◆ Significant problems with the ability to think clearly and maintain attention.

- ◆ Impaired memory.

- ◆ Faltering of emotional controls. People are more emotionally sensitive and reactive, and they tend to take things more personally and have poorer frustration tolerance.

These problems are most pronounced when people do not get enough deep sleep (also referred to as restorative sleep). A night of sleep is no simple change in brain activity. In fact, the brain goes through a number of dramatically different stages of sleep each night. These are generally referred to as …

- ◆ Light sleep: twilight sleep, halfway between asleep and awake.

- ◆ Deep sleep: considered to be restorative sleep. Deep sleep is especially important for reducing daytime fatigue and maintaining good emotional control.

- ◆ REM sleep: REM is short for "rapid eye movement" sleep. Here the brain is very active; it is during REM sleep that most dreaming occurs.

Unfortunately even minor stress can disrupt sleep. When people are going through hard times, several forms of sleep disturbance can occur:

- ◆ Trouble falling asleep.

- ◆ Restless sleep: tossing and turning all night, with frequent awakenings.

- ◆ Early-morning awakening: waking up two to three hours before you want to wake up, (e.g. waking up at 4:30) and being unable to return to sleep even though feeling exhausted.

- ◆ *Hypersomnia*: Sleeping too much (10, 12, or 14 hours a day). Despite sleeping so much, most people with hypersomnia still feel very tired during the day.

Difficulty falling asleep is very common in people who are encountering stress in general or in those with anxiety disorders. Often when they try to go to sleep, despite feeling tired, the mind is still up and running. Generally here, people tend to worry, and the worries keep them awake and anxious. So they feel tired and wired. Stress and anxiety can also, at times, cause restless sleep.

Restless sleep also occurs during episodes of depression. Early-morning awakening is a classic and very common symptom of depression. Hypersomnia also occurs with depression.

def•i•ni•tion

Hypersomnia is sleeping too much. Although hypersomnia can occur in typical, garden-variety depressions, it is frequently associated with bipolar depression (a depressive episode seen in the context of bipolar illness). Hypersomnia is a red flag signaling the need to be evaluated for possible bipolar illness. This is especially important because many depressed people are treated with antidepressants. Antidepressant medications can be highly effective in treating most forms of depression. However, there are risks in using these drugs in individuals with bipolar disorder. Here antidepressants can make things worse by either triggering mania or making the overall disorder more severe.

Sleep Disturbances: The Usual Suspects

As mentioned, anxiety and stress in general, and depression, disrupt sleep. In fact, if you can successfully improve the quality of sleep, many stress symptoms subside. A number of stress symptoms are directly related to the sleep disturbance. In the last chapter, we saw how making sure that you don't have medical conditions or use drugs that cause stress symptoms is the first order of business in managing negative moods. The second crucial step is to aggressively deal with sleep problems. To do so is a very high-yield coping strategy.

In addition, many other factors commonly have a very negative impact on sleep. Most of these take their greatest toll on deep sleep, with the consequences we listed previously.

Drugs That Ruin Sleep

The following drugs can dramatically interfere with sleep:

◆ Alcohol

◆ Tranquilizers (e.g. Xanax, Valium, Klonopin, Ativan)

◆ Most prescription sleeping pills (believe it or not!)

◆ Caffeine

◆ Decongestants (pseudoephedrine, nasal sprays, and many over-the-counter cold medications)

◆ Steroids

◆ Broncodilators (used to treat asthma and other respiratory disorders)

Alcohol, tranquilizers, and prescription sleeping pills are all very potent in knocking a person out; they really put people to sleep. They are all central-nervous-system depressants. However, the problem with these drugs is that they are notorious for causing a particular sleep disturbance: reduced time spent in deep sleep. No kidding!

These drugs are seductive since they clearly help people to fall asleep (giving the impression that they actually help sleep disorders). However, most people simply do not realize that the price paid is decreased total time in deep, restorative sleep. So they may sleep, but it is poor quality sleep and the next day they have fatigue, poor concentration, irritability, and such. Alas, for some people, if these drugs are used daily for more than a month, two additional problems can occur: the drugs are habit forming (you can become dependent on them), and these drugs directly can cause depression.

> **Bet You Didn't Know**
>
> Two recently released prescription medications, Lunesta and Rozerem, appear to not adversely affect deep sleep and may not be habit forming. Check with your doctor.

Caffeine: The Real Sleeper

Caffeine use is widespread in our country. People like it because it has a rapid onset of positively experienced effects:

- Increases alertness.

- Combats fatigue.

- Caffeine also has mild, albeit transient antidepressant effects (depressed people feel a little less depressed for 20 minutes or so after ingesting caffeine).

No wonder it's such a popular drug. But then there are the downsides:

- It can cause anxiety.

- Has a negative impact on your sleep.

- Discontinuation can cause caffeine withdrawal symptoms.

The Problems Associated with Caffeine

The first problem with caffeine is that it can cause anxiety. Caffeine use significantly increases blood levels of stress hormones such as adrenaline. People undergoing substantial stress are already anxious, so it seems counterintuitive that they would ingest something that ultimately makes anxiety worse. But the fact is that during times of high stress, people certainly feel tense and anxious, but they are often also exhausted.

Worry, tension, and anxiety wear people out. And many people going through difficult times also experience at least some degree of depression. The immediate impact of reducing fatigue and depression is just positive enough that people ingest caffeine. The more immediate effect feels positive, but during the day as caffeine levels build up in the blood stream, and so do stress hormone levels, and stress symptoms are amplified. During stressful times, many people often have a gradual increase in caffeine use.

Another problem with caffeine is the impact it has on sleep. Everyone knows that a cup of coffee in the evening may make it harder to fall asleep. And this certainly is a fact. However, what is not widely known is the effect of caffeine on the quality of sleep. This is the major problem with caffeine. Moderate amounts of caffeine taken during the day can dramatically reduce the amount of time spent in deep sleep and contribute to frequent awakenings.

Then guess what? There is more fatigue the next day, and subsequently, people tend to gravitate toward more caffeine use to combat the fatigue. Now we have a very common vicious cycle.

And the third problem with caffeine is that if you consume even modest amounts of caffeine per day, "cold-turkey" discontinuation can cause caffeine withdrawal that includes headaches, jitteriness, and, oddly enough, difficulty falling asleep. Thus a very gradual withdrawal approach is important, for example, reducing your caffeine by 20 percent each week.

But watch out. As you begin to reduce caffeine use, guess what? A wave of fatigue will probably hit you (since your brain has been accustomed to using caffeine to stay energized.) However, after several weeks, the fatigue should diminish as you begin to have improvement in the quality of sleep. By then your brain is doing a better job at regulating itself rather than relying on drugs.

How Much Is Too Much?

Generally, caffeine amounts that exceed 500 mg per day are problematic. In some people (especially in those over the age of 60) amounts more than 250 mg per day can be problematic. The questionnaire below will help you determine your caffeine intake.

Caffeine Consumption Questionnaire

		Average number of ounces/ doses/ tablets per day	Average total per day
Beverages/Foods			
Coffee (6 oz)	125 mg	X _____	_____
Decaf coffee (6 oz)	5 mg	X _____	_____
Tea (6 oz)	50 mg	X _____	_____
Green tea (6 oz)	20 mg	X _____	_____
Hot cocoa (6 oz)	15 mg	X _____	_____
Caffeinated soft drinks (12 oz)	40–60 mg	X _____	_____
Chocolate candy bar	20 mg	X _____	_____
Over-the-Counter Medications			
Anacin	32 mg	X _____	_____
Appetite-control pills	100–200 mg	X _____	_____
Dristan	16 mg	X _____	_____
Excedrin	65 mg	X _____	_____
Extra-Strength Excedrin	100 mg	X _____	_____
Midol	132 mg	X _____	_____
NoDoz	100 mg	X _____	_____
Triaminicin	30 mg	X _____	_____
Vanquish	33 mg	X _____	_____
Vivarin	200 mg	X _____	_____
Prescription Medications			
Cafergot	100 mg	X _____	_____
Fiorinal	40 mg	X _____	_____
Darvon compound	32 mg	X _____	_____

Total mg caffeine per day _____

>250 mg per day may interfere with deep sleep

When people are going through a very difficult time in their lives, it may seem silly or trivial to think that reducing caffeine can make any meaningful kind of difference. Please do not take this suggestion lightly. Sleep is tremendously important for maintaining good emotional functioning. I have had numerous psychotherapy clients who have found out the truth. Reducing caffeine, especially if it is done gradually, can be a very effective way to help your brain to more effectively regulate itself and reduce negative mood symptoms.

Other Common Causes of Sleep Disturbance

The following medical conditions can greatly disrupt the quality of sleep:

- ◆ Chronic pain conditions
- ◆ Congestive heart failure
- ◆ Respiratory diseases
- ◆ Acid reflux
- ◆ Hot flashes associated with perimenopause
- ◆ Restless legs syndrome
- ◆ Sleep apnea
- ◆ Exercise, if it occurs within three hours before retiring to bed

Sleep apnea deserves special attention, because it is often not recognized by the sufferer. Apnea affects 13 million people in the United States, it can continue for years undetected, and yet be responsible for fatigue and considerable emotional suffering. Let's see what this is all about.

> **Bet You Didn't Know**
>
> The impact of marijuana and nicotine on sleep are not well understood. Major illicit drugs, especially cocaine and methamphetamine, absolutely destroy sleep. Among prescription drugs, antidepressants and the anticonvulsant drug, Gabatril, may increase the amount of time spent in deep sleep.

Gasping for Breath: Sleep Apnea

Apnea is where a person stops breathing for a brief period of time during the night. Most people do this three or four times a night and it's no big deal. But with clinical sleep apnea, the episodes occur 200 to 400 times per night. Spells of apnea may last 10 seconds, and up to 2 minutes. This greatly interferes with getting quality sleep.

The most common cause is what is referred to as obstructive sleep apnea. Here the muscles in the throat and upper airway relax too much, collapsing and blocking the airway. The person cannot breathe. As oxygen levels in the blood get lower and lower, the person will then begin to gasp. The gasping may sound like snoring or may include odd noises as inhalation tries to open up the blocked airway.

Many people who have sleep apnea never know it, and may suffer for years or even decades. However, it is hard to miss if you happen to be sleeping with someone who has apnea. The bed partner will surely recognize the loud snoring and other manifestations of apnea. If emotional stress symptoms are accompanied by noticeable daytime fatigue, it is always very important to determine if you snore. It may be a red flag for apnea.

Lots of people who snore may keep the whole neighborhood awake at night, and yet they do not know they snore or may strongly deny it. So asking your bed partner about the presence of snoring is important. Not everyone who snores has apnea, but all people who have apnea snore.

Fatigue + snoring = possible apnea.

If you suspect sleep apnea, talk to your doctor about seeing a sleep disorder specialist. Millions of people have apnea (about 4 percent of the population), don't know it, and suffer needlessly. There are medical treatments for apnea. I have had a number of my psychotherapy clients who suffered for years with fatigue and depression get diagnosed as having apnea. They didn't need psychotherapy. They didn't need antidepressants. They needed and responded to medical treatments for sleep apnea. After treatment, the change can often be remarkable!

Think About It

The simplest approach to treating apnea is to sew a tennis ball into the middle of the back of your pajamas. When people turn over on to their backs during sleep, the ball will cause a bit of discomfort and result in their rolling over on to their sides. Apnea is more pronounced if you sleep on your back. Medical treatments include the use of a devise called CPAP (continuous positive air pressure). It is a mask worn over the nose that pushes air into the airway under pressure. This is often quite effective. Should CPAP not be effective, there are some surgical procedures that may treat severe sleep apnea.

Exercise: For Better and For Worse

In Chapter 11, we will see the many benefits of exercise, including how it can significantly improve the quality of sleep. However, it is important to know that moderate-to-strenuous exercise occurring during a period of three hours before going to bed can interfere with the ability to go to sleep. Exercise has many positive effects; however, it does result in temporary increases in stress hormones, which stay in the body for two or three hours and may cause difficulties in falling asleep. So plan exercise for earlier in the day.

In the next chapter, we will explore a number of additional strategies that can very effectively enhance sleep and thus aid in coping with difficult moods.

The Least You Need to Know

- Good quality sleep is absolutely essential for effective emotional coping.

- Sleep can be easily disrupted by even moderate amounts of stress.

- Tranquilizers, prescription sleeping pills, and alcohol actually ruin quality sleep.

- Caffeine can cause a marked decrease in the amount of time spent in deep, restorative sleep.

- Sleep apnea is often not diagnosed and results in years or even decades of fatigue and emotional suffering.

Chapter 10

Potent Solutions for Improving Sleep

In This Chapter

◆ The importance of improving sleep

◆ Techniques used to enhance sleep

◆ High-yield strategies to calming down the stressed-out body

◆ The role of exercise in improving sleep

Deep in the brain stem are nerve centers that activate the brain. Every waking moment, these nerve centers spritz the brain with chemicals that maintain alertness and keep you awake. In order to fall asleep, you must shut down the activities in these brain-stem centers.

Four factors are known to activate these alerting nerve cells, all of which are directly play a role in preventing sleep:

◆ Stimulating drugs, such as caffeine.

◆ The presences of stress hormones in circulation.

◆ Activation from the body (especially pain and/or muscle tension).

◆ A busy brain: despite feeling tired, many of us find it very difficult to shut off worries. Often we just can't stop this thinking over and over again about various problems in our lives.

In this chapter, we will look at specific approaches that together can help you more easily go to sleep and stay asleep.

Preparing the Body and Mind for Sleep

Physicians call it *sleep hygiene*. Some of the critical factors in sleep hygiene include preparation for sleep that should actually begin about 6 P.M. For the brain to make a shift into a more quiet state, essential for falling asleep, it is important to begin reducing stimulation in the early evening. Most important is to avoid exposure to bright light (such as sunlight) after 6 P.M. Very bright light is an important environmental stimulus that has a profound impact on brain chemistry, the circadian rhythm, and sleep-wake cycles. Bright light enters the eyes, and then nerve impulses go directly from the retina to a part of the brain that is the primary control center for regulating sleep.

def•i•ni•tion

Sleep hygiene refers to a number of specific steps that one can take to improve the quality of sleep.

Other sources of stimulation to avoid include the following:

◆ Intense exercise for a period of time at least three hours before retiring to bed. As mentioned in the previous chapter, an immediate effect of exercise is to dump some stress hormones into the bloodstream, and it takes two to three hours for these to be eliminated from the body. Exercise needs to be done earlier in the day.

◆ Loud music and emotionally charged entertainment (such as Monday night football or exciting or intense movies). Coping effectively must include finding a balance in life (see Chapter 17), and, clearly, doing fun activities is a part of this. However, intense entertainment, despite its value in increasing happiness, generates the release of stress hormones, especially adrenaline and cortisol (both of which significantly interfere with the ability to sleep). Thus the key is to plan more exciting activities for earlier in the day. To maximize quality sleep, the evening must be devoted to more calming activities, such as listening to relaxing music or reading that does not generate a lot of emotional intensity.

◆ Engaging in emotional arguments with others. The evening is not the time to do this. Again, the problem is that these kinds of encounters increase the level of circulating stress hormones. Obviously, lots of times people can't really schedule arguments. But, you can make some choices about when to bring up certain on-going problems such as worries about finances or heated discussions with your teenagers.

Keep in mind that any activity (even positive ones) that generates stress hormones require two to three hours for these hormones to be broken down and excreted by the body.

Calming the Body

Oftentimes, muscle tension is very noticeable and even painful. Tension headaches and tight shoulders are common for many of us. However, it's a surprising fact that even significant muscle tension often becomes so pervasive, chronic, and continuous that people can actually, in a sense, get used to it, and fail to really notice it after a while.

I've seen many people who are clearly gritting their teeth, clenching their fists, and have tension written all over their faces, and when asked how they are feeling, they reply "Fine." The tension has become such a habitual part of daily life that they don't even notice it. It can be present every minute of the day, even when they're asleep. Many people constantly clinch their jaws and grind their teeth during the night. This muscle tension is a very common cause of sleep problems (it also can damage teeth). It just keeps pushing the buttons in the brain stem. People may sleep, but only go in to light sleep, getting little deep sleep.

We will now take a look at a very effective muscle relaxation exercise that can quickly reduce bodily tension. However, first a word or two about relaxation.

Many (if not most) people going through very stressful times have been given this form of useless advice: "Just relax." Such counsel is about as helpful as telling a depressed person to "Just cheer up." Keep in mind that the approach I am recommending is not about "just relaxing." This is a technique designed specifically to reduce activation in the brain stem and thus facilitate the ability to fall asleep.

It may be hard to will yourself into a state of relaxation. However, one particular systematic procedure has been shown to be highly effectively in reducing muscle tension, even in highly stressed individuals. The technique accomplishes this largely by mechanically manipulating tense muscles. Here is how it works.

During times of stress, particular muscles and muscle groups tend to become tense automatically. Progressive muscle relaxation techniques are designed to reduce tension in all the body's major muscle groups.

The relaxation procedure requires a period of time (about 10 minutes), and you need to find a time and a place where you will not be disturbed. Sit in a comfortable chair or recline on a couch, bed, or carpeted floor. Loosen any tight clothing and take off your shoes.

Close your eyes and take two slow, deep breaths. As you exhale slowly, notice the gradual release of tension in your chest and shoulder muscles. Feel the weight of your body against the chair (couch, floor) and the gentle pull of gravity as you settle into the chair. After a few moments, you can begin a series of simple exercises, tensing particular muscles, holding the tension for 10 seconds, and then releasing. Each time you tense and then release, you can enhance the effect by paying special attention to the experience of relaxation and letting go that occurs immediately after release.

Allow 15 to 20 seconds between each muscle group before proceeding to the next. The tensing exercises begin with the feet and progress like this:

1. Feet/toes (like you are making a fist with your feet)

2. Calves/lower legs

3. Thighs

4. Buttocks (squeeze together)

5. Abdomen

6. Lower back (arch)

7. Chest (accomplish this by taking in a deep breath and holding it hold it for a count of three)

8. Hands (make fists)

9. Upper arms

10. Shoulders (shrug)

11. Face (squeeze eyes and purse lips)

12. Face (open eyes and mouth)

Many experts on relaxation techniques recommend 10 to 15 minutes twice a day to go through this exercise, especially when you're first learning the procedure. It is best to take plenty of time when first learning the procedure. However, after about a week, many people find that they can move through the various muscle groups more quickly, reducing the time it takes to four to five minutes. This simple and effective technique can, of course, be done several times during the day to promote relaxation, but it is right before going to sleep that it is most effective in promoting better-quality sleep.

Another effective way to reduce muscle tension will come as no surprise: soaking in a tub of hot water. This easy way to reduce tension can also be a pleasant way to be good to yourself. However, there is an important point to keep in mind. To enter deep sleep, the human body needs to cool off. Thus getting overheated in a bath or a hot tub should be done 1 to 1 $\frac{1}{2}$ hours before bed. This allows muscles to begin relaxing, and yet there is plenty of time to cool down before retiring.

Also if you are waking up in the middle of the night and having a hard time going back to sleep, this brief exercise can be very useful in helping you fall back asleep.

Remember, tense muscles keep the brain on alert and interfere with sleep. These techniques are not just about "relaxing"; they have been designed to directly shut off this source of arousal, loosening the muscles and calming the brain.

Calming Bedtime Snacks

Dietary approaches to stress management are discussed in more detail in Chapter 11. Here we'll take a brief look at evening snacks that can help you relax and, conversely, at snacks that can keep you awake (and thus should be avoided).

In general, carbohydrates (without proteins) are often calming. These include certain fruits: bananas, plums, grapes, cherries, apples, pears, oranges, peaches, high-fiber breakfast cereals, or oatmeal. Simple carbohydrates (simple sugars) such as candy bars, donuts, and ice-cream taste great, but may cause some activation rather than calm. The trouble with simple sugars is that they may in fact soothe and calm rather quickly, but shortly thereafter, have a rebound effect, and can cause increased activation or moodiness. They can also contribute to middle-of-the-night awakening.

Think About It

Remember to stay away from things that contain caffeine (not just coffee, tea, and sodas, but also chocolate).

Try to avoid snacks that include large amounts of protein (e.g. eggs, meat, nuts, and cheese). It has been clearly demonstrated that protein tends to cause activation.

Creating the Right Bedroom Environment

There are five key factors to making your bedroom environment conducive to sleep. Some of these are pretty obvious, but take them seriously. To get good sleep you must pull out all of the stops and tackle sleep problems on several different levels.

◆ Reducing noise. If you live near a busy street or in an apartment where neighbors are often loud, earplugs or a sound machine (one creating white noise—sometimes a fan can accomplish the same thing) will help to drown out noise.

◆ Make sure you have a comfortable mattress (not too soft and not too hard).

◆ Keep the room temperature comfortable, and a bit on the cool side. Cooler temperatures help people get into deeper sleep.

◆ Use blackout shades to prevent early-morning light from waking you up too early.

◆ It's best not to watch TV or read exciting novels in bed. Time spent in bed should be reserved for only two activities: sleep and sex. If you become accustomed to watching intense TV shows in bed, the brain gets programmed to be more activated when getting into bed (as if anticipating excitement). This kind of conditioning really does occur.

Some people have tried to quiet their busy brains by counting sheep. The concept of counting sheep seems sound; after all, what could be more boring than to count sheep? Replacing stressful thoughts with boring ones can reduce arousal, but the sheep-counting approach often just doesn't work. Why? When people are intensely preoccupied with stressful life events, it can be very difficult to shut off these troublesome thoughts long enough to even imagine a sheep. One British study actually demonstrated this when they found that stressed-out people can't visually imagine sheep for more than about a minute.

A more effective approach is to read a boring book or watch a boring TV show. These are external stimuli that can, at times, pull one's thoughts away from worries. If this works, great. However, for many, even this is not terribly effective. Three other approaches hold more promise.

Avoid Evening Conflicts

Not infrequently, worrisome thoughts are sparked by stressful interactions or conflicts with others in the hours prior to bedtime (such as an argument with your children or spouse, or an anxiety-ridden discussion about finances). A first helpful strategy we've already considered is to avoid getting into arguments or conflicts later in the evening. This is not just about avoiding activities that can increase stress hormones. It is also designed to reduce provocative situations that stir up both strong emotions and stress hormones.

Communicate Your Stresses

A second approach takes aim at recurring worries, those thoughts that bounce around in your mind, accomplish nothing, and provoke stress. Noted psychologist James Pennebaker has demonstrated that two simple approaches are often surprisingly effective in shutting off worry. The first is this. As soon as you notice that you are into worrying mode, get out of bed, sit down at a table, and write out on a piece of paper exactly what thoughts have been reverberating in your mind. There is something about getting these thoughts out of your head and onto paper that reduces internal worry.

It may seem hard to believe that something this simple could actually work. All you need to do is to experiment. Just do this one or two times and judge for yourself.

Another version of this, recommended by Dr. Pennebaker, is that, instead of writing the worries down, speak into a small hand-held micro-cassette recorder. Again, the intent is to get these troublesome thoughts out of your head. You speak them out loud and record the thoughts. One of Pennebaker's research subjects referred to his micro-cassette recorder as a "psychic vacuum cleaner" … it is as if the troublesome thoughts were being sucked out of his mind.

The "Eyes Have It"

Another powerful technique has been shown by studies over the past 10 years to be surprisingly effective. The technique involves back-and-forth eye movements. This approach takes two minutes, it's painless, and it is thought to rapidly reduce stress by disrupting and shutting off repetitive thoughts. I must admit that on first glance this may seem bizarre.

Dr. Stickgold, a researcher from Harvard, has demonstrated that back-and-forth eye movements appear to turn on what's known as the parasympathetic nervous system (PNS). When the PNS turns on, it reduces physical stress. It is the primary biological mechanism for turning on the relaxation response in the body and in the brain. There is a decrease in heart rate, blood pressure, and muscle tension.

This technique also (for reasons that are not well understood) shuts off repetitive worry. Often without wanting to or choosing to think about stressful things, thoughts automatically whiz through a person's mind. Some researchers have hypothesized that the brain has neural circuits or loops that get activated and appear to reverberate. The result is repetitive, troublesome thoughts that seem to serve little useful purposes and generate stress and interfere with sleep.

The eye-movement technique described here can often shut off such recurrent thoughts and may do so by some direct effect on these neural brain circuits. Here's how the technique works:

1. Sit in a comfortable chair or in your bed and take a moment to relax. Then, while holding your neck and head still, begin moving your eyes from side to side (as if watching the ball go back and forth in a ping-pong game), taking about 1 second to shift your eyes from right to left and back to the right.

2. Repeat this back-and-forth movement about 20 times. Then stop, close your eyes, and relax.

3. For a moment, scan through your body and simply be aware of any particular sensations of tension or discomfort. Simply notice it. When you do, you'll likely notice that there is less tension.

4. Repeat step one; take a calming, deep breath, and then begin back-and-forth eyes movements. When finished, close your eyes and relax. A few seconds later, do it again, a third time. About 75 percent of people will clearly notice a calming of mental activity and a feeling of relaxation.

After going through this exercise a few times, you'll likely get the hang of it. Thereafter you can do eye movements as you get into bed at night, repeating them two or three times. Some people find that they can eventually achieve the same results by doing the eye movements with their eyes closed.

This approach (especially when combined with the relaxation exercise mentioned previously) is often quite effective in promoting drowsiness and sleep. Additionally, eye movements can also be used during the day to reduce stress and promote tension reduction.

I wouldn't be surprised if this technique sounds pretty weird to you. It certainly did to me when I first heard about it. However, eye movements (and other repetitive body movements, as previously described) as an anxiety-reduction technique have caught on among many mental-health therapists both in the United States and in Europe and currently are the focus of intense study by neuroscientists.

One thing that is good about this approach is that, when positive results occur, they generally are immediate. Try it even once and see how it works for you.

Possible Meltdown

Those who wear contact lenses are advised to remove contacts before using eye-movement techniques.

Stabilizing Your Circadian Rhythm

The *circadian rhythm* involves a complex number of biological changes that occur in a highly regular basis during each day. They include the release of a number of hormones at particular times of the day (for example, growth hormone is released at night during deep sleep). Other physical aspects of the circadian rhythm include changes in digestion, the functioning of the immune system, variations in body temperature, and the chemical regulation of the brain.

Optimal sleep and the ability to maintain adaptive emotional control depend heavily on the stability of the circadian rhythm. Two primary factors are responsible for maintaining the appropriate function of the circadian rhythm. And these two activities have a powerful impact on establishing and preserving good-quality sleep.

The first is a highly effective technique, but quite frankly, is something that many people just simply do not want to do. It is to establish very regular bedtimes and regular times for waking up each day. This high degree of regularity helps to stabilize the circadian rhythm. The key to this approach is to decide on a specific half-hour window of time for going to bed and for waking up, let's say, getting to bed between 10 and 10:30 P.M. and waking up between 6:30 and 7 A.M. For this to be effective, it needs to be the rule of thumb every day—weekdays, weekends, and holidays.

def•i•ni•tion

The term **circadian** comes from the root words circa (meaning about or approximately) and dies (meaning a day) … thus "about a day." The circadian rhythm is controlled in the brain by what is known as the "endogenous circadian pacemaker." This is the internal biological clock that regulates the release of many hormones, influences sleep and awake times, and controls body temperature. All of these fluctuations in the body occur at approximately the same time each day. And the rhythm repeats itself every 24 hours.

Lots of people, understandably, do not want to do this. It interferes with their lifestyle. I can appreciate this, however it is important to emphasize: this approach is extremely effective in enhancing the ability to handle strong emotions. The results are not seen immediately. It generally takes a month of this routine to start to see results.

The second approach is to get at least 10 minutes of bright light exposure early in the morning (preferably during the first half hour after waking up. In order to accomplish this, the light has to be high intensity. This can only be achieved by either going outside (without sunglasses) or by the use of a commercially available light box. Light boxes and what is referred to as high-intensity light therapy for treating stress will be discussed later in Chapter 11.

Exercise in Order to Sleep Better

Although exercising right before bed can interfere with sleep, as noted previously, there is more than 25 years of solid research demonstrating that one of the most powerful ways to improve sleep is to engage in regular exercise. In Chapter 11 we'll take a closer look at the multitude of benefits from exercise, but for now, just a few comments about exercise and sleep.

The good news is that the type of exercise that works need not be high-intensity aerobic exercise. You don't have to be a jock to have exercise help with sleep. What is required is some form of exercise each day. Even walking 15 minutes a day can accomplish this. Other types of exercise may also do the trick such as gardening or cleaning the house. If people are very fit, then jogging, swimming, running, and such, of course are beneficial.

The main gain from exercise is that after three months of regular daily exercise, you should see a noticeable increase in the amount of time spent in deep (restorative) sleep and less-frequent middle-of-the-night awakenings.

The Least You Need to Know

- People often dismiss the techniques of sleep hygiene because they seem trivial in the light of current, significant life stresses, yet maintaining good quality sleep is critically dependent on preserving good quality sleep.

- Several things commonly interfere with getting quality sleep. The best approach is to attack this problem on several fronts using a combination of simple, effective strategies.

- Most approaches to improving sleep can have rather immediate benefits.

- Regular exercise (even walking) has been shown to significantly increase the amount of deep, restorative sleep.

11

Additional Strategies to Calm the Body and the Mind

In This Chapter

- How exercise quickly changes levels of brain chemicals that regulate mood

- Using exercise to solve feelings of anger or intense irritability

- The effectiveness of exercise in treating depression

- Dietary strategies and bright light exposure

In this chapter, we are going to expand our repertoire of strategies to calm your body and reduce stress. The focus here will be on the role of exercise, diet, and exposure to bright light (which is a surprisingly robust way to alter brain chemistry).

The Benefits of Exercise

Among all self-help approaches, exercise is one of the most potent approaches to reducing nervousness, irritability, moodiness, and depression. Although it's a real challenge for many people to start and maintain exercise, the benefits are substantial.

Anthropologists have determined that early humans, surviving by hunting and gathering, had to be moderately physically active for about two or three hours per day. This was true for the earliest humans; it persisted for five million years, and has changed only in very recent times. Especially during the past century, Americans have become increasingly sedentary.

Movement directly changes brain functioning by increasing levels of neurotransmitters that regulate moods such as serotonin (90 minutes of exercise doubles the amount of serotonin in the brain). Increased levels of brain serotonin reduce anxiety, irritability, and depression. Exercise also activates the release of morphine-like chemicals in the brain, endorphins. These brain molecules produce a calming effect.

In addition to direct mood-enhancing effects, exercise has been shown to significantly affect one's perspective. Southern California psychologist, Dr. Robert Thayer, has conducted research that demonstrates that high levels of physical tension combined with low levels of energy result in a noticeable increase in negative and pessimistic thinking.

Possible Meltdown

Exercise generally is safe and has many positive health benefits. However, beginning a new exercise program and pushing yourself too hard can result in injuries. Additionally, if you have diabetes, heart disease, lung disease, or other significant health problems, please be sure to consult with your physician before beginning a program of exercise.

During high-tension/low-energy times of the day, people are much more likely to view current life problems from an especially negative point of view. They are more prone to feel helpless and pessimistic about relationship problems, financial worries, or any number of other distressing life occurrences.

Interestingly, Dr. Thayer has been able to show that decreasing physical-tension levels (exercise in general may do this, but especially helpful are stretching exercises or yoga), and increasing energy quickly shifts thinking from negative to more positive and optimistic. Increasing energy can be achieved by consuming caffeine, but as we have seen in previous chapters, this is not generally a wise choice to make. What works well, and has few if any side effects, is exercise.

What Dose of Exercise Works?

An important point to make is that getting control over negative thinking need not involve prolonged or strenuous exercise. Even 2 minutes of stretching and a 10- to 15-minute brisk walk will often do the trick.

This level and duration of exercise is something realistic that many people are, in fact, able to do. It's not like the prolonged commitment of preparing for the Olympics or the more time-consuming exercise that is a part of an athlete's life.

This form of exercise is a "quick fix"; it works rapidly, doesn't take a lot of time, and the results last about an hour to an hour and a half. Once people try this and find out how easy and effective it can be, it can easily be woven into the fabric of everyday life. It is an especially good technique to use strategically during times of the day when you feel exhausted or when you notice that you are worrying or brooding. Try it out twice and see what you think!

Bet You Didn't Know

In the brain, low levels of serotonin appear to be directly related to increased irritability and anger. Once again, 10 minutes of fairly intense exercise is often a very effective solution for turning down the volume on anger. A 10-minute brisk walk, jog, or run (depending on your level of fitness), or chopping wood, or digging holes in your garden with a shovel, can be action strategies that take direct aim at reducing the intensity of anger or irritation.

Longer-Term Benefits of Exercise

Researchers have taken lab rats and corporate executives as subjects to test the impact of exercise on stress reactions (presumably no connection between the rats and the CEOs … well, maybe not). They hooked them up to devices that measure heart rate, blood pressure, and other physical aspects of anxiety and set off a loud "bang." All subjects have an immediate startle reaction; the significance was in measuring the intensity of the reaction and how long it took both people and rats to calm down.

Then they had both groups of subjects exercise daily for 4 months (the rats were made to exercise on a treadmill device where they had to walk for 20 minutes a day). Four months later they repeated the experiment. The loud "bang" still produced an immediate startle reaction. But the increase in physical arousal (e.g. blood pressure) was a lot less. Also, both groups calmed down more quickly. Psychologists referred to this as *emotional recovery*, how long it takes to regain composure.

def•i•ni•tion

Emotional recovery is the amount of time it takes a person to calm down after a stressful event. The calming generally refers to decreased physical activation, but also includes emotionally feeling relaxed and in control.

The exercise "therapy" had a direct impact on the brain, resulting in much-less-intense reactivity. Certainly not a quick fix, but a rather dramatic testimony to the benefits of exercise and how it helps people cope more effectively.

How Exercise Can Strengthen and Repair the Brain

Brains can be damaged over a period of time due to the effects of aging, drug overuse or abuse, and exposure to severe chronic stress. Yet the nervous system has an exceptional ability to repair itself. In certain nerve cells, a protein is made and secreted: *brain-derived neurotrophic factor* (BDNF, for short). This protein helps to repair damaged nerve cells, and in one part of the brain it helps to activate a process called neurogenesis. Neurogenesis is the birth of new nerve cells (prior to 2001, this was a fact unknown to neuroscientists).

Guess what? Three things are potent activators of this protein, BDNF. Two are psychiatric medications: lithium and antidepressants. The third is, as you may have guessed, exercise. Exercise can actually help your brain maintain and repair itself. BDNF turns on neurogenesis in a part of the brain, the hippocampus, which is an important brain structure that helps to control strong emotions.

def•i•ni•tion

Brain-derived neurotropic factor (BDNF) is a protein that is considered to be "neuro-protective." It helps facilitate the repair and maintenance of nerve cells in the brain. It also can activate neurogenesis, which is the birth of new nerve cells.

Exercise, Moodiness, and Depression

In a review of recent research on the impact of exercise on moodiness and depression, Professor Larry Leith found that 80 percent of studies report significant reductions in depression occurring just a few weeks after beginning a program of regular exercise. Some studies have compared the effect of exercise to treatment outcomes with prescription antidepressant medications. The results are that regular exercise can reduce depression symptoms just as effectively as antidepressants.

This varies from study to study. Probably the best approach is 10 minutes of brisk walking, jogging, or running, twice a day, every day. Other studies recommend 20 to 30 minutes, three or four times per week. The remarkable finding is that the intensity of exercise need not be unrealistically high. People can simply exercise in keeping with their level of fitness (e.g. those who are not too fit can walk; those very fit can run or swim vigorously). The key is, however, to have it be aerobic exercise (getting you to breathe more rapidly and increasing the heart rate).

More intense exercise may be required for maximizing cardio-vascular health. But these smaller "doses" of exercise are generally effective for improving mood.

The Big Hurdle

Exercise may be the single-most potent strategy for defeating the biological aspects of stress, anxiety, and depression. But let's be honest—it can be very difficult to get motivated to go and exercise. In my experience, one viable approach to this problem is to hire a trainer at a sports club or enlist a "buddy" to join you, to encourage you, and to insist that you follow through.

If you can start a program of regular exercise and stick with it, the benefits can be enormous. You'll not only reduce your stress, but also will improve your overall health, enhance the quality of your sleep, and increase your feelings of self-esteem.

Bet You Didn't Know
As mentioned in Chapter 9, regular exercise has been clearly associated with improving the quality of sleep (especially increasing the amounts of time spent in deep, restorative sleep). As a result, people cope better with difficult life circumstances. Exercise has been shown to also improve health by decreasing cholesterol, decreasing blood pressure, improving circulation, reducing constipation, promoting weight loss or preventing of weight gain, enhancing pain tolerance, and reducing muscle tension.

Relaxation Rocks

Repetitive movements have also been shown to reduce stress. These include some forms of exercise, like walking. But it also includes rhythmic and repetitive motions such as rocking in a rocking chair, knitting, chewing gum, and even bouncing your leg up and down—over and over again. This last approach may be seen as an annoying, nervous habit, but guess what? Like other repetitive movements, it increases brain serotonin levels and provides some calming effects.

You Are What You Eat: Dietary Strategies

Brain chemistry depends, in part, on the availability of certain essential amino acids. These molecules, which must be derived from your diet, are the building blocks of key brain chemicals (such as serotonin, dopamine, and norepinephrine). A substantial body

Think About It _____

The human body makes a number of amino acids. However, essential amino acids are not produced in your body and must be derived from your diet. Several of these are the key ingredients in the manufacturing of brain neurotransmitters that regulate mood. Two that you may have heard of are tryptophan and tyrosine.

of research has supported the fact that many people suffering from depression and chronic stress have diminished levels of one or more of these important brain chemicals.

A normal, reasonably healthy diet generally supplies adequate amino acids for the body, although these molecules (owing to their size and chemical properties) only cross into the brain in fairly small amounts. The primary strategy in using dietary approaches to treating negative moods is to increase the amount and availability of selected amino acids in the brain. When they are available in adequate amounts in the brain, they are taken into nerve cells and transformed into mood-regulating neurotransmitters.

Dietary Strategies

You may find that specific dietary approaches may make a noticeable change in your mood. The two target symptoms for dietary "treatment" are the following:

- anxiety (restlessness, nervousness, irritability, tension, agitation, difficulty falling asleep)

- fatigue (lethargy, exhaustion, lack of energy, lack of motivation, impaired concentration)

Before getting to specifics, I'd like to point out some limitations to dietary strategies. First, not everyone responds. For some people, the effects are substantial and ultimately very helpful. But for others, there may be no noticeable effects. People vary a lot in terms of their individual biology and metabolism. There is simply no way to know ahead of time if this will be effective for you. But it's a simple experiment to conduct, and if the approaches work, you should feel the difference right away.

Limitation number two is that these approaches are "quick fixes." They are not the cure for significant mood problems, although they can be successfully used on a day-to-day basis to have some control over those especially stressful times of the day. Being able to do something, to take action, and feel a positive result cannot only change one's mood but can also feel empowering.

Targeting Nervousness, Irritability, and Anxiety

As we have seen previously, one of the most important brain chemicals for regulating mood is serotonin. With increases in serotonin, nervousness, irritability, and anxiety often diminish. The amino-acid building block for serotonin is tryptophan. Generally a normal diet provides adequate amounts of tryptophan to the blood stream. The trick is getting it into the brain (tryptophan is a large molecule that has some difficulty passing through the *blood-brain barrier* and into the brain).

One way to facilitate the entry of tryptophan into the brain is to increase the amount of insulin in the blood stream. With increased insulin, a window opens into the blood-brain barrier, and tryptophan can more easily enter. An effective way to increase insulin is to eat carbohydrates. For this to work, the snack or meal should ideally include low-glucose carbohydrates such as beans, some grains and whole-grain breads, peaches, apples, bran, pears, cherries, grapes, plums, and oranges. Low-glucose carbohydrates more slowly increase the amount of glucose (sugar) levels to enter the blood stream.

Simple carbohydrates like sugars and some starches (high-glucose carbohydrates) can produce a very temporary improvement in mood (one reason that people often choose such snacks). But this is often followed by a "sugar crash," causing an intensification of anxiety and sometimes depression (plus, of course, lots of calories and weight gain). A sugar crash can leave people feeling like they are on an emotional roller coaster. Thus avoid the following: donuts, french fries, candy, and (unfortunately) chocolate (I hate having to deliver that bit of bad news). One exception is if you eat simple carbohydrates and immediately follow it with vigorous exercise, then it will not result in the sugar crash.

def•i•ni•tion

The **blood-brain barrier** is a complex arrangement of tightly packet cells in the brain that operate to keep certain potentially dangerous chemicals out of the brain. The blood-brain barrier also, to some degree, can make it difficult for certain large molecules to enter brain tissue.

Targeting Fatigue and Low Motivation

The brain chemicals that increase energy, motivation, and mental alertness are dopamine and norepinephrine. Both require the amino acid tyrosine as a building block.

Proteins are made up of long chains of amino acids, including tyrosine. Protein snacks have been used for a number of years by the armed forces as a way for pilots to maintain energy and alertness. However, for this strategy to work, the protein snack needs to be eaten alone or with only a very small amount of carbohydrates (if proteins are eaten along with substantial amounts of carbohydrates, the energizing effect is lost). The best proteins include protein powder, tofu, eggs, fish, chicken, turkey, Gouda cheese, Monterey jack cheese, nonfat cottage cheese, buttermilk, and lean beef.

Here's a reminder: be careful not to eat protein snacks too close to bedtime, as the increased energy and alertness can, at times, interfere with sleep.

Something Fishy Is Going On Here

One dietary option currently holds promise for providing more long-term effects on mood: omega-3 fatty acids. The main dietary source for omega-3 fatty acids is fish. Fish-oil capsules can also be purchased as an over-the-counter product at health-food stores. Preliminary studies have suggested a lower incidence of mood disorders in cultures that have omega-3 fatty acids as a regular part of their diets.

Some promising studies at the National Institute of Health tend to support the finding that treatment with supplemental dietary omega-3 fatty acids can reduce negative mood swings in people who are depressed or suffer from bipolar disorder. A few studies have shown that omega-3 fatty acids also can reduce moodiness in people who do not suffer from these more severe disorders. Omega-3 is a critical ingredient in nerve-cell membranes, and a diet including this fatty acid may actually help repair or build healthy brain cells.

The most effective approach to the use of omega-e fatty acids is to take 1 to 2 grams per day. It is also very helpful to, at the same time, reduce intake of omega-6 fatty acids. The balance of these two fatty acids is important in the brain. The main source of omega-6 fatty acids is from animal tissue (meat and lard, which, unfortunately, is used in many junk foods).

This dietary approach does not produce a rapid change in mood, but rather is usually successful after several weeks to several months of the new diet. The best sources of omega-3 fatty acids are fish and fish oil. Flaxseed oil may also be helpful in stabilizing mood.

Combating Fatigue

Fatigue associated with chronic stress, moodiness, and depression can be overpowering. It's unpleasant, it interferes with work and school, and it contributes to withdrawal and emotional paralysis. I'd like to offer an "energize-yourself" checklist (strategies aimed at restoring energy and combating fatigue).

Upon awakening:

- ◆ Get up, once up, and do not lie back down (no matter what!).

- ◆ Eat a protein-rich breakfast with little or no carbs.

- ◆ Shower and dress.

- ◆ Keep caffeine use at a minimum.

- ◆ Energize yourself with one to two minutes of stretching.

- ◆ Take a 10-to-15-minute walk outside.

- ◆ Get bright-light exposure during your walk; don't wear sunglasses (unless you have a diagnosed disease of the eyes and have been instructed by your doctor to wear sunglasses).

During the day:

- ◆ Keep involved with others.

- ◆ At all costs, avoid lying down during the day.

- ◆ Avoid naps (most times, naps will actually increase fatigue and lower mood in people who are depressed).

- ◆ Eat a mid-afternoon protein snack.

- ◆ Choose the late afternoon for more intense exercise.

In the evening:

- ◆ A meal higher in carbohydrates may promote relaxation as you begin to wind down prior to bedtime

- ◆ Use sleep-enhancement approaches outlined in the previous chapters.

What can you expect from the strategies mentioned here? Noticable increase in day time energy, more productivity, an increased sense of motivation to complete tasks and less moodiness. These strategies are a recipe for a productive day.

Catching Some Rays

All animals studied, from snails to humans, have shown that certain environmental stimuli can have a powerful influence on internal biological processes, affecting hormone levels, body temperature, sleep cycles, activity levels, and brain chemistry. Most anthropologists agree that the human race first emerged in equatorial Africa some 5 to 6 million years ago. For hundreds of thousands of years, primitive humans lived and evolved in this ecological niche that is characterized by 12 hours of sunlight, 365 days per year—no seasonal variations in the amount of daily sunlight. Across eons, all species must biologically adapt to local environmental conditions to survive, and this undoubtedly occurred for our ancient ancestors.

There is a growing body of research suggesting that bright-light stimulation does have a significant impact on the functioning of the human brain (our brains likely evolved over the millennia accustomed to getting 12 hours per day of such stimulation). And it appears that maintaining normal levels of brain chemicals, such as serotonin, has come to rely, in part, on getting a certain amount of bright-light stimulation each day.

Most of us, these days, are exposed to substantially less than 12 hours a day of bright light. For 20 percent of the population, reduced light exposure creates low energy and mild mood changes, such as low motivation and irritability. For others (about 10 percent of the population), it can provoke serious depression, commonly referred to as *seasonal affective disorder*. Decreased exposure to bright light can also provoke episodes of depression in people suffering from bipolar disorders. As the name of the disorder implies, this depression is often associated with the decreased light exposure seen during winter months. However, it's also commonly seen in people who routinely work night shifts.

def•i•ni•tion

Seasonal affective disorder is a type of depression that is caused primarily by reduced photic stimulation (decreased amounts of light entering the eye). This type of depression is most frequently accompanied by increased appetite, weight gain, lethargy, fatigue, low motivation, and hypersomnia (sleeping too much).

Light therapy may be the solution. The key to successful light therapy has nothing to do with light hitting the skin, but actually with light entering the eye. Light energy entering the eye and striking the retina activates a nerve pathway that penetrates deep into the brain. It is here that the stimulation influences levels of neurotransmitters, especially serotonin. The amount of light entering the eye matters: it must be at least 2500 lux of light energy. Regular indoor lighting may be able to produce 400-500 lux. Thus ordinary lighting will not do the trick.

Bright-light exposure can be accomplished by two means. One is by purchasing and using a commercially available "light box." Light boxes emit about 10,000 lux of light energy. The second approach is by getting exposure to sunlight by going outdoors. Even on a cloudy day there is enough bright light to stimulate the brain (10,000 lux on a cloudy day; 100,000 lux on a sunny day).

How much exposure is required? The length of exposure varies tremendously from one individual to another. For some people, as little as 10 minutes per day is all that is needed. Others may require up to two hours. Probably a half-hour is the average.

If you've considered using a light box, you'll need to place it in a convenient spot, such as on your desk. For adequate amounts of light to stimulate the retina, you must sit within $2\frac{1}{2}$ feet of the light source. Those who use light boxes do not stare directly into the light. Rather, they sit in front of the light and often read, pay bills, or make phone calls.

If you prefer to try out natural sunlight, be sure to use sunscreen to avoid excessive UV-ray exposure, and go outside (bright sunlight and a 15-minute walk are a good combination). Remember, all that is required is light entering the eyes. So leave the sunglasses off!

Possible Meltdown

Recent studies have shown that 25 percent of people suffering from severe seasonal affective disorder have bipolar illness. If you are experiencing a moderate to severe seasonal depression, please consult a physician or mental-health professional before using high-intensity light therapy. In people suffering from bipolar disorder, excessive light exposure can trigger a manic episode. This is not likely to occur if the mood changes are only mild.

Bright-light exposure can have other benefits as well. First thing in the morning, bright-light exposure can help you feel more energized. It may also help to normalize sleep patterns and stabilize your circadian rhythm. Early-morning light exposure is especially helpful if it is combined with exercise (for example, taking a short walk outdoors).

One additional note of caution is this: bright-light exposure may not be safe for individuals with certain eye disorders. (If you suffer from any diseases of the eye, please consult with your eye doctor before using light therapy.)

The Least You Need to Know

- ◆ Exercise is beneficial in reducing a large array of distressing emotions.

- ◆ Longer-term programs of exercise can substantially reduce emotional reactivity. It is a way of not only conditioning the body but also conditioning the emotional brain to better handle stress.

- ◆ Long-term use of omega-3 fatty acids can reduce moodiness and increase stress tolerance.

- ◆ High-intensity light therapy can reduce moodiness and lethargy.

12

Over-the-Counter and Herbal Products for Managing Moods

In This Chapter

- ◆ Herbals and other over-the-counter (OTC) mood regulators
- ◆ OTC products that have been found to contain toxic contaminates
- ◆ Why natural does not necessarily mean safe
- ◆ Caution about the use of St. John's Wort

For many years people have sought nonmedical remedies for mood problems. Health food stores are filled with many products purporting to reduce stress or depression. Many such claims are not supported by scientific research. However, a few over-the-counter and herbal products have been shown to have positive effects on mood. We'll take a close look at such products in this chapter and consider the risks and benefits.

"Natural Products"

The herbal industry generates billions of dollars per year. These products are widely used in both the United States and in many European countries. Many people have an understandable desire to use herbal and other so-called natural dietary supplements. Some of the products we will consider in this chapter do have research support for safety and efficacy in managing moods such as nervousness, anxiety, and depression. And many are not plagued by the numerous side effects often associated with prescription psychiatric drugs.

There are three main precautions regarding the use of over-the-counter (OTC) products to treat your mood:

 ◆ **Not all OTC products are created equal.** Because herbal and other OTC products are not monitored by the Food and Drug Administration, there are no uniform standards for either quality or strength. Even though certain products may claim to have a particular milligram dosage, there are instances in which some products actually have little active ingredient. Some have been found to contain contaminants, and, on occasion, even toxic plants. Remember, natural does not necessarily mean safe. Thus, it's important to purchase OTC medications from reputable health-food stores, or buy products manufactured by well-established pharmaceutical companies. (Many of the more well-known drug companies have gotten into the herbal business in recent years.) Should you choose to use these products, be sure to check the labels to see if they have a stamp of approval from one of two independent agencies: USP (U.S. Pharmacopia) or NSF (National Sanitation Foundation). These organizations evaluate OTC herbal products to make sure they contain the advertised ingredients at the appropriate doses, and they test for the presence of contaminants. Approval of products by these organizations does not attest to effectiveness of the products, just quality control with regard to ingredients.

 ◆ **Not all OTC products are safe.** Although most are safe if taken as directed or taken alone, excessive doses can cause problems. Also, many serious difficulties can arise if OTC drugs or herbals are taken by people also taking prescription drugs. There can be significant, and sometimes dangerous, drug interactions. This is especially the case with St. John's Wort. St. John's Wort is quite safe if taken at normal doses. However, if combined with certain prescription drugs, drug interactions can be dangerous! Always consult with your physician or pharmacist when taking herbals along with other medications.

♦ **The choice to treat yourself with OTC products may interfere with seeking professional treatment.** It's not uncommon for people experiencing severe anxiety or depression to attempt self-treatment with OTC drugs instead of seeking professional treatment, which could be more potent and effective. Especially for those with bipolar disorder, some OTC or bipolar-illness products can actually cause the condition to become more severe.

Possible Meltdown

Any effective treatment for depression can cause severe moods swings or mania in people suffering from bipolar disorder. This includes OTC products discussed in this chapter.

OTC Products Effective in Treating Depression

The following products have some research support as effective treatments for depression:

♦ **St. John's Wort (hypericum)** May be effective in treating mild-to-moderate depression. Three large-scale reviews of 89 studies comparing St. John's Wort to standard-prescription antidepressants have shown that, in general, St. John's Wort is effective in treating mild depression. It also may be effective in treating the depression and anxiety associated with premenstrual dysphoria. Typical dosing ranges from 900 to 1800 mg per day. It generally takes six weeks of treatment before the first signs of improvement are noted. St. John's Wort appears to have few side effects, and it is non-habit-forming and well tolerated. St. John's Wort should not be taken at the same time that one is taking prescription antidepressants, because dangerous interactions can occur. Additionally St. John's Wort can cause drug-interaction problems with the following medications: warfarin, theophylin, digoxin, birth-control pills, and drugs used to treat AIDS and migraine headaches. There may be potentially serious drug interactions with other prescription medications. Thus it is essential to ask your pharmacist or physician about the compatibility of St. John's Wort and any prescription medication you are taking.

♦ **SAM-e** May be effective in treating mild-to-severe depression. There are few side effects, and it is non-habit-forming and well tolerated. A review of the world literature by Dr. Papakostas, including 76 studies of SAM-e, strongly suggests its efficacy in treating some forms of depression. Doses range from 400 to 1600 mg per day. Some improvement in symptoms can be seen after two to four weeks of treatment. SAM-e should always be taken with a vitamin-B-complex supplement.

OTC Products That May Be Effective

The following products considered may be effective, although there is more limited research on effectiveness, compared to studies of St. John's Wort and SAM-e:

- ◆ **5-HTP (5-hydroxytryptophan)**   May be effective in treating mild-to-severe depression. There are few side effects, and it is non-habit-forming and well tolerated. The typical daily dose is 300 mg a day, and you might see some symptom improvement within two to four weeks.

- ◆ **DHEA (dehydro-epiandrosterone)**   A hormone that may treat depression (there is some research support, albeit limited, for this treatment).

- ◆ **Kava (a.k.a. kava kava)**   Comes from the root of the kava plant and has been used for hundreds of years in Polynesian cultures. The main benefits are reduced anxiety, worry, and insomnia. Kava has been widely used in Germany and Switzerland. It appears to have an effect on the nervous system similar to that of tranquilizers (such as Valium or Xanax). The advantage over prescription tranquilizers is that it does not appear to be habit-forming (as prescription tranquilizers can be).

   The dose of kava that is effective depends on the amount of the active ingredient (kava lactones) in the capsule. It varies from one brand to another, from 30–70 percent kava lactones. The effective dose of kava is three to four divided doses a day of 250 mg of kava lactones. So you'll have to do the math. Thus a 200 mg capsule of kava containing 30 percent kava lactones would only total 60 mg kava lactones. Thus you would need to take four capsules, three to four times a day, to approximate a normal daily dose.

   High doses of kava may cause drowsiness, impaired alertness, and even intoxication. Caution should be exercised in driving when using kava. There have been arrests for kava-related DUIs.

Possible Meltdown

Kava has been safely used for hundreds of years. However, in 2002, some kava users reported cases of severe liver damage. It turns out that certain companies producing kava not only used kava root but their products also contained stems and leaves. The stems and leaves of kava plants are known to contain toxic chemicals. This underscores the need to only consider products with USP or NSF endorsement. The jury is still out on this safety issue with kava, thus caution is warranted, especially for those with any history of liver disease.

♦ **Valerian (Valerian Root)**   Valerian is an herbal sedative that can reduce anxiety and help prevent insomnia (primarily helping people to fall asleep). The advantage of valerian over prescription sleeping pills and tranquilizers is that it appears to be non-habit-forming. Effective doses range from 200–400 mg for treating anxiety during the day and 400–800 mg for sleep. The general consensus is people should avoid daily use of valerian over a period of months, and should never take it in combination with prescription tranquilizers or sleeping pills. Alcohol use should also be avoided with valerian.

♦ **Melatonin**   Melatonin is a naturally occurring hormone produced in the brain. It starts to be released into the blood stream in small amounts in the early evening and in larger concentrations during sleep. Melatonin does not directly produce sleep, but it quiets the body and the mind in ways that help prepare a person for sleep. Melatonin is felt to activate the *parasympathetic nervous system*, which relaxes the body in general, and helps to lower body temperature. A lower body temperature is necessary for entering into stages of deep, restorative sleep.

def•i•ni•tion

The **parasympathetic nervous system** sends nerves throughout the body, and when it is activated, it rapidly produces a calming effect.

Possible Meltdown

There is some indication that high doses of melatonin, e.g. 5 mg, may aggravate depression. Thus if you have been experiencing depression, you should avoid these higher melatonin doses.

People eager to get to sleep may find that doses of 2–5 mg can produce drowsiness. However, many sleep experts recommend that such dosing is too high. A safer strategy is to take $\frac{1}{2}$ mg between 6 and 7 P.M. You will not feel any noticeable impact, but rather, melatonin at this dosage level will begin to gradually shift the body and the mind in the direction of more relaxation. This may translate in improved ability to go to sleep later in the evening.

OTC Products Still Under Investigation

Numerous herbal and other OTC products have been touted as effective in regulating mood symptoms. Well-conducted research on safety and effectiveness is limited. It bears keeping this in mind until they have been subject to more rigorous investigation. If you are considering the use of these products, please consult with your physician. These products include:

♦ Hops, for promoting relaxation.

♦ B vitamin, to combat stress and increase energy.

♦ GABA (gamma amino butyric acid), an amino acid for reducing anxiety.

♦ Tyrosine, an amino acid for reducing depression.

♦ Tryptophan, an amino acid for reducing nervousness, anxiety, and irritability.

♦ Chamomile, an herb that may reduce anxiety.

♦ Passionflower, an herb that has a calming effect.

♦ Ginseng, a dietary supplement that increases energy.

Once again, please keep in mind that natural does not necessarily mean safe. Make sure that the use of OTC and herbal products carry a seal of approval from either USP or NSF. And, it is always a good idea to keep your physician informed about any and all natural products you are using.

The Least You Need to Know

♦ Certain over-the-counter products may help regulate moods.

♦ Remember, however, that natural does not necessarily mean safe. Some of these products have been found to contain toxic contaminants and cause drug-interaction problems.

♦ Caution: over-the-counter products that reduce depression can cause serious mood swings in people who suffer from bipolar disorder.

♦ Most OTC and herbal remedies are used for treating milder versions of anxiety, insomnia, or depression. They generally are not effective in the treatment of more severe emotional problems.

Part

Psychological Self-Help Strategies

In Part 3 we will first consider something I refer to as "solutions that back-fire." Many people during very stressful times try their best to cope, but may inadvertently do things that ultimately make stress worse. It is important to spot these "solutions" and stop or change them.

Then we will launch into a host of different coping strategies that have been developed during the past 25 years that can help you gain control over distressing moods.

Chapter

13

Common Solutions That Backfire

In This Chapter

- ◆ Coping strategies that ultimately create more problems
- ◆ Spotting "solutions that backfire"
- ◆ Excessive blocking of authentic emotions
- ◆ Thinking that can magnify a perception of powerlessness

The first rule of medicine is to "do no harm." The same thing is good advice when you are going through emotionally difficult times. At any given moment, as people are struggling with difficult life circumstances, most people actually are giving it their best shot. Sometimes people collapse into complete passivity, but most of the time, human beings are doing the best they can to cope. However, doing your best doesn't necessarily mean that what you're doing is effective. People often feel overwhelmed or at least somewhat powerless when life gets really hard. A problem is that people often inadvertently do things during stressful times that make it worse.

A concept in psychology is *self-regulation*. Self-regulation involves actions that people make (often habitually or unconsciously) that have the immediate impact of reducing stress or tension, at least somewhat. Here are some very common examples. You are sitting watching TV, and after 15 minutes or so, your back feels stiff, so you shift your posture and immediately feel at least a bit more comfortable. Or how about the following examples? Going to the freezer for one more bowl of ice cream, or drinking an extra cup of coffee during a demanding day, or deciding "What the hell" and drinking a third can of beer.

def•i•ni•tion

Self-regulation refers to a number of actions people take to reduce tension. Most of the time these are done without conscious awareness. They include benign actions like stretching and yawning, and extend to more problematic behaviors such as excessive consumption of alcohol.

All of this is so common and so natural. However, some forms of self-regulation feel good in the moment, but come back to haunt you. The message in this chapter is to become alert to those largely automatic forms of self-regulation that end up causing more problems down the line. In this chapter, we'll look at common types of actions that people take that are high risk for increasing negative moods. Once recognized, you can then take steps to reduce or eliminate them.

Emotionally Gritting Your Teeth

I'd like to use a metaphor. If you burn yourself on your hand, and it's a significant burn, one way of responding is to put a bandage on the wound. This may sound logical. The bandage can keep germs out and provide a buffer so that it will not hurt too much if you bump your hand into something. But what if you over-bandage the wound and keep it completely covered up for a month? Well, of course, when you remove the bandage, the burn has not fully healed. In fact, it may be worse. Wounds need protection from bacteria and additional injury, but at some point they need exposure to the air. Lots of distressing emotions are like this, too.

In Chapter 7 we spoke of excessive emotional control and how common it is for people, especially in Western culture, to be very reluctant to open up and share painful, deep, or very personal emotions. At the same time, most mental-health professionals agree that to some extent people need to open up and talk about difficult emotional experiences to facilitate emotional coping and healing. Psychologically gritting your teeth is often a short-term solution that leads to more difficult problems with coping.

Having said this, I must also strongly state that people vary tremendously regarding this issue of "opening up." Some people are very private; it is not in their nature to openly share strong feelings with others. Many people feel quite uneasy about showing emotions, and this is primarily due to the influence of their past experiences. Lots of people feel embarrassed, ashamed, or too vulnerable to open up with others, even with people they love and trust.

It is, of course, important to be very discriminating in deciding whom to open up to. Some friends or family members may not be able to really listen. Some may be shaken if you express strong emotions (especially if you never have before); they have become accustomed to seeing you in a different light. Some may respond in a judgmental way, showing some form of criticism for the emotions you feel. Some will offer quick remedies, trying to get you over feeling bad as soon as possible. Some will want to rush in with advice about how to "fix" your life problems. Often people say, "I understand," and although their intentions may be good, often they do not fully understand.

All of these responses may come from those who know you well and love you. But these kinds of responses rarely help, and often hurt. They usually drive emotions back underground.

Solutions

If you have been prone to keeping a lot of feelings bottled up inside and it feels intuitively right to start opening up with a friend or loved one, it might be very helpful first to have a frank discussion with them. This might include acknowledging that you characteristically don't get emotional or share more private feelings. However, life has been very difficult lately, and you want to be able to talk with them.

It is also generally helpful to express any reservations or fears that you have, before sharing your distressing emotions. Just stating this out loud can often reduce the anxiety you are feeling about opening up. For example …

- ◆ "I want to talk with you, but it's hard for me to do."
- ◆ "It's just hard for me to get started telling you this."
- ◆ "I think that many times during my life I have just been ashamed or embarrassed to be really open with my emotions. I am telling you this mainly because I want you to know how hard it is for me to say these things."

These kinds of comments often make a significant difference in reducing distress about opening up. Often the other person will be quite understanding regarding these initial remarks, and will offer reassurances and support.

Validation

One of the single-most powerful human experiences is what is commonly referred to as *validation*. When a person expresses personal feelings, how the other person reacts is critically important. Most of the time when people share personal emotions, confiding in a friend or loved one, they really are not looking for advice about how to resolve their problems. Even if they directly say, "What should I do?" many times this is not actually a question; rather, it is an expression of their sense of powerlessness or exasperation. What they want and need is to truly be heard and understood. What often matters so much more than "advice" is to have the experience of having another human being really care about their suffering.

def•i•ni•tion

Validation is a term often used in psychology to describe the experience of sharing a thought or a feeling with another and seeing that what you have said has been accepted, understood, and not judged.

Validation is acceptance of the truth of another person's distress. It is acknowledgment and belief. Unfortunately, many of us growing up did express strong feelings to our parents or to others only to have them trivialize our experience ("For God's sakes … it's not that big a deal"), criticize us ("You are too sensitive"), or even worse, to be oblivious and unconcerned.

These same experiences can certainly continue into adult life, as well. This once again underscores the need for you to choose wisely whom you will be open with. For many people, a benefit from going into psychotherapy is finding a safe place to be open.

Invalidation from the Inside

People can experience a lack of genuine validation from others. But perhaps more insidious and damaging is when we do it to ourselves. This is a very common solution that backfires. The person who is overwhelmed with sadness may think to herself, "Don't be so emotional! What's wrong with me?!" The aim of such an internal comment might be to help her maintain her emotional composure. That's the "solution" part. However the backfire is a double whammy: first, she is invalidating her authentic inner feeling, and second, she is scolding herself. She is being harsh toward herself for having an emotion.

This kind of internal "self-talk," as we have seen, is a major factor increasing unnecessary pain.

How can you deal with this in a helpful way? The first step requires some introspection. You need to look inward to see what you are telling yourself during times when you feel frustrated, sad, nervous, etc. Most people who make a point to start noticing self-talk usually find it simple to spot these inner sources of criticism and self-invalidation. In Chapter 14, we will look more closely at a number of specific approaches designed to help you spot and stop negative self-talk.

Opening Up in Privacy: Therapeutic Writing

Psychologist and researcher Dr. James Pennebaker has conducted extensive studies revealing that pent-up emotions contribute to both physical health problems (such as high blood pressure) and an increased incidence of anxiety, depression, and sleep disorders. Dr. Pennebaker's breakthrough strategy can facilitate "opening up," and involves what he calls therapeutic writing. Try the following:

1. Find a time and place where you will not be disturbed. Have pen and paper available. And take a moment to relax.

2. Begin to write. Write about important, difficult, and painful events that are on your mind. These may also include events that happened a long time ago. What is necessary for this strategy to work is to write about these experiences expressing your deepest emotions. This is not like a cut-and-dry newspaper article, but rather writing in a very personal, honest, and emotional way.

3. Write for about 20 minutes. Really get into it; don't worry about spelling or grammar. No one else will ever read it. Repeat this each day for at least five days in a row.

Remarkably, many people who are otherwise cut off from inner feelings or find it hard to confide in others often find therapeutic writing to be a powerful way to access and experience inner, pent-up, or buried emotions.

Pennebaker (in numerous, ingenious studies) has demonstrated that this technique alone can have impressive results. Such outcomes include improved health, decreased blood pressure, an enhanced immune system, better sleep, and reduced emotional suffering.

Like other techniques we've explored in this book, therapeutic writing at first glance may seem simplistic. However, do not underestimate the power of this strategy. It's a direct and effective approach that helps people acknowledge and come to terms with inner "necessary pain."

Shame: The Great Inhibiting Emotion

Perhaps the most common reason people hold back their feelings (hold back from sharing with others and hold back from really even noticing their own inner feelings) has to do with shame.

At the heart of shame is a fear of rejection or abandonment. When little kids are criticized, scolded, or humiliated by others, it's easy to see that face of shame … downcast eyes, bowed head. Across cultures, all children are taught to obey certain rules and social customs. One of the most potent and harmful ways to shape a child's character is to shame them. Of course children must learn to be socialized and to behave. But shaming is something that goes beyond normal "shoulds" and "shouldn'ts." It is a message that says, "There is something deeply wrong with you." It is an attack on the basic worth of a child that conveys a powerful message, "Shape up or get out of my sight!"

Shame also gets internalized. People can feel deeply ashamed of themselves even when completely alone. Also, shame operates like an early warning signal. In those moments before shedding a tear or expressing some strong emotion, shame works like a stopper. The person automatically anticipates rejection or some other negative reaction from the person he is with. Shame gets activated and the person swallows his feelings.

Pat Conroy, in his popular novel *The Prince of Tides*, tells the story of an entire family who feel too scared and too ashamed to speak about terrible events that happened years ago. His main character, Tom Wingo, says, "… in silence we would honor our private shame and make it unspeakable." This is what shame does … it's like a black cloud that comes over people and forces them to hide a part of their humanity.

We have all heard, "Confession is good for the soul." If and when people find the right person to confide in and muster the courage to speak out about inner emotional struggles, often shame begins to evaporate. The primary underlying emotions such as sadness, anger, or what have you, are there; they are expressed, and there is relief. A lot of this relief comes from the experience in the moment of being heard and not rejected.

Substance Use and Abuse

Although we have spoken a good deal about substance use (e.g. alcohol and caffeine), it is worth mentioning here in the context of solutions that backfire. We already know the negative impact of substance abuse and how most recreational drugs ultimately make anxiety, moodiness, and depression worse. Let's add to this list that a common consequence of drug abuse is to block feelings.

Josh was a very devoted high school teacher. He worked for an inner-city high school. He met with his kids before school and with children and parents well into the evening.

He went above and beyond the call of duty, trying to help these troubled teenagers. After work he drove home, vigorously worked out by running on his treadmill for an hour, and then poured himself a huge drink of bourbon. He drank his drink and passed out until the next morning.

This has not always been Josh's lifestyle. It started six months ago when his young wife died from breast cancer. The over-focus on work, the intense exercise, and his substantial alcohol use were distracting him from his intense inner feelings of grief. He kept his anguish at bay, was rarely aware of his internal suffering, and was also heading straight toward an addiction to alcohol.

Again may I say, this is not a moral issue. This is about intense emotional suffering and Josh's desperate attempt to avoid the enormous pain of his loss. No one wants to suffer this much. But, ultimately, the alcohol use took its toll. His sleep became more and more impaired. And at some point he crashed into a severe depression.

It took involvement in an alcohol recovery program and psychotherapy to resolve his drinking problem and the depression. Once these problems were dealt with, he became more aware of what was eating him up inside. The healing of his broken heart then required opening up to his grief.

Stinkin' Thinkin'

Confronted by stressful times, people must think clearly—planning, problem solving, carefully coming to an understanding about what's happening, formulating strategies for coping, and anticipating what will happen.

Unfortunately, significant stress often takes a toll on clear-headed thinking. When emotions overwhelm people, it is not uncommon to experience some degree of confusion, indecisiveness, and, especially, a loss of perspective. A common experience is also to *ruminate* and engage in nonproductive worry. In addition, when human beings are severely distressed, they frequently begin to make particular errors in thinking that psychologists refer to as cognitive distortions. In some 12-step programs, they call it stinkin' thinkin'. These problems in thinking always intensify distress and especially turn up the volume on feelings of powerlessness.

Let's look at five common versions of stinkin' thinkin':

def•i•ni•tion

Rumination is the tendency to have troublesome thoughts going through your mind again and again. It is also a kind of worrying that never leads to any real solutions. In common vernacular, rumination is sometimes called "stewing in your own juices."

♦ **Jumping to conclusions.** You call someone and leave a message for her to return your call, but you receive no reply. You conclude, "She doesn't even care enough about me to call me back." This is a conclusion. It may be accurate, but there are lots of other, plausible explanations. Maybe the message did not get recorded properly on her answering machine; maybe she is out of town and has not picked up messages. The conclusion was based on little concrete data.

♦ **Negative labeling.** "I am such a loser!" Usually such pejorative labels are based on a person's reaction to a mistake that he has made or experiencing a major disappointment. These labels are too global, overly harsh, and not completely accurate. And rather than motivate people, they result in low self-esteem, a loss of self-confidence, and even self-hatred.

♦ **The "shoulds."** Insisting that life or people should or should not be a certain way. "She should know how I feel!" or "This shouldn't be happening to me!" The effect of "shoulds" is always to take whatever emotion you are experiencing, and turn up the volume on it. It always increases your sense of powerlessness. This kind of thinking never fosters emotional well-being or enhances effective coping.

♦ **All-or-none thinking.** "I can't do anything right!" Again, this global way of thinking may feel accurate, but is almost never 100 percent true. Again, it erodes self-confidence and increases feelings of powerlessness.

♦ **Negative predictions.** "I'll never get the job I want," "No one will ever love me." People are notoriously bad at being able to predict the future. Negative predictions increase feelings of hopelessness.

Why do these maladaptive ways of thinking occur? Sometimes they are influenced by long-held negative self-concepts (like we discussed in Chapter 6). Thinking "I'm a loser" or "I can't do anything right" might occur due to the impact of underlying negative core beliefs.

Many times these types of distorted thinking occur because when people are overwhelmed, they lose perspective. For most people, very negative moods are like the tides. They come in for a while and eventually recede. Yet this loss of perspective often leaves people unable to really look at life from a broader point of view. People get swallowed up in the moment, and have trouble seeing beyond their current suffering.

Finally, stinkin' thinkin' occurs often when people are depressed. There is a good deal of research to suggest that this is tied to chemical changes occurring in the brain.

Do No Harm: Revisited

You must take stock of these common factors that inadvertently increase stress and misery, and make an all-out effort to stop them. In our next chapter, we'll take a look at some very effective ways to target distorted thinking.

The Least You Need to Know

- Expressing inner emotions can be very helpful for many people, but it is important to be discriminating in choosing with whom you share inner feelings.

- Therapeutic writing is a powerful way to cope with stressful life circumstances.

- Substance use and abuse is one of the most common ways that people anesthetize painful emotions.

- Spotting distorted thinking can significantly reduce distress.

14

Keeping a Clear Head and a Realistic Perspective

In This Chapter

- ◆ Biased and distorted thinking
- ◆ Why distorted thinking can lead to feeling more powerless
- ◆ Quickly reducing the intensity of negative emotions
- ◆ How "shoulds" are a pathway to feeling like a victim

The most successful approaches to coping with difficult times are to keep a realistic perspective and be able to think and problem solve effectively. This can be hard to do when life stresses begin to mount. In this chapter, we'll consider some powerful techniques that can help you keep a clear head during stressful times.

Loss of Perspective and Distorted Thinking

As we saw in the previous chapter, significant stress affects thinking. It's important to underscore that this can happen to anyone, regardless of how intelligent you are.

Stress in general can provoke cognitive distortions such as all-or-none thinking and jumping to conclusions. In addition, particular mood states selectively bias thinking. People who have experienced losses (e.g. the break-up of a relationship, the loss of a job), recent failures, or who are feeling depressed, are very likely to begin seeing the world in a particular way where negative events are keenly noticed and positive events are ignored. Some psychologists have referred to this as tunnel vision. Here is an example:

Samantha has been depressed for two months. One day she goes to the circus with her husband and her two young children. It is a beautiful spring day and her kids are thrilled about going to their first circus. Moments after walking through the front gate of the circus and on the way to the circus tent, Samantha says to her husband, "It's so dusty here … you'd think they could have found a better place to have the circus." One minute later she says, "These circus people look so filthy." Another minute and she says, "God, it smells bad here" (there were circus animals and, of course, manure happens). Her husband turns to her and says, "Are we having fun yet?"

Samantha perceives the world through depressed eyes. Her attention and thoughts are drawn to some negative aspects of the current situation. She is not intentionally focusing on bad things—it's just automatic. And she's not imagining or hallucinating these perceptions. They are completely accurate bits of reality. But what she is not doing is noticing the beautiful weather or the happiness her kids are feeling as they anticipate the excitement of this new experience. Her perceptions and thoughts are not balanced … she is not taking in the whole picture.

Think About It

Psychologists Lyn Abramson and Lauren Alloy conducted a study and found that when depressed people were compared to nondepressed people, the depressed individuals actually were more accurate in perceiving negative events in the environment. The researchers' conclusion was that most of us who are able to avoid depression do this, in part, by not noticing bad stuff. The ability to deny or screen out negative events may be an effective coping skill for many people.

Let's face it, life is often hard and if you pay attention, you'll notice a lot of unpleasant, negative, and often terrible things happening in the world. Most people are able to ward off excessive pessimism by seeing both the positive and the negative … taking in the whole picture. I am not talking about looking at the world through rose-colored glasses or living in Pollyannaish denial. Balanced thinking includes facing painful realities while also seeing the hope and beauty in the world.

Danger Everywhere

When people have experienced very frightening or traumatic experiences, a different kind of distorted thinking occurs. What happens here is a keen and exaggerated state of vigilance, scanning the environment for possible dangers.

Dan was involved in a serious traffic accident. A drunk driver rear-ended him. Dan sustained minor injuries, but the intoxicated man and his wife, who was a passenger in the car, were killed. It was a horrible and very frightening experience. In the weeks following the accident, Dan found himself often tense and anxious, especially while driving (of course!). He was in a constant state of hyper-alertness and small things, like a car passing him, caused him to startle … he would grip the steering wheel tightly, perspire, and feel his heart pound.

The impact of exposure to frightening events biases thinking by making it much more likely to think …

♦ Something bad will happen, and

♦ When it does, it will be catastrophic.

The emphasis is on the thought, "bad things will happen," not "bad things may happen" or "may be catastrophic." It is a strongly felt conviction that disaster will strike and it will be terrible.

These versions of negative and distorted thinking are sometimes obvious, easy to spot, and hard to ignore. However, during especially stressful times, most stinkin' thinkin' is not in conscious awareness. Like an almost-silent voice constantly whispering, "Everything is terrible," "I'm completely out of control," "I'll never get over this," "I better watch out," or "I feel like a loser."

Let's Take Action

This kind of distorted thinking and negative self-talk is at the root of almost all unnecessary suffering. This kind of internal thinking is a powerful misery amplifier. But the good news is that certain strategies have been developed that can help people spot negative self-talk and put a stop to it. These are very high-yield coping strategies. Let's take a look.

Sara has been going through a time of significant distress following the break-up of a romantic relationship. One night, sitting alone in her apartment, she became more and more discouraged.

In the past few weeks she has had similar experiences, and each time felt helpless to do anything to ease her suffering. She'd often get into a downhill spiral of depression, feeling worse as the evening went on.

Various forms of the thought record have been developed and used since the late 1970s. This straightforward self-help technique generally requires about 10 to 15 minutes to complete, and often in this brief period of time, intense negative feelings can be noticeably reduced. Try it even once and judge for yourself.

People who have never truly experienced major stresses often will suggest, "Don't be so negative," or, "Look on the bright side of life." These admonitions almost never help a person who is feeling depressed. If people could, somehow, by willpower alone, simply stop seeing things from a negative perspective, they would have done it long ago.

Specialized strategies are required to alter negative thinking. It's important to emphasize that the thought record, described here, has nothing to do with the notion of "positive thinking." Rather, its goal is to keep your thinking accurate, balanced, and realistic, and to help you maintain perspective. This perspective aims to increase the clarity of perceptions of both the positive and negative events or aspects of life.

Step 1: Notice Negative Signals

Use your negative feeling (sadness, frustration, nervousness, irritability, etc.) as a signal. Next time (or any time) you notice an especially intense, unpleasant feeling, let it serve as a cue to do a thought record (take this action rather than just endure the unpleasant emotion).

Step 2: Record Your Emotions

Briefly write down the emotion(s) you are feeling (sad, upset, angry, disappointed, discouraged…) in the "mood" column (see the following example), and next to the emotion, rate the intensity of the feeling (from 0, meaning the emotion is not present at all, to 100, meaning the worst you have ever experienced it in your entire life). Interestingly, simply rating the intensity of your mood, itself, has been shown to reduce emotional distress somewhat.

Step 3: Reflect

Reflect for a moment, and then ask yourself, "I am feeling _____ (sad, tense, hopeless) right now. What is going through my mind?" Almost always, strong feelings are accompanied by or associated with underlying thoughts (although often we are not fully aware of thinking during moments of emotion unless a conscious effort is made to notice these thoughts). Whatever thoughts come to mind, jot them down. To make this exercise effective but easy, write down your thought only briefly.

Let's see how Sara approached this technique. Instead of sinking into an increasingly down mood one evening, she decided to take action and use her thought record for the first time. She wrote the following:

Mood	Thoughts
Sad (75)	Tom left me for another woman.
Hopeless (80)	I'll never get over this. No one will ever want to be with me, and I'll be lonely for the rest of my life.

She was able to fairly easily pinpoint the particular thoughts that were provoking her emotional pain and it only took her a couple of minutes to do this step.

Step 4: Evidence Supporting the Thoughts

Please note, this step can be emotionally difficult, but it is very important. The step requires honestly asking yourself for any and all proof that the thought noted in step 3 may be at least somewhat true. In other words, ask yourself what evidence supports your thoughts. Let's see how Sara approached this:

Thought	Evidence Supporting the Thoughts
Tom left me for another woman.	This accurate. He told me so, and I have seen him with her.
I'll never get over this.	There is no absolute evidence that I'll never get over this upsetting time in my life. All I know for sure is that I feel bad now.
No one will ever want to be with me.	This is hard to know for sure.
I'll be lonely for the rest of my life.	I can't tell the future for sure.

Step 5: Be Objective

Negative thoughts are compelling; they feel real, accurate, and certain. However, you must try to be very objective, and one way to do this is to ask yourself, as you write down your response, "Is this thought (or belief or statement) absolutely true? Is it the whole truth and nothing but the truth?"

Again, let me emphasize that this is not an exercise in positive thinking or an attempt to pretend that things are perfectly okay or to superficially cheer yourself up. The exercise is a search for the truth and for clarity and accuracy in your thinking. For Sara, a part of this ("Tom left me for another woman") is accurate, and of course it's very painful. In contrast, the thought, "No one will ever want to be with me" may feel accurate to Sara, but it is not supported by any factual data. No one can really tell the future (it's an example of making negative predictions).

As you do this, ask yourself, "Is there any evidence that refutes or does not support my thought?" Sara wrote the following:

Thoughts	Evidence Refuting
Tom left me for another woman.	Nothing refutes this. It is accurate.
No one will ever want to be with me.	Guys have asked me out in the past. There is no solid proof that, for some reason, it will never happen again.
I'll be lonely for the rest of my life.	I am lonely now, but I am a friendly person. I like people. In general, I know a lot of people that like me. There is no evidence that I will absolutely be lonely for the rest of my life.

Step 6: Looking Back

Look back at what you have written. Look at the evidence in both columns and ask, "All things considered, how do I feel right now?" Then re-rate the intensity of your feelings.

For Sara, it was sad (65) and hopeless (35). She is sad, and she has every right to be. The break-up of a love relationship is a very painful experience. This reality needs to be faced and honored as an understandable and honest human emotion. However, Sara's overall level of distress was noticeably reduced, mainly due to decreased feelings of hopelessness. This exercise simultaneously helped her acknowledge her legitimate sadness and regain realistic perspective.

> *"Well, maybe it helped Sara, but it won't help me."*

The thought record may seem too simplistic (at first glance); it does to most people who are going through very difficult times. It is very easy to simply dismiss this as another quick-fix tip, characteristic of pop psychology. However, don't let its apparent simplicity deceive you. During the past 25 years, this approach has been shown to be one of the most useful techniques for correcting unrealistic negative thinking and for reducing the intensity of distressing moods.

During very distressing times, thinking clearly and accurately without using the thought record can be extremely difficult. The process of writing thoughts and evidence down and the ability to see your thoughts in black and white greatly facilitates the ability to clarify thinking and to gain realistic perspective.

Please give the thought record a try. For Sara, the alternative would have been to sink into yet another evening of depression, helpless to do anything to ease her pain. Using this approach she was able, in about 15 minutes, to significantly alter her mood. No technique completely erases unpleasant feelings, but the name of the game is taking action to gain some measure of control over your mood.

It should also be noted that the use of a thought record on a regular basis is an effective way to modify negative core beliefs (which we discussed in Chapter 6). The thought record is a tool to help you bring in the light of reason and to challenge long-held negative beliefs about yourself.

Tyranny of the "Shoulds"

Some common "shoulds" include the following:

- "I should be stronger."
- "I shouldn't let things get to me so much."
- "I shouldn't be so sensitive."
- "I should be able to pull myself out of this bad mood."
- "This shouldn't be happening to me."

"Shoulds" and "shouldn'ts" are powerful, negative thoughts that convey a strong inner desire or an insistence that you, others, or reality ought to be a certain way. They also can represent a set of unrealistic standards for your own behavior. The failure to live up to such standards results in harsh judgments and a condemning of the self.

What is so important to appreciate is that at the heart of should statements is a perception of the world that always generates a sense of powerlessness. When you think with shoulds, you are always seeing yourself as a victim of circumstances beyond your control. This perception of victimhood contributes greatly to feelings of powerlessness and helplessness. Thinking with shoulds is one of the most potent ways that human beings inadvertently turn up the volume on misery.

This very common thought pattern, unfortunately, never really helps to change situations or to motivate people. Rather, it always becomes a source of harsh self-criticism and greatly intensifies feelings of helplessness.

The most effective way to combat shoulds is to make use of your thought record. In moments of intense negative emotions, the question, "What's going through my mind?" often reveals shoulds.

Betsy's experience provides a good example. She had been feeling increasingly distressed and upset with herself. Much of her worry centered around her growing marital conflicts and a great disappointment in her husband, who had become increasingly distant during the past two years.

Betsy finally sat down, calmed herself down a bit, and wrote out a quick thought record on a tablet of paper:

Mood	Thoughts
Upset (90)	
Frustrated (95)	How can he be so cold?
Angry (80)	
Hopeless (95)	It shouldn't be this way. Marriages should bring happiness, not sorrow.
Anxious (85)	
Angry with myself (85)	I shouldn't be so upset … what's wrong with me?

Note, often questions like, "How can he be so cold?" carry hidden "shoulds" ("He shouldn't be so cold").

The most powerful way to address shoulds in a thought record is to rewrite your statement, but not in terms of shoulds or shouldn'ts. Rather, substitute the terms "I want" or "I don't want." Here is what Betsy wrote:

> *"I don't want it to be this way."*
>
> *"I wanted my marriage to be happy."*
>
> *"I don't want him to be cold toward me."*

And instead of stating, "I shouldn't be so upset," it is more helpful to simply state how you do feel:

> *"I do feel upset. This matters a lot to me, and God knows I never wanted things to turn out this way."*

What is embedded in Betsy's revised statements are the following:

- ◆ She is acknowledging the truth of how she really feels.
- ◆ Rather than being harsh or critical of herself, she is adopting an attitude of understanding and compassion for herself.

Almost always when people use such an approach, one important result is to experience significantly less feeling of powerlessness, and often this is immediately noticeable! Try it even once and you be the judge. When this is done, a shift occurs from viewing yourself as a helpless victim to seeing yourself as a human being with legitimate emotional pain.

Shoulds are everywhere. On close inspection, almost invariably, all intense emotions are accompanied by shoulds. And shoulds always have the effect of taking any painful emotion and turning up the volume.

In my experience, the simple exercise described above is one of the most rapid ways to de-escalate very intense emotional upset and regain perspective and a sense of control over strong feelings. However, for this to be truly effective, you must also then give yourself permission to acknowledge and to experience the underlying, legitimate human emotions. For Betsy, it was clear and understandable that the emotional distance she has felt from her husband is a source of sadness and disappointment.

You should try this exercise, even once! (Sorry, I mean I *want* you to give it a try.)

This, Too, Shall Pass

Another all-too-common distortion in thinking is a loss of time perspective. Here, people get caught up in the intensity of the moment and lose sight of the fact that most negative feelings come and go. We saw this with Sara, "I'll never get over this."

Here is an analogy. Say you are standing in waist-high water at the beach. A large wave comes in, and for just a moment or two, you are completely underwater. So you just hold your breath because you know that in a moment the wave will subside and you will be able breathe again. The truth is that for those one or two moments, however, you are under water and cannot breathe. When people get hit by waves of strong emotion, it often feels like, "I'll never get over this." It does feel bad, but this perception involves a loss of awareness of time. It is helpful to deepen this perspective that almost all forms of strong feeling, like waves, have ebbs and flows. No one stays completely depressed forever; no one feels a perpetual state of panic.

The strategy here is to acknowledge and accept, "In this moment I feel bad," and then remind yourself, "This won't last forever … just hang on and this intensity, too, shall pass." Please be clear: I am not recommending complete passivity in the face of distress, because there are many actions you can take to reduce emotional suffering. However, in these moments of intensely painful feelings, this kind of acceptance, combined with the ability to see beyond it, can substantially reduce the level of distress.

The Least You Need to Know

◆ Negative and distorted thinking can occur for almost anyone, and usually it goes completely unnoticed. You must take action to spot these misery amplifiers.

◆ The thought record is one of the most effective and rapid techniques for reducing the intensity of negative feelings.

◆ Taking aim at eliminating shoulds and shouldn'ts reduces unnecessary emotional pain and helps to reduce feelings of powerlessness.

◆ The techniques addressed in this chapter, because they seem so simple, are often not used by people going through difficult times. The good news is that you can experiment with them. Often, if people will try these approaches even once, they discover how helpful they are for rapidly reducing distress.

Chapter 15

Combating Shame, Guilt, and Low Self-Esteem

In This Chapter

- ◆ Shame, inappropriate guilt, and low self-esteem
- ◆ Action strategies for combating guilt and shame
- ◆ Carefully evaluating sources of low self-esteem
- ◆ Developing a more positive inner voice of self-support

Shame, guilt, loss of confidence, low self-esteem, and even self-hatred … these are the inner emotions that often plague people for a lifetime. In this chapter, we'll see how to reduce these unnecessary sources of human misery.

Shame and Guilt

Ginny says, "Since I've been so overwhelmed with my work, I've had this increasing feeling of worthlessness. I so often feel like I'm to blame for all the problems in my family … especially about how I neglect my kids. It's all my fault."

A certain amount of guilt or feeling of responsibility is often appropriate. It's a sort of internal barometer that tells you when you have transgressed others or inadvertently caused harm to another. However, the finger of blame can often become excessively harsh and unrealistic when you're in the throes of a significant life crisis. There may be a tendency for you to assume more than your fair share of responsibility for problems that may in fact be due to a number of factors, including the actions of others.

Getting Clear About Your Thoughts and the Facts

Excessive, unrealistic self-criticism and shaming always intensify misery and rarely help improve circumstances. If you are experiencing these feelings, try out the following:

Step 1: Get It Down on Paper

Often the voice of self-blame is subtle and only on the edge of awareness. Thus it's important to first make this inner thinking conscious and clear. One of the best ways to do this is to take five minutes or so and write your self-critical thoughts down on paper.

- ◆ What do I think about myself?
- ◆ What am I telling myself?
- ◆ In what ways do I feel to blame?
- ◆ What things do I feel a sense of shame about?

Step 2: What's the Evidence?

In keeping with the thought record discussed in the previous chapter, next consider two things: Is there any solid evidence that you are directly to blame or any evidence that refutes this? As mentioned before, these questions are most effectively addressed by writing down such evidence, rather than just thinking about it.

Step 3: Find Explanations

Looking at the evidence in both columns, carefully reflect, and ask yourself, "Is this 100 percent true?" and "Are there any other explanations, any other factors or other people who have contributed to the particular problems or events?" Without being overly critical of others, you can simply approach such questions in a matter-of-fact manner. The goal is not to attack or blame, but rather to find explanations. "Just the facts, ma'am …."

Step 4: Take Stock

After a careful analysis of the facts in step 3, if there clearly are mistakes you've made or inadvertent hurt caused to others, then consider the following ways of looking at it:

◆ It is often helpful to honestly "own" the part you may have played in creating hurt or problems, offering apologies when appropriate.

◆ Carefully consider your intentions. Often, people never intend to hurt others or create difficulties. It became clear to Ginny that she did often ignore her children as she was working overtime in desperate pursuit of a job promotion. She wanted the promotion and she loves her kids. She honestly admitted to herself that she was away from her children, and to a degree that may have been emotionally hard on them. In this spirit of honesty she was also quite certain that, "I never intended to cause them any emotional pain. I just got overly focused on my job." This ability to own her part of the problem while making it clear and conscious that she had absolutely no intention to cause her children pain, helped Ginny turn down the volume on what had been intense self-blame and, at times, self-hatred.

◆ Change guilt to regret. Guilt often carries a dual message: feeling bad about something you have done and a sense of "badness of self." It is this second element that is often unwarranted and is the source of unrealistic self-loathing. An alternative is to give yourself permission to own and feel a sincere sense of regret, but move away from the more global sense of being a bad person that guilt often implies.

◆ The experience of shame digs even deeper into one's sense of self: a self that is fundamentally flawed, somehow defective, unworthy, or deserving of scorn. Shame, in a sense, embodies a global and condemning view of yourself. Most people who experience significant amounts of shame make such conclusions based on limited data. Such data may certainly include mistakes that have been made, some of which may have had a clearly negative impact on others. Yet, typically, the shame conclusions fail to take into consideration a multitude of other data, for example, numerous times that the person has been kind, helpful, loving, and available to others.

If you are plagued by feelings of shame, it is essential to think carefully about yourself as a whole human being. This must involve honest acceptance of shortcomings, owning one's mistakes, and humbly acknowledging your membership in the human race where no one is without fault. But it is also very important to give careful consideration to other aspects of yourself and of your life.

Ginny took careful stock of herself and acknowledged things for which she felt regret. And then she also wrote the following list of her personal attributes:

- I deeply care for my husband and children. If it were required, I know in my heart that I would die for them.

- I am a good and loyal friend.

- My friends and family trust me. I keep confidences and I follow through with promises.

- I may have made mistakes, but I know that I have never intentionally hurt other people.

- There are causes that I believe in. I contribute money to my church, and I speak out about things that I believe in.

- When my kids have needed me to take a stand on their behalf, I've done it and never let them down.

Without conscious effort and the specific technique outlined here, Ginny, and others like her, could continue for months to be eaten alive by the consuming, destructive force of shame. Again this approach to coping rests heavily on thinking clearly and in a balanced fashion.

Combating Low Self-Esteem

Some people go through their entire lifetimes burdened by feelings of worthlessness, inferiority, and low self-esteem. Often, this is a natural outcome from being mistreated, unloved, unappreciated, unsupported, neglected, or abused as a child (the feelings are closely tied to their enduring, negative core beliefs that we discussed in Chapter 6). However, many people may generally feel okay about themselves until major stressful life events hit. This is manifested in a number of ways:

- Feeling inferior or inadequate

- Lacking self-confidence

- ◆ Indecisiveness (doubting your ability to make good decisions)

- ◆ Unrealistic or harsh self-criticism, self-blame, guilt, and shame

- ◆ Viewing yourself in a very negative light; seeing yourself as stupid, incompetent, ugly, unlovable, worthless

- ◆ Self-hatred

In this chapter of the book, we will look at some strategies for reducing low self-esteem.

Getting Clear About What Matters

Self-esteem for most of us certainly is influenced by the opinions of others. If we are valued by our boss, loved by our spouse, and respected by colleagues, then self-worth is bolstered. Conversely, being ridiculed, criticized, or belittled by others can be very emotionally wounding. Being the recipient of such negative messages from others may be a contributing and ongoing cause of low self-esteem.

At times, critical remarks from others are simply an expression of differences of opinion or perspective. However, it's not uncommon for such words to be spoken out of anger or in an attempt to hurt or control another.

Julie's example is all too common: "My husband, Ken, is constantly putting me down or looking at me with a 'God, you're stupid' expression on his face. It hurts a lot, and most times I find myself believing that his criticisms are true."

Some people are especially sensitive to even mildly critical comments, taking them to heart and feeling terribly hurt even when critical comments were not intended to be hurtful or even to be taken seriously.

One way to strengthen yourself, to erect a buffer against criticism, and to tackle the problem of low self-esteem is to find ways to clarify and strengthen inner values and beliefs. The following steps may help.

Step 1: Get Your Ideas Clear

Get this idea clear in your mind: "I am separate from others. No law states that I must agree with everyone, and I have a right to find my own way through life, to discover what I truly believe to be important values, goals, and beliefs for myself. I can learn to respect others' opinions while also honoring my own. In many relationships, ideas, beliefs, and lifestyles may be different; neither right or wrong, but simply different. Human beings often do not see eye to eye."

Step 2: Get It on Paper

Write down those things that you feel define who you are, the things that really matter to you. These may include some of the following areas of life:

1. Things you hold to be important characteristics of good relationships (trust, openness, and so on).

2. Your spiritual values.

3. Values and beliefs that you hold so dearly that you would be willing to defend them with your life.

4. The people in your life that mean the most to you.

5. Qualities that you require in a good friend or in an intimate relationship.

6. Activities that make your life enjoyable and worthwhile.

7. Social or political issues that matter to you.

8. Small things that you enjoy.

9. Your favorite places.

10. Things about you that other people value.

Step 3: Connect With Your Authentic Self

Often in very old age, people develop a new perspective on life. Looking back over the years and coming closer to the end of life, many older and wiser people come to appreciate the folly in living life in accord with others' expectations. At some point in life, it simply doesn't matter that much anymore what other people think of you. Letting go of the pressure to conform or to please others, you may be better able to live more according to your own inner needs, values, and beliefs.

A useful exercise is to imagine yourself as a very old person, perhaps someone who has only a short time to live. Play with this image a bit—get into it enough to really experience how things might seem from such a perspective. Then ask yourself, "What things am I ready to let go of? What felt obligations can I gratefully release? How does it feel to divorce myself from others' judgments and expectations?"

This exercise can help you more clearly connect with your more private and authentic self. It can also help to identify current sources of felt criticism or judgment.

Step 4: Support Yourself

Once you have clearly identified important beliefs and values, the next step is to focus on giving yourself support for being who you are. You have a right to live your life on your own terms, even if others may not fully agree. And you certainly have the right to suspend self-criticism and accept and honor your true self. As Popeye says, "I yam what I yam."

Often when people are under enormous stress or are depressed, they begin to lose contact with the self. Especially during difficult times, it's important to refresh your memory regarding your inner and unique self, to anchor yourself in your own beliefs, values, activities, and sources of enjoyment, and to embrace (rather than discount) these personal sources of meaning and aliveness.

Step 5: List Your Supporters and Nonsupporters

Finally, it can be helpful to make a list with two columns, one listing "Those who support me for who I am," and "Those who do not." Once this list is made, it might be good to consider the following metaphor.

If you had a precious yet fragile family heirloom and you wanted to entrust it to someone for safekeeping, you wouldn't give it to just anyone, and you certainly wouldn't hand it over to someone who would damage or neglect it. You would choose someone whom you can really trust, someone who can appreciate the value and preciousness of the object. Likewise, it's a good idea to be careful about revealing yourself only to those whom you really trust. To whom do you entrust your private thoughts, feelings, needs, wishes, and fears? With whom is emotional vulnerability safe? When self-esteem is low, you need to surround yourself with companions who can appreciate and support you, not those who throw salt in the wound.

Developing an Inner Language of Self-Support

As we've seen in the previous chapter, internal thoughts (self-talk) often underlie negative moods. This is also true when it comes to low self-esteem. Whether it is obvious or subtle, inner voices of criticism, self-hatred, judgment, unrealistic standards, and condemnation always fuel the fires of low self-worth. Pay attention to your inner voice and see if any of the following statements might provide kinder, gentler, and more realistic support for yourself.

If you are thinking, "I can't do anything right," then consider these alternatives:

♦ I do a number of things right, and I also make mistakes.

♦ I am doing the best that I can at this moment.

♦ Accomplishing things is difficult for all people experiencing stressful life circumstances.

♦ Even if I am struggling, I should not lose awareness of the many difficulties I have faced and overcome before.

♦ Especially during times of significant stress, it is important to not be hard on myself.

If you are thinking, "I shouldn't be feeling so bad," consider this alternative:

♦ It's not a matter of shoulds or shouldn'ts. The fact is, I'm distressed and when human beings go through hard times, it is natural to experience strong, painful emotions.

If you are thinking, "I should be better able to control my emotions," then consider this alternative:

♦ Again, it's not a matter of shoulds or shouldn'ts. It's just a fact that I am having a difficult time now, and I am committed to doing whatever I can to overcome my emotional suffering.

If you are self-labeling, "I'm a loser … I'm a failure … I am unlovable … I'm a terrible mother … I'm a lousy husband," consider these alternatives:

♦ Self-damning never helps. I've got to be kind and decent to myself (especially during this difficult time).

♦ Negative labels are inaccurate, gross generalizations. I can't afford to fall prey to this kind of distorted thinking. It's unrealistic, and it only makes people worse.

Here are some useful self-statements that may also provide support:

♦ Take one day at a time.

♦ Whenever possible, take action and avoid passivity or withdrawal.

♦ Just do it!

- I must treat myself in a compassionate way.

- For now, I can choose to adjust my standards for performance and reevaluate my standards after the negative mood begins to subside.

- No matter what others may think, I am trying to do my best.

- To experience frustrations, to suffer disappointments, and to mourn losses are part of the human experience. Often life is hard. That's a fact. I can take some comfort in knowing that fellow human beings have also traveled this road. It's part of the human experience.

- Some life decisions might be best put off until I get emotionally back on my feet again. Not everything has to be done now. I can give myself permission to deal with some issues later.

- It's okay to have limits on what I am able to do just now. It's okay to prioritize. It's okay to say "no."

More Strategies to Combat Low Self-Esteem

In this proactive vein, let's also consider the following strategies for defeating low self-esteem:

- Accept compliments. When others offer a compliment, don't reject, minimize, or pooh-pooh it. Say "thanks" and let it sink in. Allow yourself to consider the compliment as an honest and sincere gift. Give yourself permission to consider that the positive comment is true.

- Avoid minimizing. Give yourself credit for accomplishments, acts of kindness, or friendship with others. Do not minimize what you do.

- Reframe. Reframe your mistakes. After making a mistake, you can choose to rake yourself over the coals. But a better approach is to:

  Own it. Admit that you did, in fact, make a mistake. Humbly acknowledge that, as a human being, you are not perfect.

  Rather than punish yourself, ask, "What can I learn from this mistake that could help me in the future?"

> **Bet You Didn't Know**
>
> It is amazing that when people are going through hard times, most energy gets focused on coping and surviving, and people just simply forget to do things that are self-nurturing (we will talk more about this in Chapter 17, which addresses how to create balance in your life).

Consider that often mistakes are not due solely to personal error.

♦ Take good care of yourself. Make an all-out commitment to nurture yourself. Make a list of those life activities that almost always provide some degree of pleasure and do them—often! Some examples are the following:

1. Going to the movies

2. Taking a bubble bath

3. Buying take-out food rather than cooking

4. Taking a day off from work to drive in the country

5. Renting a silly video and watching it

6. Drinking a root-beer float

7. Listening to great music

♦ Get involved. Pursue hobbies, crafts, volunteer work, continuing education, or sports that you have had some interest in but have never done. Stretch yourself, take some risks, and go for it! Reinvent your life, building in more fun and personally meaningful activities.

♦ Avoid toxic people. Seek out people who are good to you, and stay away from jerks.

The Least You Need to Know

♦ Many times guilt and shame are inappropriate reactions to events for which you are not to blame.

♦ Carefully considering your intentions can help you gain a new perspective that can reduce feelings of guilt or shame.

♦ Owning your mistakes and asking for forgiveness often reduces the burden of feelings of guilt.

♦ Again, realistic and balanced thinking is important for reducing unnecessary feelings of shame, guilt, and low self-esteem.

Chapter 16

Anger Management

In This Chapter

- ◆ Some anger is adaptive and some can destroy lives
- ◆ Anger can be a smoke screen hiding other painful feelings
- ◆ Often severe depression is the cause of anger
- ◆ Effective ways to gain control over anger

Sometimes anger is the energy behind self-defense and can empower people to stand up for themselves. But, as you will learn in this chapter, anger can also destroy lives. Inappropriate and overly intense anger is a major source of emotional suffering for both the person expressing anger and for those who live with him or her. It is important to understand what anger is all about and to develop effective strategies for managing it.

Understanding Anger

Fundamentally anger comes out of that instinctually driven response to danger: the fight-or-flight reaction. It can oftentimes be a form of instrumental coping, mobilizing people to take direct action to change current circumstances. Examples are attacking someone who is harming your child, or voicing your anger toward someone who has taken advantage of you.

Anger often supplies the energy and the backbone for assertive behavior as you confront others and ask them to stop hurting or using you (see Chapter 19).

However, anger frequently is misdirected, inappropriately intense, and the source of enormous harm. People can get seriously injured or even killed during volcanic eruptions of anger. In the midst of an anger meltdown, people can say very cruel and hurtful things to others that they later deeply regret. Domestic violence, road rage, explosive behaviors that get a person fired, and anger fueling the fires of political tension, suicidal bombers, and war. Out-of-control anger ruins relationships and careers. Pent-up anger has been associated with significantly increased risk of heart disease, strokes, and high blood pressure.

Lighting the Fuse

A number of life events can trigger anger as well as many internally generated feelings and thoughts. Consider the following:

- Strongly wanting to finish a project or arrive at a destination and being blocked from reaching your goal (frustration).

- Being used, abused, or taken advantage of by another person or place of business.

- Broken promises, lies, or betrayal in an important relationship.

- Being treated in ways that you consider to be unfair or unjust.

- Being cut off in traffic or in other ways unnecessarily put in danger by other drivers.

- Not getting what you feel you deserve (for example, a job promotion).

- Missing an airline flight or an important appointment.

- Being harshly criticized (especially unjustified criticism), humiliated, or teased in a hurtful way by another person.

- Re-circulating (mentally) past hurts or injustices. Going over and over again unpleasant events that are long past.

- Witnessing bad things happening to innocent people (such as racial prejudice) or cruelty to animals.

- Seeing that corporate greed has resulted in great harm to innocent people.

- Being let down by someone you were counting on.

- Counter-aggression when you or a loved one has been emotionally or physically attacked.

- Feeling anger if you have failed or made a mistake. This anger may be directed toward yourself or toward others (this is referred to as externalization of blame). One example is when people who are frustrated kick their dog.

Anger as a Distraction

Often when people inwardly feel afraid, vulnerable, or powerless, a way to manage such feelings is to get angry. Almost always this happens automatically and unconsciously; rarely is this a conscious choice. This may be somewhat more common in men in our culture, where social values state that men should not feel weak or vulnerable. Some men who have lost their wives may certainly experience grief, but what is even more apparent is that they become grumpy, irritable, and chronically bitter, angry at life. Some of this anger may be legitimate, but a lot of it may be a defense against experiencing inner, more deeply buried feelings of sadness, neediness, or vulnerability.

Some children torture animals. This is often the first outward sign of a serious personality disorder. These kids most times have been subject to brutality and severe abuse by their parents. Only by torturing and thus having ultimate control over helpless animals can they reassure themselves that they are powerful, they are not weak, they are in control. In this way, violence and hostility is a defense against inner fears of powerlessness.

This same dynamic is also likely to be a common cause for adults who seek out powerful positions. Examples might be CEOs, politicians, dictators, and such, who sometimes exhibit a sadistic pleasure in seeing others fail. In many cases of domestic violence, this defense against powerlessness may fuel the fires of abuse. And a very common manifestation of this is aggressive driving and road rage.

Why do people cut in front of others or intimidate by tailgating? Everyone knows that this behavior rarely gets you to your destination sooner. But people who do this need the ongoing reassurances that they are powerful and in control. Next time you encounter this on the freeway, remind yourself that very likely the aggressive driver inwardly feels insecure, powerless, and impotent. They are trying to prove something by driving recklessly. Guess what? No matter how successfully they were at intimidating you on the roadway, they will still go home tonight and struggle to ward off their inner feelings of powerlessness.

Anger and Depression

When most people think about depression, the first thing that comes to mind is the look of sadness, dejection, and despair. However, it is very important to know that many people who suffer from depression (both minor and severe forms) show irritability and anger outbursts as the primary mood change. When this occurs and there are no other obvious signs of depression, most times friends, co-workers, and family misunderstand what is going on.

When irritability is due to depression, it is also very likely that the person also experiences some of the following: sleep disturbances, weight loss or gain, apathy, and a loss of interest in usual life activities. If asked, "Are you sad or depressed?" she is likely to say "no," but if asked, "Are you happy?" the answer is probably also "no."

Think About It _____

Many people suffering from depression of course feel sad and depressed, but a rather large minority of very depressed individuals primarily show mood changes that include impatience, frustration, irritability or outright anger. In many, if not most, of these cases other people may never see outward signs of what clearly would reflect depression. Yet inwardly, many of these irritable, depressed people feel hopeless, helpless, and very unhappy.

Shades of Red

Expressions of anger come in many different forms. There are levels of intensity:

- annoyance
- frustration
- irritation
- exasperation
- anger
- hatred
- rage

Anger is also often combined with other feelings such as anger and resentment or anger and jealousy. It can be largely internalized and felt only at a private level or it may leak out in behavior by being grumpy or impatient. It can be directed toward others in clear-cut ways, by comments of biting sarcasm, words to induce guilt, or in passive-aggressive ways. Or in the extreme, anger gets expressed as hostility and even violence toward others. At times suicides or suicide attempts are ways to punish others or to induce guilt, fueled by intense anger toward them.

Finally, anger can be directed toward oneself. This can take the form of angry and condemning self-talk, such as, "You stupid idiot," or the form of self-hatred and sometimes suicide or suicide attempts.

Anger Management

The first step to successfully managing anger requires taking a careful look at the sources of anger.

Anger can be a maladaptive and very hurtful emotion, something that needs management; however, it can also be an understandable and adaptive response to some types of life circumstances. Legitimate anger, as we saw earlier, may lead to the honest expression of feelings that are a reaction to being used or abused. And it can provide the impetus for initiating action, such as taking a stand, saying "no," or negotiating for changes in relationships.

Careful reflection may reveal the sources of anger. This can often be done on your own; however, many people find it helpful to see a therapist or counselor in order to explore the underlying causes for anger.

Should it be clear that if the anger emanates from such problems in an interpersonal relationship, then making a plan to address this in an assertive way is a wise choice (this will be covered in detail in Chapter 19). Couples counseling may also be helpful.

Anger Escalators

Intense feelings of anger sometimes occur abruptly; however, many begin and then gradually build up into more intense feelings. An important step in managing anger is to become watchful for common ways that irritation escalates into anger. The following can serve as a checklist:

◆ At the root of intense anger, almost always you will find should or shouldn't statements. "She shouldn't do this … for God sakes, she knows this irritates me!" "He should know how I feel!"

◆ Another common element is suggested in these two examples: thinking in ways that bring up old issues, old hurts; and repetitive patterns of conflict. This then is a reaction to something happening in the here and now, and the ruminating about past conflicts or injustices. Replaying these troublesome memories does nothing more than amplify anger.

◆ Be especially mindful of thoughts regarding what is right versus wrong, fair versus unfair, or justifications for your anger based on the "principle" of it. "She did _____, thus I am entitled to be angry." Many relationships crash on the rocks of these kinds of arguments. Many ongoing conflicts between countries or ethnic groups may be associated with the belief, "We have been wronged and therefore we deserve to _____" and thus aggression is justified.

◆ Jumping to conclusions or mind reading. Many times if someone has been hurt, ignored, or inconvenienced, a critical ingredient stroking the fires of anger is making assumptions about the other person's motives. "He doesn't give a damn about me," or "She is just doing this to get back at me." Sometimes such conclusions may be accurate, but acting and reacting as if you know for sure about someone's motives is risky. It's better to first directly inquire about reasons that somebody did or did not do something. Remember how inaccurate mind reading often is.

◆ Substance use or abuse is a common contributing factor in anger outburst. Intoxicating drugs impair judgment and critical thinking and increase impulsive behavior (abruptly speaking or striking out without first thinking about it).

Think About It

Most cases of anger, if thought about carefully, are at least somewhat understandable. However, there are cases in which people are plagued by abrupt, out-of-the-blue, and completely inappropriate anger and aggression. One form is referred to as anger attacks. This generally is not provoked by particular environmental triggers, but rather, it erupts spontaneously. This is a relatively rare psychiatric disorder that can respond to psychiatric medication treatment. Explosive personality is another condition where there is no slow burn or buildup of anger. Someone may accidentally bump into this person, and wham! There is a very abrupt outburst of anger or aggression. Finally, there is pathological alcoholism. Here, certain individuals consume a minor amount of alcohol and become very uncharacteristically explosive. Each of these conditions are believed to have a neurological cause and can be treated medically.

Turning Down the Volume on Anger

If anger escalates into out-of-control rage or violence, it is essential to take steps to quickly de-escalate it. This is described in detail in Chapter 18. In less-intense episodes of anger, it is helpful to engage in what I call avalanche control.

Along mountain roads with steep inclines, on the side of the highway you'll often see small wire fences. These generally are 2 to 3 feet high and are positioned about every 50 feet or so from the top of the incline to the shoulder of the road. The intent is to quickly stop rockslides, stopping rocks from swiftly coming down the incline and causing a landslide.

Anger often also starts with small irritants or frustration. It gets fed by should statements, thoughts about past injustices, getting caught up in arguments about what is fair, and provocative interactions (such as blaming or name-calling). Just like stopping rockslides early to prevent a full-blown avalanche, anger also must be nipped in the bud. The best way to do this is to first anticipate when you are about to walk into a high-risk situation, knowing ahead of time that an interaction is likely to bring up feelings that can spark anger.

Knowing this sometimes can lead to strategic avoidance. Like they say, it's important to choose your battles. Ask this question ahead of time, "Is this really worth it … is it a big enough issue to risk getting into an argument?" Consider this realistically. Some situations, especially in the grand scheme of things, are simply not that crucial. However, don't also let yourself minimize or deny what might be a significant relationship issue.

If you decide to bring up a problematic or touchy issue with someone, it is always best to plan ahead and develop a sound strategy (we'll look at this in more detail in Chapter 19). Also keep clearly in mind your goals in bringing something up. For example:

- Is it to prove a point?

- Is it to strike out and punish someone or induce guilt?

- Is it aimed at solving a particular problem?

- Is it born of the desire to simply speak your peace or get something off your chest?

- Is it a step taken toward getting some specific outcome (for example, to stop someone from abusing or neglecting you)?

I cannot overemphasize how important planning ahead is. Rather than coming off half-cocked, this beforehand consideration for your motives is likely to help you be more successful in delivering your message effectively.

Although in the heat of anger it may feel good to blow off steam, if done in an inappropriately hostile or impulsive way, people may win the battle but lose the war … it can get you fired, can seriously damage or end a relationship, or even land you in jail.

In preventing avalanches, it is especially important to think about these four questions:

1. Specifically, what do I want to say? (Write it down on paper ahead of time.)

2. What change am I hoping for by bringing this up?

3. Do I also want to preserve the relationship?

4. When this is over, will my approach leave me feeling guilty or result in a loss of self-respect?

Noting the Signs of Escalating Anger

Be especially attuned to these behaviors and physical cues that your anger is becoming more intense:

- Feeling agitated
- Clenching your fists or gritting your teeth
- Raising your voice
- Feeling like swearing, name-calling, or the urge to hit someone
- Increasing muscle tension
- Racing heart
- Feeling shaky
- Glaring at the other person
- Driving faster or more aggressively

The earlier you can recognize these signs of escalating anger, the better. Once recognized, there are actions you can take to reduce the intensity of your anger. These concrete steps are spelled out in detail in Chapter 18.

Anger That Hides Hurt or Vulnerability

One of the most potent steps to take to reduce anger is to first get clear about any underlying feelings (e.g. sadness, neediness, fear, worries, loss, a fear of loss of control, or vulnerability). Then, approach a friend or loved one and confide in them regarding these underlying emotions.

Stan was irritable, impatient, and easily frustrated most of the time. His pervasive crankiness was driving a wedge between him and his wife. He always got hot under the collar when having to wait at a stoplight. He frequently snapped at his kids. One night he spoke very candidly with his wife Wendy and said, "Wendy this is very hard for me to even talk about," (he looked very uneasy as he spoke these words) "but something has been eating away at me. I am so sorry I am always edgy, but I think the real problem is that I'm terribly worried about being laid off from my job. You know I've been with the company for 24 years, but they are downsizing and laying off lots of good, long-term employees. I'm just scared and worried … especially worried that if I get laid off, I'll feel like a failure."

It was hard for Stan to find the courage to bring this up. But as he did you could visibly see the tension in both Stan and Wendy melt away. He became somewhat tearful and his wife lovingly comforted him. Stan felt a great sense of relief. This was the beginning point for the two of them to reconnect. His buried worries and fears were festering and he had become estranged from both his wife and his children. Anger was just the surface emotion. It disappeared when he began to truly give voice to his inner worries.

> **Think About It**
>
> It is also so often the case that people harbor strong and legitimate anger, yet feel anxious about their own feelings of anger. Some people cry instead of getting outwardly angry.

Owning It

One of the most important steps to take in managing anger is to have the courage to own your feelings. Certainly other people may play a big role in provoking conflicts and hurt, but often it is tempting to do what psychologists call "externalizing blame": "She forced me to do it," "I couldn't help it … I just exploded … it's not my fault," or "The devil made me do it." Some people are strongly averse to admitting to their own role in anger problems. Stubbornness, pride, or the need to punish the other person can lead to impasses or escalating anger that can ruin lives or create emotional tension that can last decades. It happens with individuals and it happens with nations.

The Least You Need to Know

◆ Many people misunderstand the true sources of anger, which can include depression, grief, fear, and vulnerability.

◆ Understanding the root of anger is essential in effective anger management.

◆ It is very difficult, if not impossible, for people to think with a clear mind when they are boiling with anger. Often, the first step to take in such situations is to use effective techniques to de-escalate emotional intensity.

◆ Often it takes an enormous act of courage to "own" your role in conflicts with others or problems with out-of-control anger.

Chapter 17

When Life Gets Out of Balance

In This Chapter

- ◆ A life seriously out of balance can be a common cause for distress
- ◆ Stressed-out people commonly just stop doing life-sustaining activities
- ◆ Getting clear about how you are spending the time of your life
- ◆ Set limits and develop effective ways to say "no"

When people experience significant life crises, it makes sense to feel stressed out. However for many of us there may not be any particular, major stressors going on. The cause is living a life out of balance. In this chapter, we take a close look at this and see how you can perform a balancing act.

Koyaanisqatsi

Koyaanisqatsi is a Hopi word meaning "life out of balance." Does this ring a bell for you? It certainly does for me. For many people a life that is overloaded with work or obligations may be a day-in and day-out source of significant stress. Picking up the kids, paying bills, returning phone calls, work, work, work! Many of us live this way for decades, living lives devoid of pursuits or experiences that create balance. Certainly many people manage to take a vacation each year, but after one or two weeks at the seashore, they return to the grind of everyday life. Does a week or two a year really restore people?

When people are experiencing very significant distress or depressing times, often so much focus and energy gets poured into struggling and emotional survival that there is little time left to engage in activities that might restore some balance and sanity. For people besieged by stress, it may not even dawn on them that their life has become so one-sided. When people are going through very difficult times, one of the first things that drops by the wayside are activities that are self-nurturing.

At the heart of unbalanced lives are three common factors. The first is a loss of a sense of choice. Many folks that live a chronic life out of balance believe that it has to be this way; they feel trapped and at the mercy of life's demands. Second is simply not noticing it. It is easy to become so consumed with daily life, that people may go for decades not fully realizing how empty their lives have become. Third is that some people do not feel like they deserve to make time for themselves. Either they feel unworthy of self-care activities or they may habitually think that others come first. Their lives have become devoted to caring for others 24/7.

Are You Running Out of Gas?

The prices paid for living a life out of balance are numerous: exhaustion, burn-out, pent-up resentment, feelings of emptiness or meaninglessness, depression, a loss of intimacy in marriages or other meaningful relationships …. Solutions can also ruin lives, such as alcohol abuse, gambling, and marital infidelity (and other symptoms of a "midlife crisis").

Think About It _____

As the saying goes, "It's not so much about adding years to your life as it is adding life to your years."

A story I have heard too many times from elders is that they look back on their lives with regret. They now realize that they never liked their job, but felt trapped in it without other viable options. Or they realize the folly of working all the time and never stopping to smell the roses. It's never too late to reinvent your life, but as the old saying goes, "You better enjoy yourself … it is later than you think."

Taking Stock of Your Life

The first step to take in creating a healthier balance in your life is to take an honest look at how you are living your life on a day-to-day basis.

Try this exercise. Draw this table on a legal pad and jot down everything you do for a period of one week. Obviously this would not include very minor events such as a trip to the bathroom or taking a drink of water. But develop a shorthand way to briefly record your activities that take 15 minutes or more of your time and record the amount of time you spend doing each activity. On this sheet you will see nine boxes where you can list activities according to two dimensions: necessary for life and quality of life.

Prioritizing Activities

Necessary for Life	Quality of Life		
	High	Medium	Low
High	A	B	C
Medium	D	E	F
Low	G	H	I

For example, box C might include such activities as "washing the laundry." Unless you really get off on this activity, it's likely to be in box C because (at least eventually) it is necessary to do. However, for most people it does not rank high in terms of enhancing the quality of life. Box G might include "soaking in a hot bath while listening to peaceful music, just to unwind." This is not a necessity, but it may feel good and contribute to self-nurturing and relaxation. You will likely find that activities in box I turn out to be either unpleasant obligations or habits. For lots of people, this box gets filled with many activities.

At first glance, recording all of your activities for a week might seem like a daunting or tedious task. But this exercise can be an eye-opener. People often discover how much of their time and their lives they are giving away, doing things that may not be at all necessary and certainly not rewarding. We all have certain obligations, and it would not be realistic to simply stop doing all such actions; however, the goal of this exercise is to increase conscious awareness of how you are living your life.

You will probably discover some things in box I that you'd really like to let go of (we'll be talking about how to say "no," and negotiation for changes in relationships, in

Chapter 19). Changing your life by letting go of some undesirable obligations is one step to take toward reinventing your life. Saying no and setting limits on how much time you are obligated to do certain activities will almost certainly free up time and energy that you can devote to other pursuits.

I want to be very clear. This exercise and these suggestions are not about becoming totally self-centered or selfish. We all feel the need to give to others (and, in fact, reaching out to and helping others is often a very important part of living a balanced life). But the point is that many people overdo it and the suggestion here is to carefully take stock of what you are doing and consider establishing some limits on box I activities.

Who Is In Charge of My Life?

Do you feel trapped in a job you do not like, or a relationship that is not a good fit? An important element in this kind of experience is a perception of powerlessness. "There is no way I can find another job that has good pay and good benefits!" How often is this belief what contributes to that trapped feeling?

I know an attorney who got fed up with his career and quit, and started driving 18-wheeler trucks. And we've all heard stories about the CEO who gets burned out, leaves his wife, and moves to an artist colony in Arizona. Some people can and do make these dramatic life changes. But let's be realistic. Most people are not inclined to take these kinds of huge steps to change their lives. Yet there are ways to initiate changes and reduce the experience of powerlessness.

Think About It _____

So many times people conclude that they simply cannot make significant changes in their lives; for example, moving to a different part of the country or changing jobs or careers. Yet, years and years later, as an older person, many look back with regret and think, "Why didn't I just go for it years ago? Gosh, how I'd like to go back and have another chance to change my life!"

Julie was in a dead-end job. She felt no challenge, and most days she had to drag herself to work. Her passion was playing the violin and she had dreamt of a career as a musician. But she was a single mom and needed to support herself and her two children. Getting a job as a musician seemed a complete impossibility. She decided to go to counseling, and after a period of time where she carefully looked at her life, she became much clearer about how her life was almost completely devoted to her job and her kids. She came to see how this lifestyle was about survival, but not really living. Eventually, she decided to join a musical group that played several times a month at various nursing homes. She started to feel more alive. One day in her counseling session she remarked, "I still have my day job … but it's just work … my career is a musician, and my people at the nursing homes are probably the oldest 'groupies' around!"

Julie's retooling of her life was not a radical 180-degree change of life. But it clearly was a course correction that mattered. Her life now feels different. She experiences more aliveness. In addition, she also started feeling less trapped, less powerless. She has the same job and she is not wild about it, but she feels more the author of her own life. Rather than feel like a leaf passively being blown around by the wind, she has restored a sense of choice.

Over-Obligated

Charity and service to others can bring a sense of meaning to our lives. Compassion for others, sacrifice, or just being helpful toward others is important in living a balanced life. This can involve caring for a sick relative, doing volunteer work, serving on a committee at church, coaching a soccer team, spending time on the phone consoling a friend who is going through a divorce. These are decent things to do. The problem is, however, that many people have trouble setting limits.

When one's life becomes increasingly out of balance with too much time consumed by obligations, it can begin to wear on a person. Often what starts out as an act of love or kindness can gradually transform into a felt sense of obligation and a burden, and may eventually result in both burnout and inner feelings of resentment.

Another complication is, once again, feeling trapped. The key to change is to get to a place where you can feel okay about saying "no" and setting limits.

Joel had earned a lot of respect and admiration for the work be did on numerous committees at his synagogue. People constantly praised him for everything he did. Many weeks he would spend all day Sunday and three nights during the week with various activities. He did genuinely like what he was doing. He was also getting worn out. At times he considered cutting back, but was worried that he would disappoint others. A turning point for Joel was when his rabbi got him aside one day and said, "I want you to know how much I appreciate what you do, but I must tell you that I think you may be taking on too much."

This opened the door to an important discussion. The two of them talked, and Joel was, for the first time, able to speak freely about the conflict he felt. Thankfully his rabbi, who had also experienced this same dilemma himself, really supported Joel in his decision to cut back. Joel imagined that if he resigned from some of his committees, his friends would be disappointed or possibly upset with him. In trying to predict the future, it was this conclusion that lended to his feeling of being trapped. But with his rabbi's encouragement, he decided to speak with his fellow committee members. To Joel's surprise, when he spoke with his friends on the various committees, all he experienced were expressions of appreciation for what he had done and complete support for his decision to pare back his activities. One word described his reaction: relief.

Think About It

Over-obligated is not just for adults. In recent times, many young people also take on too much. Sometimes this is to win the approval of friends. Often, it is to please parents or, at times, to live out their parent's unmet dreams. Not infrequently this is seen when a child or teenager becomes very involved in sports or dance, largely because they feel pressured by parents to take on these activities. Of course, many kids like such activities, but I've known many who have been pushed into the activities by their parents. We have all heard about some child movie stars or Olympic athletes who experience incredible stress as their lives begin to be dominated by a parent's need to see them succeed.

Back to the Future

Imagine yourself as a very old person nearing the end of your life. Try to really get into this image. Look back at your life. What are those memories that you values and cherish? Are there regrets? This perspective can help you carefully consider the decisions you make each day that lend either to balance or to Koyaanisqatsi.

Think About It

Comedian George Carlin has wisely said, "Life is not measured by the number of breaths we take, but by the moments that take our breath away."

I saw a cartoon in which a woman was sitting at the bedside of her dying husband. He spoke to her about his regrets, "I should have bought more stuff." I kinda doubt that anyone has really thought of that on his or her deathbed.

Cultivating Balance and Inner Peace

Throughout history people have struggled with this issue of balance. The ancient Dominicans had a tradition called the "Seven Actions for a Whole Life." They recommended that each and every day time be carved out for all of these seven important actions:

1. Stimulation of the intellect

2. Appreciation for nature

3. Physical exercise

4. Play and recreation

5. Employment: this could be a job or being involved in activities that benefit the family or community

6. Charity

7. Prayer

A more modern version of this prescription for balance has been recommended by psychiatrist Paul Fleischman. He suggests these following elements that contribute to inner peace:

1. Seek out peaceful people.

2. Give peace a priority.

3. Select out obstacles (reduce those life activities, habits, and obligations that may be an unnecessary burden).

4. Commune with creatures of nature.

5. Expose yourself to beauty, art, and nature.

6. Befriend sorrow. Fleeing sorrow, in the long run, never leads to inner peace.

7. Find the sacred in everyday life.

Elizabeth Barrett Browning underscores this final point with her short verse:

> "Earth is crammed with heaven,
> and every common bush afire
> with God, but only he who sees,
> takes off his shoes; the rest sit
> around it and pick blackberries."

For many of us, it may take years, if not a lifetime, to discover that unique formula for living a whole and balanced life (and such a formula may be very different as a 25-year-old versus a 53-year-old … priorities and wisdom change). The biggest obstacle to finding it for yourself may simply be that you have not taken time to look closely at your life. This inspection of your priorities and lifestyle can certainly be done on your own and by using some of the exercises suggested in this chapter. For many people, however, it is much more effectively explored in counseling or psychotherapy. Some people may think that therapy is only for people with serious problems. However, please know that going to a therapist to sort through your life and get clarity about your choices and priorities is an absolutely legitimate reason for going to see a psychotherapist.

Thinking Back and Reflecting

Think back to when you were younger, when you yearned for things in your life such as a college degree, a profession, a loving relationship, a sense of freedom and independence in choosing a style of life, owning your home, and so on. Remember how much you longed for these sought-after goals. Then, acknowledge the goals that have now been realized. Sit with this awareness for a while. People often take goals that have been achieved for granted and lose sight of how important such things can be in one's life. This exercise in remembrance and reflection can often help you experience a greater sense of gratitude for goals achieved.

Taking Stock of the Moment

Throughout the day, as many times as possible, stop yourself for a second or two and consciously take stock of the moment. Intentionally focus on yourself and the environment in the here and now, and see if there is anything you can notice that is nice, sweet, beautiful, upbeat, humorous, or peaceful. For example, "Right this moment, I feel calm and there is a cool breeze," or you notice a beautiful tree, a blue sky, a smile on a child's face, a friendly or courteous interaction with a clerk at the grocery store, a great-tasting lunch, a funny joke on a TV program, and so on. Right in this moment as I am typing this page, I stopped for a moment and looked at a picture I have in my office of my beloved grandfather holding me on his lap when I was 3 years old.

Some people in the midst of significant life crises may have thoughts like, "This is silly," "I don't feel in the mood to stop and smell the roses," or "How could this possibly help me feel better?" Also, this strategy may be something that simply does not dawn on you to do.

Like a lot of exercises and suggestions in this book, this particular suggestion, in itself, is not a cure for emotional suffering. But it is an action you can choose to do that can have an impact. One of my clients, Chuck, told me: "I've realized that to get through this very difficult time, I must adopt an attitude in which I am decent to myself, where I give myself permission to enjoy what I can and notice small positive things whenever I am able." This approach is not Pollyannaish; you are not denying serious problems in your life. But you are willfully choosing to expand your vision of the world and strive for a more realistic and balanced perspective.

Writing in a Diary

Each night, take a minute before bed and write in a diary, listing at least two things for which you feel grateful today. Then sit and reflect for just a moment. Chuck did this as well, and told me, "When I look over my list of gratitudes, I remind myself that, especially when I am depressed and overwhelmed, I cannot afford to ever forget these things in my life for which I feel grateful."

Encouraging Yourself with Positive Statements

Scan the following list of positive statements (often referred to as affirmations), and see if any feel appropriate and sincere to you. The chanting of unauthentic affirmations rarely helps anyone. However, you may find that one or two of these do strike a positive chord. If so, it may be helpful to write them on an index card and, several times a day, pull it out and read it to yourself (even out loud, if you are alone).

The following are words of encouragement and reassurance, and they are a way of providing ongoing support for yourself as you take action overcome emotional distress:

- I may not be perfect, but in this moment I am doing the best I can.

- I deserve to treat myself in a decent way.

- I am only human and, like others, I have strengths and limitations.

- I need to stick by my guns, believe in myself, take a stand, and hold on to things I believe in.

- I need to trust myself—trust my instincts and intuitions.

- Keep focused on what matters: don't get bogged down by trivial stuff or by others' opinions.

- It's okay for me to live life at my own pace.

- To thine own self be true: it's okay to live life in accord with my own values and beliefs.

- ◆ It is human to grieve and mourn losses.
- ◆ (For Christians) Even Jesus Christ wept tears of anguish when he faced very difficult times.
- ◆ I won't be so hard on myself.

Getting Positive About Pleasure

Psychologist Peter Lewinsohn and colleagues discovered something in the 1970s that seems so obvious and yet so powerful. Depression, feelings of emptiness, and a loss of enthusiasm and aliveness often are due to the fact that, for various reasons, people have drifted into lives devoid of pleasant and life-enhancing activities.

Many people, especially those who feel down, discouraged, or pessimistic may certainly know that if they did more pleasurable things, they would feel better. It just makes sense. However, there are two common problems:

1. Especially if you are feeling down, it may be very hard to think of fun things to do.

2. Even if you had ideas about particular enjoyable activities, frequently people just feel so worn-out and so exhausted, they think, "I just don't feel motivated to do anything except collapse on the couch."

Lewinsohn compiled a long list of social, recreational, and fun activities. He then conducted research with people experiencing serious depression. In this study, the therapist and the research subject looked at the list and came up with a dozen or so potential, positive activities. Then they were instructed (actually pushed) to engage in these activities several times a week. Many offered initial complaints, "I just don't feel like doing it." Of course they didn't. They had depression and virtually no sense of motivation. Noted psychiatrist Dr. David Burns says, "Motivation follows action." When you don't feel motivated, just do it anyway, or have a friend or family member push you to do it. Most of the time, once you have started the activity, it begins to feel easier and even pleasant.

Guess what? After three months, most of this large group of very depressed people had recovered from their depression. No psychotherapy, no antidepressant medications. Just being forced to engage in life. During times of significant stress or blue moods people shut down and withdraw. As noted before, commonly the first activities that are sacrificed are these energizing and life-sustaining pleasurable activities. Positive-activity therapy, if you want to call it that, may sound overly simplistic; however, there is solid research evidence to demonstrate that it can have a powerful impact on restoring life to people who are struggling. Take it seriously.

Think About It

For many people, they must *feel* motivated in order to get moving and engage in a pleasant activity. When times are hard, when you are exhausted, when you feel blue, if you wait to feel motivated before doing something, you'll be waiting a long time. As the Nike motto goes, "Just do it!" Once you start moving and begin to do things, that's often the time that you begin to feel the energy and motivation.

In Appendix C, we have a list of positive activities, many of which you may not have even considered. Spend some time looking at this list and come up with your own smaller list of activities. Then speak with a friend or family member and say something like this, "I'm having a rough time in my life right now. I want and need to do some things to bring more balance and more pleasure into my life. But I need your help to motivate me. Otherwise I'm afraid I just won't follow through." Often this is the key to having this work.

Ask for your friend or spouse to kick you in the butt, encourage you, or actually join you in the activity. It often really helps to reach out for this kind of help.

The Least You Need to Know

- A life out of balance is a very common source of significant distress.
- When life gets hard, people often stop engaging in self-nurturing activities.
- Feeling trapped and believing that you have no options for changing your lifestyle adds considerably to feelings of distress and powerlessness.
- Sometimes relatively small changes in your life can make a difference.

Chapter 18

Strategies for Managing and Overcoming Very Intense Emotions

In This Chapter

- ◆ Expressing very intense emotions can lessen their intensity
- ◆ Thinking clearly in the midst of very strong feelings
- ◆ Regaining a realistic perspective
- ◆ Be with someone you love and trust, and confide in them

Sometimes life stresses push people to the breaking point. The consequence may be to feel quite overwhelmed. Not only do these times cause enormous suffering but they can also compel people to do and say things that they later regret. In this chapter, we'll look at a number of effective strategies for rapidly de-escalating overwhelming feelings in order to regain a degree of emotional control.

When Enough Is Too Much

It makes sense that people would do anything to avoid excruciatingly unpleasant emotions. And I do not believe that there is anything inherently noble about facing painful feelings. However, this struggle against feeling understandable, authentic human emotions often can make things worse.

In psychoanalytic writings, the words neurosis and neurotic refer to the tendency for people to fight against feeling their emotions (over-control as described in Chapter 7). Famed Swiss psychoanalyst Carl Jung said, "Neurosis is always a substitute for legitimate suffering." As we've seen in Chapter 13, psychologically gritting your teeth too much can lead to significant psychological symptoms such as depression and anxiety attacks, and stress-related illnesses such as high blood pressure and tension headaches. People going through psychotherapy often experience a very common outcome. They eventually loosen up tight, inner emotional controls and begin to feel these underlying legitimate feelings (such as anger or grief). These emotions can be felt as very intense or painful, but are often accompanied by relief.

Jungian analyst, Marion Woodman says, "Real suffering burns clean. Neurotic suffering creates more and more soot." The struggle to bottle up feelings often actually leads to an intensification of suffering. It may seem paradoxical, but often expressing heart-felt emotions leads to relief and less emotional intensity.

Think About It _____

Buddha said, "Muddy water ... let stand ... become clear." The insistence, "I shouldn't be feeling so bad ... I'm too sensitive," or "This shouldn't be happening to me!" is like shaking up a jar of water with silt in it ... muddy water. Yet being able to stop the battle against feelings, surrender to them, sit with your feelings, and let yourself feel, can lead not only to relief but also to greater clarity about what is happening in your life and in your heart.

Rapid Solutions for Tolerating and Managing Intense Emotions

During times of great emotional distress, many people experience moments of extremely intense, painful emotions: anxiety, panic, sadness, despair, anger, and so on. We have just considered the value in feeling and expressing emotions. But let's be honest. Sometimes emotional distress just feels too overpowering. When you are beset by waves of intense emotion, it will be helpful to use effective strategies to manage such feelings in order to reduce suffering and regain some control. This chapter takes a look at seven approaches that are often successful in turning down the volume on painful feelings.

Tears of Relief

Previously (in Chapter 2) we looked at research conducted by neurobiologist William Frey. His studies reveal that many people begin to cry, feel ashamed, and then choke back tears. But when people give themselves permission to cry—no shaming, no self-criticism—the experience of crying rapidly reduces a wide range of intense emotions (from sadness to anger). Recall that a rapid reduction of painful emotions often follows an average crying spell, which generally lasts only three to six minutes.

Thus we human beings have built into our biology this incredibly effective way of rapidly reducing emotional intensity. The key is to give yourself permission to cry without self-condemnation or shaming.

> **Bet You Didn't Know**
>
> The stress hormone cortisol is activated by a hormone: ACTH. When people cry, ACTH is released in tears and actually results in a decrease in cortisol levels.

Taking a Time Out

Often, intense emotions erupt in the context of a heated encounter with another person. Sometimes the back-and-forth interaction throws gas on the fire, and negative emotions escalate. During these times it may be difficult to keep a realistic perspective, and people sometimes say and do things that they later regret.

The approach to dealing with this kind of situation is to give yourself a "time out." This is a strategy often used with children to help them calm down. Well, believe it or not, it works with adults, too. Getting away from the provocative interaction can reduce emotional intensity. And as you simmer down, it's then easier to think things through and regain a realistic perspective. People just don't think clearly when emotions are intense.

In the heat of an argument, lots of folks get caught up in winning, making a point, or trying to convince the other person that he is being unrealistic or unfair. These issues may be important, but frequently, if approached with excessive intensity, may

---

> **Bet You Didn't Know**
>
> The rapid increase in serotonin that accompanies intense physical exercise operates to inhibit a wide array of emotions. Do it even once and judge for yourself.

just lead to more conflict or hurt feelings. Going into another room, into the back yard, or better yet, going for a 10-minute brisk walk, the volume is likely to get turned down on strong feelings, at least somewhat. Then it may be easier to think, "What really matters?"—possibly, despite the upset, you'll realize that maintaining the relationship, or maintaining self-respect, now seems ultimately more important than winning an argument.

The Sixty-Second Reality Check

The 60-second reality check is a strategy that can help you quickly gain perspective and rapidly reduce emotional distress. It is best to do this when you can think more clearly, thus it's important to first de-escalate some of the intense emotions (as noted above). If you're feeling upset, follow these six instructions:

1. Ask yourself, "What has just happened? What are my feelings and are they understandable?"

2. In the grand scheme of things, how important is this?

3. Ask yourself, "Given my strong feelings now, am I likely to be this upset about it 24 hours from now? Or 48 hours from now?"

4. Quickly scan your mind for "shoulds/shouldn'ts," especially "This shouldn't be happening," "I shouldn't feel this way," or "They shouldn't be treating me this way." If these are present, say to yourself, "It's not a matter of should or shouldn't. These upsetting events/experiences are happening. And I do feel bad (sad, irritated, etc.). It's just the truth."

5. If the intense emotion is anxiety or nervousness, do two sets of eye movements or breathing techniques (as described in Chapter 10).

6. Remind yourself: "No matter what, I will not be hard on myself. I must be decent, gentle, and compassionate toward myself."

Okay, maybe it takes 90 seconds, but try it—even once. Most people experience an immediate de-escalation in strong emotions.

Countering Catastrophic Thinking

During moments of very intense emotions, the mind tends to generate catastrophic thinking, thoughts that scare people and accentuate the sense of being out of control. "I feel like I'm going crazy" … "I can't stand this!" … "Oh my God, I'm losing it." These thoughts just throw gasoline on the fire.

One way to help reduce some of the intensity of emotion is to actively avoid catastrophic thinking. Tell yourself that these thoughts are not helping. And replace them with one or more of the following (in your mind or, even better, by saying them out loud if you are in a private place):

♦ I've survived this before; I'll survive this time, too.

♦ Strong feelings are unpleasant, but they are not dangerous.

♦ This is a strong wave of emotion … just ride with it … it will subside.

♦ Fighting this emotion won't help … just hang on and know it won't last forever.

♦ I hate feeling this way, but I can accept it.

♦ These strong emotions are a reminder for me to use my coping skills (e.g. relaxation techniques, eye movements, etc.).

> **Bet You Didn't Know**
>
> Many Americans are chronically dehydrated. This can have an impact on emotions. Likewise, feeling hungry may contribute to more emotional reactivity. When feeling overwhelmed, drinking a large glass of water can help. Try it out. Soothing foods (as we discussed in Chapter 11) can also be a helpful quick fix.

Engaging in Nondestructive Distractions

Actively focusing your mind on nondestructive distractions can often effectively turn down the volume on intense emotions. Consider the following options:

1. Listen to music or a CD of Gregorian chants.

2. Read a ridiculously stupid tabloid.

3. Exercise.

4. Do something mundane, such as doing a load of laundry.

5. Take a hot shower or bath.

6. Use lilac- or lemon-balm-fragranced incense or lotion (which can have a calming effect for some people).

7. Drink warm milk.

8. Do muscle relaxation exercises (as described in Chapter 10).

9. Walk outside and look carefully at something beautiful, such as a flower or clouds in the sky.

10. Look at photographs from important, memorable, or fun times in your life. Remind yourself of these good times (it's best to have a handful of these pictures readily available ahead of time).

11. Experience powerful sensations, e.g. eat a lemon, or hurt yourself (a little bit). This last suggestion needs some explaining. Sometimes very brief and nonharmful physical pain will snap people out of an emotional meltdown. Here the goal absolutely is not self-harm; it is distraction. Two easy ways to do this are to snap your wrist smartly a couple of times with a rubber band or hold ice cubes in your hand. This doesn't work for everyone, but it does for some, and you can find out by trying it even once when you are in a state of significant overwhelm.

12. If a part of your distress is intense nervousness or anxiety and you feel a smothering sensation or shortness of breath, place a bag (lunch-sack-size) over your mouth and nose, and repeatedly breathe in and out. For this to be effective, continue breathing for several minutes until you are noticeably calmed down. This is an effective and rapid technique for reducing anxiety.

Bet You Didn't Know

When people feel very anxious they often experience a shortness of breath or smothering sensation. It feels like you are not getting enough oxygen, and this can be very frightening. The truth is that the kind of breathing that occurs with anxiety (rapid shallow breathing or sighing) actually super saturates your blood with oxygen. The problem is that this radical change in oxygen in the bloodstream causes red blood cells to hold on to oxygen molecules more tightly and the oxygen does not get readily released into your body and brain (thus the *sensation* of shortness of breath). Breathing more (hyperventilation) actually makes it worse. In addition to breathing back and forth into a paper bag, running for a few minutes, or other forms of exercise can quickly change the blood chemistry back to normal.

Riding the Waves of Emotion: Radical Acceptance

It may be hard to believe, but often people are calmed by what is known as radical acceptance. Here is how this works: no one likes intensely painful emotions. Yet the path of radical acceptance asks you not to fight the feeling; rather, notice it, acknowledge the truth, "This is very difficult (or painful)," and then say to yourself, "I don't have to like this, but I can simply accept that this is how I feel in the moment. These are honest human emotions. And, like all emotions, they come in waves. Soon the intensity of this feeling will begin to subside."

Staying Connected

Possibly the most important step to take when in a state of emotional overload is to reach out to other people or (if you are so inclined) to God. Talking with a friend or getting a hug from a loved one can be stabilizing and calming. This may also be accomplished by writing letters or emails to friends or loved ones.

Likewise, praying (especially praying out loud) can be helpful. Sometimes people pray for their life to be dramatically different, and then experience disappointment. The Navajo have a particular spiritual tradition called "the Hozro way." If they experience a severe drought, for instance, they don't pray for rain. Rather they pray for the courage and strength to endure this hardship.

Think About It

If you have a digital camera and Internet access, sending photos to a friend or relative can be an activity that can serve to distract you from strong feelings. This is also a way to make contact with people you like or love.

The Least You Need to Know

- Paradoxically, expressing difficult feelings often provides relief and reduces the intensity of painful emotions.

- As you encounter overwhelmingly intense emotions, a number of strategies can help to reduce that out-of-control feeling. Crying and a few minutes of exercise may be the quickest route to de-escalating strong emotions.

- A number of easy and nondestructive distractions can also help you regain emotional control.

- Reaching out for comfort and connection with others or your higher power likely is the most effective way to manage very intense emotions.

Chapter **19**

Taking Action in Your Life

In This Chapter

- ◆ Simplify your life and remove some sources of ongoing stress
- ◆ There are ways to proactively speak out and to repair relationships
- ◆ Increasing the likelihood of successfully changing problematic relationships
- ◆ Become very clear about those things that you cannot change

In much of this book, we have looked at facing and dealing with distressing moods internally … coping and healing from within. This chapter focuses on actions you may choose to take to change problematic situations in your life.

We will consider four areas of change: simplifying your life, repairing damaged relationships, learning to be assertive, and accepting what you cannot change.

Simplifying Your Life

Lives get cluttered with activities and stuff (possessions). Often this clutter contributes significantly to a sense of chaos and loss of balance in life. One approach to coping more effectively with life is to let go and simplify your life. Here are some suggestions:

◆ Say no or let go of life activities that are not truly meaningful or necessary for you and that exact a toll in terms of time and exhaustion (what we talked about in Chapter 17).

◆ Get clear about your own natural rhythms and pace of life. This can help you evaluate the way you choose to use your time each day ... each week. Honor your own pace.

◆ Develop rituals. Psychiatrist Robert Arnot has written that human beings generally do not respond well to change or chaos. He says that developing routines and rituals in your life can help to simplify and create order, familiarity, and symmetry. Routines and rituals are like anchors in your life that help provide stability during stormy, high-stress times. Additionally, it has been shown that certain highly regular routines help to stabilize the brain's biological clock (the circadian rhythm). This is especially so regarding times of day that you eat, exercise, relax, and sleep. Regularity is the key to stabilizing our biology.

◆ Numerous phone calls and emails, coming in all day long, can interrupt the flow of your life and create chaos. It is often helpful to set aside a specific time each day to return phone calls and respond to e-mails.

◆ Every day should also make room for regular stress breaks (e.g. 10 minutes where you stretch and walk outside for a few minutes).

◆ Delegate. Many people feel that they must do it all. Sometimes this comes from the belief that if you have someone else do it, they won't do it right. One solution is to have your children do routine chores. Or hire someone to come in and clean your house or yard. Many people believe that this last proposition is just too expensive, so they do it themselves. If you enjoy mowing the lawn, that's a different thing. But if it is a tedious chore, think again. Lots of people spend a number of hours doing these tasks when they could easily hire a neighborhood teenager to do it for small cost. Even having someone come in once a month to clean the house can help.

◆ Look at your clutter and if there are things you never use, then sell them or give them away.

- Get an answering machine and screen calls. You do not have to answer the phone every time it rings.

- Make fewer trips to the grocery store.

- Stop junk mail. Contact Stop the Mail at PO Box 9008, Farmingdale, N.Y., 11735, and ask that your name be removed from mailing lists. This is likely to reduce junk mail by 50 percent.

Repairing Damaged Relationships

Many people carry the burden of long-held regrets, grudges, and unspoken words. Maybe these issues are not constantly in conscious awareness, but they eat away at people in subtle and insidious ways. People may know this but put off doing anything about it for years. A choice you can make is to proactively address these areas of unfinished business. This might involve writing a letter or making a phone call to a friend or relative, and speaking out openly about your feelings.

Two months before my father died from lung cancer, I wrote him a heartfelt letter letting him know about many positive memories that I had with him as I was growing up. I had wanted to do this for a long time but felt bashful about doing it since he was not a very sentimental man. But to this day I am grateful that I wrote that letter. It meant a lot to him and to me, and I know now, many years after his death, I am not living with regret. So many times people do feel this need to share feelings (positive or negative) with a friend or family member, yet time runs out. They die and what is left is regret.

Forgiveness may be one thing that can help bring closure to long-held hurt, anger, or bitterness. However, forgiveness is a complicated thing. "Forgive and forget" is hard to do and may not be the answer for some people. Drs. Sidney and Suzanne Simon in their book *Forgiveness* point out what forgiveness is not: it is not excusing or giving absolution to someone for past hurtful behavior and it is not giving in. It is something people do as a way to let go of toxic, buried feelings. It is a refusal to let painful memories ruin your life. To forgive requires letting go of the wish that one's past life could have been different. It means facing the reality that life often is not fair.

Scott Peck, the author of *The Road Less Traveled* says that before you can pardon people, you must first find them guilty. I think what he means is that for forgiveness to truly make a difference, it is crucial to first face the whole truth about what happened to you and how you were hurt. If at that time you choose to forgive, it is more likely to really matter.

Remember, authentic forgiveness always includes the acknowledgement that what was done was wrong—absolutely not okay. And you are making the decision to let go of this memory that continues to hurt you. Forgiveness might involve speaking directly to or writing to the person who has hurt you. But it can also be a private action. In your own mind you may forgive someone without that person ever knowing. Finally, I want to say that forgiveness is not the pathway for everyone. It is one choice you can make, but choosing not to forgive is in no way a fault or weakness.

Think About It

"When you hold resentment toward another, you are bound to that person or condition by an emotion that is stronger than steel. Forgiveness is the only way to dissolve that link and get free." —Catherine Ponder

"To forgive is to set a prisoner free and discover that that prisoner was you." —Lewis B. Smedes

"Always forgive your enemies … nothing annoys them so much." —Oscar Wilde

Repairing problematic or damaged relationships often requires directly confronting another person and asking for some kind of change. This can be done most effectively by learning how to be more assertive.

Learning to Be Assertive

The term *assertion* is often misunderstood to mean or imply being aggressive. Assertion and *aggression* have only one thing in common: expressing feelings or opinions without holding back. But that is where the commonalty ends. Assertiveness tempers honest communication with concern, sensitivity, and respect for the other person's feelings. Dealing with conflicts in relationships in an assertive way may seem to come naturally to some people. But this is not simply something you are born with. Even very passive or *nonassertive* people can learn the skills of assertion.

There are two goals of assertive behavior. One is to ask for a change in another person's behavior. For example, if someone is being hurtful or abusive toward you, the goal might be to ask her to stop treating you this way. The second goal is to speak out about how you feel or what you believe, to increase your own sense of self-respect. I would like to strongly suggest that this second goal actually be your primary goal. There may be times when you speak directly to another and ask for a change in his behavior and, despite your best efforts, he says "no." Before approaching someone, it will be helpful for you to remind yourself, "I want him to change how he is treating me, but regardless of the outcome, my primary goal is to speak out and be heard."

def•i•ni•tion _____

Assertion is communicating in an honest and direct way, telling someone how you feel and/or asking for a change in her behavior. It is tempered by a respect for her feelings. **Nonassertion** is being passive or timid. When acting in a nonassertive way, people do not speak out and may allow someone to repeatedly use or abuse them. **Aggression** never truly takes other people's feelings into consideration. Often, aggressive remarks contain comments that attack the other person, such as belittling, humiliating, intimidating, or threatening comments.

Choosing to approach someone in an assertive way involves careful thinking about four issues. First, is this truly an important issue? This is a matter of choosing your battles. Second, what do I anticipate are the potential risks if I choose to be assertive? Third, plan ahead of time what you want to say and how you want to say it. And finally, think about back-up plans ahead of time should the assertion fail to get the desired results.

Considering the Risks

Many people put off honest confrontation with others because they anticipate all sorts of unpleasant reactions from the other person, such as the other person becoming angry in response, or hurt, or rejecting. By and large, if you approach someone in a respectful way with sensitivity for her feelings, then the risk of upsetting her is reduced. Very often if there is some upset, it diminishes quickly, in an hour or two or a day or two. And you have taken the first step toward a more permanent solution to the problematic relationship.

It is also wise to be careful. Some infantile people, especially someone in a position of power over you, such as a supervisor, may not be able or willing to hear what you have to say, even if what you are addressing is completely legitimate. Look at that person's track record. Has there been a history of inappropriate lashing out at others (verbally or physically)? Is this person typically not likely to listen to others or does he have a strong need to be in control or to dominate others? If so, this certainly does not preclude you from speaking with him, but it is something to carefully consider.

Another risk is that the assertion may fail. You may ask for a change in behavior that is completely reasonable and the person may say "no." If this occurs, you might consider a response such as, "I'm sorry you feel that way. This issue is very important to me and I hope you'll give some thought to what I've said." This is also where back-up plans come in handy, and we'll take a look at these shortly.

Critical Elements in Assertive Action

There are three key ingredients that increase the likelihood that assertive actions will be successful:

1. Verbal content. The content in what you say. Two guidelines are as follows:

   KISS (Keep It Short and Simple). Many times as people attempt to communicate in an assertive way, they get bogged down by apologies, explanations, or excuses. It is best to get right to the point. Here are some examples. "John, in the past six months you have been coming home later and later from work. It would mean a lot to me if you could make a point to spend more time with me in the evenings," or "Sally, you may not realize it, but frequently you interrupt me when I am talking. At these times I feel frustrated. I would like to kindly ask you to not do this. I would really appreciate it if you would be willing to make this change."

   "I" language. Some assertions fail because of the use of what's known as "You" language, e.g. "You make me unhappy," "You are so rude to me." "You" language almost always puts people on the defensive. Here is an example of "I" language: "When this happens, I feel sad".

2. Vocal tone. The more you can speak in a firm but nonaggressive voice, the more effective the assertion will be.

3. Body language and eye contact. When people feel very uncomfortable discussing difficult issues, it's often hard to make and maintain eye contact. When talking, if you lean forward a bit and make direct eye contact, the assertion is often more effective.

Verbal content delivers the message with the vocal tone and eye contact underscoring, "I mean what I am saying."

Back-Up Plans

Sometimes people get upset if they are confronted or the assertion fails (they say "no" to your request). Here are some back-up responses. You may not need to use them, but plan ahead of time about how you'll respond, just in case. It will help you feel more confident about your assertive interaction:

They Say	You Respond
"You are just too sensitive"	"I do have strong feelings about this and I'd like to make my point again"; then restate your assertion.
Tears, upset, and guilt messages	"I know this is hard to hear, and I know it's causing you upset, but this issue is important and I want to repeat myself."
They argue with you about the legitimacy of what you have said or how you feel.	"Regardless of the reasons, this is how I feel," or, "We may not see eye to eye on this issue, but all the same, it is how I feel."
"There is no way I'll do" what you're asking.	"I am disappointed to hear you say that. Even if you are unwilling to change, I just want to go on record that I mean what I have said."

For a more in-depth look at assertion, I recommend the very popular book, *Your Perfect Right*, a best seller written by psychologists Robert Alberti and Michael Emmons.

Accepting What You Cannot Change

Despite honest efforts to negotiate for changes in relationships, at times people are unsuccessful. A spouse, a boss, a neighbor ... continue in some way to be hurtful. Sometimes upon careful inspection, people conclude that the relationship is toxic and harmful. This may lead to decisions to seek out counseling (for example, couples counseling), to leave a job or a relationship, or to set limits on the amount of time you spend with the other person. For some people, the limit setting applies to how much of your heart or personal feelings you are willing to share with the other. You may decide to stop confiding in her or stop counting on her to be there for you. Winston Churchill said, "If you must walk through the valley of the shadow of death, just don't stop." Sometimes people will ultimately decide that certain jobs or relationships are just too damaging. They decide to get out of their own valley. Admittedly, these can be very difficult decisions to make.

There is wisdom in the prayer of St. Francis:

"God grant me the ability to accept those things I cannot change"; here the word "accept" certainly does not imply that you like it, but rather that you are accepting the hard reality that some people are cold, hurtful, infantile, or mean-spirited.

The theologian Reinhold Niebuhr is cred-
ited with building on to the prayer of St.
Francis:

> "God grant me the serenity to accept
> the things that I cannot change, the
> courage to change the things I can, and
> the wisdom to know the difference."

This has been adopted as the Serenity Prayer by
many 12-step programs. It gives wise counsel.

> **Think About It** _____
>
> Back-up plans may not be
> necessary, but they are like
> carrying a spare tire in your
> trunk. Just knowing it is there will
> help you feel more confident.
> Plus you'll have a ready come-
> back if the assertion fails.

The Least You Need to Know

◆ Some rather minor lifestyle adjustments aimed at simplifying your life can provide a significant reduction in stress.

◆ Many people live for years in problematic and troubled relationships. Unspoken
words, regrets, grudges, and ongoing hurts exact a great emotional toll. There
are action strategies you can use to repair some of the relationships.

◆ Assertive behavior is an honest and straightforward way for people to ask for and
negotiate changes in relationships.

◆ Despite your best efforts, some toxic interpersonal actions may be difficult to
change or resolve. You must then either leave the relationship or find new ways
to live with it.

Chapter

20

The Role of Spirituality in Emotional Coping and Healing

In This Chapter

- ◆ Finding comfort in spiritual beliefs and practices
- ◆ Reexamining religious beliefs that we formed many years ago as young children
- ◆ Religious and spiritual traditions that complement models of emotional healing
- ◆ Finding ways to face and respond to existential issues

Since the beginning of recorded time, people have developed spiritual traditions that serve as a source of comfort and support, especially during hard times. In this chapter, we'll take a look at the role of spirituality and emotional coping.

A Common Human Need

Across cultures and across the millennia, all societies have embraced some sort of religious or spiritual belief system. Oftentimes this is in the context of an organized religion; however, for many, spiritual beliefs are highly personalized. Spirituality likely addresses universal longings to feel cared for or looked after by a higher power. And most traditions also attempt to offer some answers to existential questions that plague all people from time to time:

◆ Why were we born if only eventually to die?

◆ What happens to us after death?

◆ Why do bad things happen to good people?

Think About It

Religious and spiritual beliefs and practices, in the words of authors Edward Shaframske and Len Sperry, "... appear to be especially valuable when suffering tests one's ability to sustain hope in the face of extraordinary hardship ... when people are pushed to the limits of their resources."

For many people, spiritual practices or participating in religious activities are woven into the fabric of daily life. It can help sustain people during hard times, offer support and hope, and provide a way to make and sustain contact with others. Here such beliefs may be an integral part of one's life.

For others, people primarily turn to religion and spiritual pondering during painful losses and severely traumatic experiences, the kind of which often drive people to their knees. During these times, ordinary sources of support and coping skills may not be enough to provide adequate comfort.

The Role of Spirituality and Religion in America

Nietzsche said, "God is dead." Most Americans disagree. Recent public opinion polls reveal that 94 percent of Americans believe in God, 69 percent belong to a religious organization, and 90 percent say that they pray (especially during difficult times). Eighty-five percent of our citizens say that because of faith, their lives have meaning and purpose.

Graffito offers a rebuttal, "Nietzsche is dead." —God.

Debate Among Mental Health Professionals

Sigmund Freud was an atheist and believed that religious beliefs were simply an illusion, a figment of human imaginations. However, his famous counterpart psychoanalyst, Carl Jung, couldn't disagree more. He believed in the importance of spiritual beliefs and held the opinion that many emotional problems could only successfully be resolved by religion. Needless to say, there have been mixed feelings among mental-health professionals regarding the role of spirituality in emotional health during the past 100 years. A part of this is likely due to the fact that while many religious beliefs, practices, and traditions can offer tremendous support, there are also times when conflicts over religion can be terribly harmful.

Psychiatrist Scott Peck has aptly stated, "Many people hurt by religious experiences throw the baby out with the bathwater. And clearly there is a lot of dirty bathwater … holy wars, inquisitions, human sacrifice, dogmatism, ignorance, hypocrisy, conformity, self-righteousness, cruelty, book-burning, witch-burning, morbid guilt, and insanity. But is all this what God has done to humans or what humans have done to God?"

In this book I do not intend to endorse a particular belief system. I have a great appreciation for how personal such things are. However, I do want to address four issues:

1. The question of "belief" … are your beliefs ones that have been prescribed by others or ones that you have chosen?

2. Aspects of organized religions that may create emotional conflict (aspects of belief systems that have been judged to run counter to effective emotional coping and growth)

3. Elements of religious beliefs that complement models of psychological growth and health

4. How spirituality may address existential issues: the unfairness of life, meaninglessness, and emptiness

Beliefs

James Fowler, who has written widely about religion, specifically addresses what he calls "stages of faith development."

From young childhood until early adolescence, most children exposed to some form of organized religion tend to take in the beliefs taught to them, largely without questioning them. Sometime during later adolescence or young adulthood, according to

Fowler's model, some people begin to question the religious dogma they have been taught. Sometimes this is spurred on by noticing paradoxes in holy writings (e.g. one place in the text it says one thing, while in another place it says something different). They begin to understand that holy writings are complex.

Others encounter difficult life experiences that directly clash with church dogma. When this happens, some abandon religion altogether, but many begin a personal quest for their own unique beliefs. Such beliefs may be largely in accord with what they have been taught, but for others, life events, reflections, and re-evaluation lead to more personal and more unique beliefs. The resulting, redefined beliefs now are not prescribed, but are chosen. Some organized religions encourage this journey of questions and personal struggle while others strongly discourage it.

As Norman Douglas has said, "There are some things you can't learn from others. You must pass through the fire."

Bet You Didn't Know

Many religious and spiritual traditions value the process of questioning, reflection, and self-discovery when it comes to each person's search for meaningful beliefs. This practice is a central part of many Native American rituals, often called "vision quests." Here the young person must discover his or her own unique totem.

The Amish provide instruction in both their religious beliefs and their cultural customs. However, when adolescents reach the age of 18 or 19, they are encouraged to leave the Amish community for a year or two and experience the outside world. After a period of time they then make a choice about whether or not to follow the Amish way. This remarkable tradition honors the ability of all young people to come to their own belief based on religious instruction, life experiences, and self-exploration.

For many people, their primary spiritual beliefs were fashioned early in life and have gone unexamined. However, in times of great emotional upset, some come to question their beliefs. Some authors have written about the concept of "de-constructing beliefs." De-constructing beliefs does not mean destroying beliefs. It simply is a careful exploration and examination of one's beliefs in light of life as it is now. Most times, initial beliefs were formed as children or adolescents and never again questioned ... what people may discover is that these existing beliefs were truly not a chosen path. For many people, this re-examination of beliefs leads to the formation of belief systems that ultimately feel more authentic.

Emotional Conflicts Surrounding Religious Issues

Although one's beliefs can often offer significant support during hard times, there certainly are times when beliefs may contribute to conflict or intensify emotional suffering. Julie Exline and colleagues suggest the following common religious-related conflicts:

1. Chronic self-blame: either seeing oneself as unworthy in the eyes of God, or interpreting negative life events as punishment from God

2. Doubt that sins can be forgiven

3. Feeling abandoned by or alienated from God

4. Inability to resolve anger at God (not uncommon in those who have experienced a tragedy such as the death of a child)

Many authors from both psychology and theology have suggested the following elements that characterize potentially toxic religions traditions:

1. Overemphasis on compliance, obeying authority, and seeing questioning as being a sign of disloyalty

2. Withholding medial or psychological treatment from children

3. Overemphasis on legalism and dogmatism

4. Exclusivity, and a holier-than-thou approach with an intolerance of other's views

5. Asking for unrealistic financial contributions

6. Discouraging leaving an abusive relationship

7. Exceedingly harsh judgments about divorce or sexual orientation

8. Encouraging hatred, vengeance, and prejudice

9. Acts of dominance or cruelty somehow justified or rationalized as being "In the name of God"; sadly not uncommon in situations of spousal abuse and domestic violence

Conversely, qualities that characterize healthy, growth-promoting beliefs include these:

1. God seen as primarily loving, forgiving, merciful, and comforting.

2. Honoring individual spiritual unfolding and personal reflection.

3. An awareness that religious literature is complex and sometimes ambiguous (open to different interpretations).

4. Respect for others' beliefs.

Religious Traditions That Complement Models of Emotional Healing

Buddhism holds as its "first noble truth" the acceptance of emotional suffering as a normal part of life ... not pathology. An even more ancient Eastern religion, Hinduism, states, "Suffering is grace, for it awakens the great heart of compassion." These traditions acknowledge the ultimate value in being open to and accepting suffering, not only for oneself but suffering in others. This is a part of the pathway to a meaningful life.

Likewise, in Christian teachings, the New Testament says, "Jesus wept," (John, Chapter 11, verse 35). He wept upon discovering that his friend Lazarus had died and when he saw the suffering of Lazarus' wife and sister. Clearly this verse gives people permission to acknowledge one's own and others' suffering.

Acceptance of human limitations is also acknowledged in the New Testament, "The spirit is willing but the flesh is weak" (Matthew, Chapter 26, verse 41).

Facing existential fears can enrich and animate life. In traditional Jewish weddings, the breaking of a wine glass at the end of the wedding, a prelude to celebration, stands as a poignant reminder of the fragility of life. In a number of West African cultures, for centuries, a sort of rattle is shaken at the time of the birth of a child. These very first baby rattles were designed to sound like the rattling of bones. At this time of great joy and new life, one must not forget how close the specter of death is.

Such traditions might seem morbid to some; facing one's own mortality can become a focus for worry or pessimism. However, conversely, it can be an ongoing reminder of how precious life is, and encourage people to live each day to the fullest.

Hope for salvation, for comfort, and for the felt presence of God can be a comfort to many people who are facing otherwise hopeless situations (such as a terminal illness). In the Jewish tradition, hope is sometimes referred to as the "anchor of the soul."

In the myth of Pandora's box, once the lid is lifted and out pours all manner of bad things, evil, pestilence, suffering … at the bottom of the box is left the spirit of hope.

Many spiritual traditions also address a common existential question. Has my life mattered? Rabbi Harold Kushner says, "It is not the fear of death, of our lives ending, that haunts our sleep so much as the fear that our lives will not have mattered."

Getting clear about what really matters in your life may be one response to these haunting existential questions. For some, this involves charity, volunteer work, and living one's life in an authentic way (as we discussed in Chapter 17). The key is to not put this off. Time is always running short; the sooner the better. Find your true calling (whether a job, a leisure-time pursuit, or a mission) and follow it. As scholar Joseph Campbell said, "Follow your bliss."

Finally, one source of great comfort is when people are able to feel some sense of connection with God. Burning bushes aside, the pathway for some is to be found in religious rituals. There is something about repetitive rituals that can, for some people, shut off the busy chatter of inner thoughts, and create an altered state, during which they feel closer to God. Different traditions have taken their own version of this, Native American sweat lodges, ritual drumming, Gregorian chants, contemplative prayer, deep meditation, or listening to favorite hymns.

Existential Suffering

Accompanying many life crises, in addition to feelings of sadness, fear, anger, intense disappointment, etc., are those very common and gut-wrenching existential anxieties. Most notable is the question, "Why do bad things happen to good people?" Rabbi Harold Kushner in his bestselling book by the same title speaks of Archibald MacLeish's play "J. B.," which is a takeoff on the book of Job from the Old Testament.

J. B., like Job, experiences extraordinary hardships. His children die, he loses all of his possessions, and is afflicted by a terrible illness. Like Job, he is a man totally devoted to God. The dilemma is how to rectify his predicament: loving God yet experiencing tragedy. In this play, he (like the rest of us) really does not fully understand what's happened or why, nor does he have a magic formula. But he does respond by saying something that may seem radical. He tells his wife that he forgives God. He forgives God for making a world where there is danger and disease, where innocent people suffer. And despite his horrific experiences, says to God that he wants more life.

Another response to existential pain comes from a very ancient tradition. In Greece, temples have been excavated and something odd has been discovered. Beneath some temples is a small dark basement. Translations of artifacts indicate that these rooms were called incubation chambers. Presumably if someone was ill (physically, emotionally, or spiritually), she would enter the underground chamber accompanied by a healer. The healer and the sick person would spend three days in the incubation chamber and emerge having been healed. Nothing is known about what happened during these three days. But I believe there are a couple of images and ideas that can be gleaned.

First, the sick person descends into darkness. This may be what many of us do when entering terribly painful times in our lives. Times that might be what some authors have called "the dark night of the soul." Let me be clear: the sick person does not flee, but rather walks into this darkness.

Secondly, she is accompanied by the healer, another human being. I believe that this kind of companionship may be what humans need (or what we can best offer to others) who are struggling with tragedy and existential despair. No one truly has answers to avoid or fix some of these painful realities. But, at least we do not have to be alone.

The word "psychotherapist" comes from the Greek words "psyche" (meaning soul) and "therapeia" (meaning caring for or tending). Literal translation is "tenders of the soul." This may certainly apply to professional therapists, but of course also can apply to pastoral counselors, clergy, and dear, trusted friends or relatives.

The Least You Need to Know

♦ Longings for comfort or protection from a higher power have been seen in every culture since antiquity. This is a huge issue for most human beings.

♦ Religious conflicts and exposure to toxic religious practices can cause great emotional harm.

♦ It matters whether one's beliefs are totally "prescribed" or if they are "personally chosen."

♦ Many spiritual and religious beliefs and practices can offer significant support for those going through very difficult life circumstances.

Part 4

Areas of Particular Concern

This section of the book focuses on four areas of particular concern: dealing with loss and grief, how to respond to exposure to very frightening or traumatic life events, discovering your true self, and how to help children who are going through difficult times. Although earlier chapters in the book have addressed a number of specific coping strategies, these particular areas of concern can be especially challenging and deserve a more thorough discussion.

21

Loss and Grief

In This Chapter

- ◆ Very painful losses are a common human experience
- ◆ Time alone does not heal wounds
- ◆ There is no prescribed pathway for mourning losses
- ◆ Complicated grief reactions often occur

If you live long enough, it is inevitable that you will experience the loss of a loved one or close friend. Modern day American culture endorses a "get over it and get on with your life" attitude regarding grief. This represents a significant misunderstanding about the nature of emotional healing following loss. We'll take a close look at this in this chapter and also see ways people can more effectively cope and heal following painful losses.

Broken Hearts

Each year in the United States, approximately 10 million people experience the death of a close family member. Each year there are more than a million new widows or widowers. Many thousands of couples lose a baby through stillbirth or miscarriage. Infertility problems rob many couples of the dream of having children. Divorces (2.5 million each year in the United

States), separations, kids leaving home, geographic relocations, the death of a beloved pet. The loss experienced when a parent realizes that his child has sustained serious brain damage or a severe type of mental illness.

The list of losses is long. And we must add to this list the loss of a dream: the dream of a happy marriage or family, the loss of a dream for a meaningful career, the loss of the dreamed-for joyous retirement when one member of a couple develops Alzheimer's disease or another similar neurological illness that causes dementia. (With such illness the losses go on and on, as the person slowly slips away.)

Misguided Notions Regarding Grief and Loss

A public-opinion poll several years ago asked a random sample of Americans, "How long does it take to get over the loss of a loved one?" The answer most often given in this poll was one year. This is wishful thinking that is clearly out of touch with the human reality. Do people, in fact, really "get over" these terrible losses?

def•i•ni•tion

Bereavement is that state of having lost someone close to you. **Grief** represents a large array of feelings that often accompany bereavement, such as sadness and loneliness. **Mourning** refers to various aspects of emotional healing that take place following a painful loss.

Most people do mourn losses and healing occurs. However, a large body of *bereavement* research indicates that broken hearts do not mend quickly. Although there are exceptions, most people continue to suffer noticeable *grief* for a period of four to seven years after the death of a spouse. And often longer, following the loss of a child. Ernest Hemingway said, "The world breaks everyone, and afterward, many are strong at the broken places." This can be one outcome. Yet many people don't mend, because complications develop.

Grief embodies a number of painful emotions that erupt in the aftermath of a significant loss, including the following:

- Sadness

- Loneliness

- Anger

- Shame (usually due to feeling emotional or vulnerable)

- Fear of loss of control

♦ Fear that other loved ones may also soon die

♦ Fear that I, too, will die soon

♦ Survivor guilt ("Why did it have to be him … it should have been me")

♦ Nervousness, anxiety attacks, and/or irritability

♦ Sometimes, prolonged periods of numbness (feeling disconnected, spacey, mildly confused, and a felt sense of unreality—this is a form of psychological shock)

Get On with Your Life!

This pervasive cultural pressure is the source of significant harm to many people who have experienced a loss. Surely there is a period of time when most friends and relatives provide support and comfort, accepting grief as a normal human response to loss. But often after six months or a year, those who are bereaved begin to encounter remarks from well-intentioned and good-hearted friends or relatives. "You look like you are still taking it hard," "You need to let go," "Your husband would have wanted you to move ahead with your life." The intentions may be sincere, but often the underlying message is, "If you are still grieving, there is something wrong with you."

As people begin to hear these comments, a very common outcome is for the bereaved person to start wondering, "Is there something wrong with me? Am I neurotic or depressed?" As we'll see shortly, about 20–25 percent of people do develop significant depression following the loss of a loved one. However, the majority of people are not clinically depressed. They are experiencing normal grief, yet they are encountering cultural standards that, in my opinion, are absurd.

In many rural Greek villages there is a social custom that prescribes a five-year period of mourning following the death of a spouse or a child. Rather than being criticized, those who have lost a loved one continue to receive support and understanding. Ongoing grief is not only accepted, but is actually encouraged. This tradition may be closer to the reality of prolonged healing following painful losses.

When Americans pick up on the "Let go and get on with your life" message, they typically begin to bury their feelings. They stop talking about or openly expressing feelings of sadness or loneliness. Their anguish goes underground. When this happens, they now are not only continuing to grieve, but must do this alone—privately in their minds without the outward acknowledgement and support for their ongoing suffering. Some people experiencing this completely natural but prolonged grief may turn to medications (tranquilizers or antidepressants) to numb their pain. Alcohol abuse is another way to anesthetize a broken heart.

The Journey of Grief

In large-scaled studies, about 10 percent of people experiencing a loss feel very little grief. Some of these people were actually never deeply attached to the person who died. If the relationship was abusive or otherwise deeply troubled, sometimes the main feeing is relief. For some, belief in the hereafter provides comfort that eases grief. Thus, for various reasons, not all humans feel intense grief. However, most do. And for some, grief does subside within that first year.

Looking at large groups of people who have had a significant loss, we can glean some common trends (although I must emphasize that from one individual to another, there may be enormous differences). Following the initial shock of the loss, most people experience four to six months of exquisitely painful sadness. This is often accompanied by pining and yearning for the lost loved one, and periodic moments of denial, "I can't believe this has really happened!"

Somewhere around the six-month time frame following the loss, a harder reality of the loss hits people. Here there is often an even deeper sense of loss. At this point, many people find that they are not handling their emotions or their lives in general as well as they were just following the loss. And yet by this time, many friends, fellow church members, and others are not as available for support as they were in the more immediate aftermath of the loss. The social isolation may now hit people hard. And long after some sadness begins to subside a bit, what stands out as especially painful is loneliness and simply missing the loved one.

I Don't Want to Let Go

Despite encouragement to let go and get on with your life, clearly two thirds of people on a regular basis continue periodically to feel the presence of their lost loved ones. They may hear their voice, smell their perfume, or feel their presence in bed next to them at night. Half of people have a strong sense that their deceased loved one is still somehow present, looking out for them. And one third of bereaved people frequently talk to their lost loved one. These experiences are very common, especially during the first two years following a loss.

Think About It _____

Despite a strong belief in the hereafter and assurance of peace for the deceased loved one, many people still are plagued by the two most common ongoing experiences of loss: missing that person and loneliness. English novelist Edward Bulwer-Lytton said it well, "Alone!—that worn-out word, So idly spoken, and so cold heard: Yet all that poets sing and grief hath known of hopes kneels in that word: Alone!" Others can never fill the emptiness left by the loss of a loved one, but companionship and human contact can offer comfort. This is especially important in the first few years following a painful loss.

Time Heals All Wounds?

This hopeful admonition is likely to be inaccurate. Just waiting for time to pass assumes passivity. What helps people to heal following major losses is not the passage of time, but rather, actively grieving the loss. Grieving is something we do (and choose to do). Let me be perfectly clear: how this is done depends entirely on the individual person. There is not a specific prescription for successful grief work. However, the following are generally accepted as essential elements in grieving that moves a person toward healing:

Shakespeare said, "Give sorrow words. Silence whispers the or' fraught heart and bids it break." Facing the painful realities of the loss is helped significantly if a person has the opportunity to speak to and to openly share emotions with another person. Grief runs so deep that almost always this sharing of emotional anguish needs to be done over and over again. Many people find it hard to seek out a friend or relative who is willing and available to hear their grief, especially if it is intense and if it is necessary to share over and over again. In such cases, bereavement groups can be very helpful. Also, many people choose to go into counseling to help them face and process their loss. Please know that therapy is not just for people with psychiatric disorders. These days, many very emotionally sturdy people seek out counseling as a way to work through their grief.

"Hold on" Versus "Letting Go"

Increasingly, experts on loss and bereavement are realizing that the cultural directive to let go of attachments to the deceased loved one may be misguided. An alternative is to do exactly the opposite. As people first encounter their grief, a lot of thinking, talking about, and feelings pertain to the suffering leading up to the death and/or the trauma of the death itself. However, at some point, many people are able to move beyond this singular focus on the death itself. As intense feelings begin to soften some, what many people then naturally do is to reminisce. At some point people may be able to let go of the pain, but not the memory of their loved one.

Reminiscing occurs in a number of ways. Repeatedly talking with others about memories of a life spent with their loved one certainly is a powerful way to reminisce. Journaling or writing about the deceased loved one can also be helpful. Putting together a scrapbook, making a collage, or taking a trip of remembrance (going back to where you first met your wife, for instance) are ways to re-experience the presence of your loved one.

Here the goal is not letting go. This approach appreciates the need people have to maintain attachments. And by reminiscing, the images and memories of the loved one actually are taken more deeply into your heart and mind.

Ongoing Connection, Ongoing Love

Rabbi Harold Kushner says, "Only human beings can defeat death by summoning up the memories of someone they loved and lost, and feeling that person close to them as they do so. Memory is what gives us power over time by keeping the past present so that it cannot fade and rob us of what we once held precious."

> **Think About It**
>
> Helen Keller suggests, "What we have once enjoyed, we can never lose. All that we love deeply becomes a part of us."

Some might argue that people do need to move on with their lives. Well, odd as it may seem, to understand, respect, and embrace this need for reminiscing often helps people more deeply heal from losses. And, in fact, they find ways to maintain their attachment while at the same time reinvesting in their new life.

Complicated Grief Reactions

It is much more likely that people will suffer complicated grief reactions if one of the following occurs:

◆ The loss was due to a murder or suicide.

◆ The death was sudden, untimely, and/or very traumatic.

◆ The bereaved person has poor or absent social supports.

◆ The death followed a very lengthy illness. In these instances, the bereaved person is very likely to have suffered for months or years caring for their loved one. This can completely wear people out emotionally.

◆ The death was a loss of a troubled or highly ambivalent relationship. An example might be that of a woman who lost her husband. They did share many years together and had happy or meaningful times together. However, the husband may also have been abusive toward her, belittling or controlling her or hurting her physically. This kind of loss is very complicated. The widow likely will be tied up in emotional knots, grieving his loss and also being relieved that the abuse has now stopped. Such ambivalent losses often result in people becoming depressed.

Twenty to 25 percent of people who lose a loved one will experience grief, but over a period of time the grief disintegrates into depression. Ten percent of people will react to the loss by developing severe anxiety (sometimes post-traumatic stress disorder). Alcohol or drug abuse often accompanies these types of complicated grief reactions. These serious outcomes are addressed in more detail in Chapter 26.

The following are signs that grief may be turning into depression:

◆ Severe sleep disturbances, especially waking up very early and being unable to return to sleep

◆ Marked weight loss

◆ A complete loss of interest in life activities; unable to derive any pleasure from life (Note: most bereaved people are dominated by sadness, but are able to have moments of happiness or enjoyment, e.g. watching a funny movie, having lunch with a friend, or playing with their grandchildren. When depression strikes, they are also robbed of these simple life pleasures.)

◆ Severe anxiety or agitation

◆ Serious thoughts about suicide

Other Losses

Losses due to separation, divorce, or geographic relocation certainly are different in many ways from the death of a loved one. However, all losses stir up strong and sometimes complex and conflicting feelings. Time alone does not heal all wounds. People have their best shot at coping with and healing from losses if they …

- Recognize that very painful emotions are a normal part of experiencing losses.

- Realize that the idea that you can "get over it" quickly is often completely unrealistic.

- Can talk about the loss over and over again. This is a central feature in healing the hurt caused by losses. You may have friends or relatives who understand this and are available to listen and support you. But if not, please consider counseling or psychotherapy.

Finally it is worth noting that some people by nature are more private. Sharing personal feelings with others is not their style. Still, it is helpful for such people to also face these painful realities and to grieve.

The Least You Need to Know

- Our culture holds misguided notions about grief. Broken hearts simply do not heal quickly.

- The majority of people experiencing very painful losses may continue to grieve for four to seven years following the loss.

- Trying to "get over it" or "let go" of attachments to a deceased loved one may actually prolong the emotional suffering that occurs in the aftermath of a loss.

- After the death of a loved one, most people experience excruciating emotional pain, but it is a part of normal grief and mourning.

- Twenty to 25 percent of people develop clinical depression or severe anxiety following painful losses. Should this occur, professional therapy can be enormously helpful.

Chapter 22

Exposure to Frightening or Traumatic Events

In This Chapter

- ◆ Most people will eventually be exposed to at least one highly traumatic event
- ◆ Most people who live through severe trauma do not develop serious psychological symptoms
- ◆ Normal reactions to traumatic events can be confusing and scary
- ◆ Post-traumatic stress disorder often responds very well to psychological treatment

In addition to the host of difficult things all of us encounter in life, exposure to very terrible and traumatic events is also quite common. In this chapter, we will look closely at the impact of severe trauma and ways to cope in the aftermath of such experiences.

Trauma: Much More Common Than You Might Think

It is estimated that 50–90 percent of people in our country will be exposed to at least one very traumatic event in their lifetime (assuming they live a normal life span). Trauma is not simply defined as an encounter with a tremendously stressful or frightening event. What defines trauma is the experience of extreme powerlessness or helplessness when confronted with a very disturbing life event.

Such events include the following:

- Natural disasters: hurricanes, floods, tornados, earthquakes …

- Rape or other form of sexual assault

- Domestic violence

- Child abuse

- Catastrophic accidents, especially those involving fatalities

- Witnessing great suffering in a loved one (e.g. a family member who is ill or injured who is experiencing significant pain and/or fear)

- Direct exposure to terrorist acts

- Combat experiences

- Robbery or assault

- Undergoing painful or very frightening medical procedures

- Elder abuse

- Torture (experienced by many refugees)

- Having a child be abducted or otherwise vanish

- Having your house catch on fire

- Traumatic exposure for police, fire fighters, health-care workers, or other emergency relief personnel

- Witnessing violence (a very common experience for those living in the inner city), seeing people injured or murdered; children watching their father physically abuse a sibling or their mother.

- Being kidnapping or having a loved one kidnapped

- School violence (including threats and severe intimidation)

- Interpersonal loss: the death of a loved one, including stillbirth and miscarriage

> **Bet You Didn't Know**
>
> In a study of adolescents in Detroit, Michigan, 42 percent of inner-city youth had seen someone shot or stabbed, and 22 percent had seen someone murdered.

It was long held by mental-health professionals that traumas, by definition, involved exposure to life-threatening events or events that are relatively rare and outside the experience of most human beings. If you take notice of the previous list, some of these traumatic events are experienced at least once in a human lifetime. Especially experienced is the death of a loved one.

An erroneous assumption was made that the death of a loved one, although tremendously painful to experience, was not traumatic except under rare circumstances (e.g. suicide, murder, severe burns). However, a recent study (The San Diego Widowhood Project) discovered that among those losing a spouse, 10 percent developed post-traumatic stress disorder (PTSD): the most severe type of psychological response to trauma. The amazing finding was that this occurred even in those people who had lost a loved one to a chronic medical illness (e.g. Alzheimer's disease, diabetes, congestive heart failure, cancer). Here the death was not sudden and often had been anticipated for months or even years.

Thus it does appear that many life events can potentially be experienced as traumatic, especially when they are accompanied by a feeling of helplessness or powerlessness.

Healthy, Adaptive Reactions to Traumatic Events

Almost all human being are terribly shaken by exposure to awful life events, like those previously noted. Almost everyone will experience what are called *intrusive symptoms* at least for a few days following the trauma (in addition to grief or a host of other understandable emotional reactions). Intrusive symptoms are memories, vivid images, thoughts, and/or nightmares that are a replay of the terrible event. They are deemed intrusive because no one wishes to have these thoughts or images; they are profoundly upsetting. Without consciously choosing to think about the events, they simply pop into a person's mind, usually accompanied by intense emotions.

def•i•ni•tion

Intrusive symptoms are highly emotionally charged and vivid memories, images, thoughts, and feelings that come into a person's mind following exposure to traumatic events. The symptoms are a replay of the traumatic event or elements of that experience. They are considered to be intrusive because they occur without conscious choice. Intrusive symptoms also include nightmares.

For about 75 percent of those exposed to traumatic events, the intrusive symptoms go away in a few days. For a long time, of course, people have distressing memories, but not of this intrusive variety.

Also, many people experience a strong need to repeatedly talk about the traumatic event, even though doing so can be very upsetting. Psychologists believe that the automatic, intrusive experiences (including nightmares) and this urge to talk about the events are a part of adaptive and natural emotional healing. It is the mind's way of repeatedly facing a horrible reality. At the heart of emotional recovery is this need to repeatedly think about and talk about what happened, until eventually some of the intense emotional charge of the experience begins to diminish.

Am I Going Crazy?

The waves of very disturbing emotions, nightmares, and memories can really scare and destabilize people. Many individuals, at least in their private thoughts, are afraid that they must be losing their minds. It does not make common sense to feel this urge to talk about something so horrible or be repeatedly haunted by intrusive memories or dreams. Yet it is very important to recognize that this is simply the mind's way to heal itself and once again find stability.

Numbed and Spaced Out

Another fairly common reaction to trauma is to experience what psychologists call *dissociation*. Dissociation is a state of psychological shock. People feel dazed, oddly numb, and devoid of what you might expect to be intense emotions. In this state, people often feel somewhat confused, report that they feel as if they have taken drugs, and may experience symptoms of derealization and/or depersonalization.

Dissociation can also feel crazy. The sensations are so odd and unfamiliar. People experiencing this type of psychological shock may be misunderstood by others. Other people may mistakenly think that the person is not distressed: either she must be handling it well, or for some reason, she must not care enough to be upset. These conclusions are absolutely inaccurate. Dissociation is an involuntary, automatic state of shock, very likely to be caused in part by significant changes in brain chemistry.

def•i•ni•tion

Dissociation is a psychological defensive reaction to emotional overwhelm. It results in a feeling of numbness and lack of strong emotions. Dissociation is often accompanied by two other psychological defenses: derealization, a peculiar feeling that the world seems unreal, and depersonalization, the sense that you are not real (feeling odd and estranged from your normal experience of self). Many experts believe that these symptoms are attributable to changes in brain chemistry that often follow emotional trauma.

Emotional Roller Coaster

The incidence of post-traumatic stress disorder (PTSD) varies depending on the nature and severity of the trauma, for example, PTSD occurs in the following:

Rape victims	48 percent
Combat experiences (Vietnam war veterans)	15 percent
Victims of natural disasters	20–30 percent
Firefighters (lifetime rate)	15 percent
Refugees who experienced torture	50–70 percent

The symptoms of PTSD are severe and, by definition, last longer than one month. In addition to intrusive experiences and dissociation, most people suffering from PTSD also have severe anxiety/panic attacks, very severe insomnia, constant arousal, and hypervigalence (for instance, the sound of a car backfiring will produce a very intense startle reaction); many develop a marked withdrawal from life activities, experience depression, and are at high risk for substance abuse (especially alcohol abuse).

Over a period of time, many who have PTSD may spend time (maybe months) in intensely disturbing intrusive phases of the disorder (e.g. anxiety each day and nightmares each night). However, the intrusive experiences sometimes give way to marked dissociation, which can last days, to weeks, to months. And then intrusions can begin again.

Psychological Treatment

Traumatic events can happen to any of us. If the symptoms are severe and last more than a couple of weeks, please seek treatment. There is a form of psychotherapy called exposure-based cognitive therapy that has a well-documented track record of effectiveness in treating PTSD. In addition, many people suffering from PTSD are successfully treated with antidepressants, in combination with psychotherapy.

> **Bet You Didn't Know**
>
> Many antidepressants (e.g. Prozac, Zoloft, Lexapro, etc.) not only treat depression, but are highly effective in treating the following PTSD symptoms: severe anxiety, intrusive experiences and even dissociation. Generally they must be taken for three or four weeks before noticeable improvement in symptoms begins to be apparent.

At least 50 percent of people with full-blown PTSD will gradually recover without treatment. However, it is a painfully slow process that greatly interferes with one's life. Also, those who do not recover can develop a much more severe, chronic version of PTSD that becomes very difficult to treat. Thus, once again, I must strongly encourage psychological treatment if symptoms continue past a couple weeks.

Our Post-9-11 World

Many children growing up during the Cold War may recall disaster drills in elementary school, preparation in the event of a nuclear war. I really never thought that hiding under one's desk at school would provide much protection. There was an ever-present threat that nuclear war could break out. Thank goodness it didn't!

Since the terrorist attacks on September 11, 2001, many of us have a new thing to worry about. On the heels of that tragedy have been devastating earthquakes, hurricanes, and tsunamis.

Some people do develop a sort of PTSD by repeated exposure to upsetting media coverage of these disasters. Probably most people do not have actual PTSD, but do carry with them, at least on the back burner of their mind, this increased awareness that these devastating events can happen to them.

For many victims of 9-11 and hurricane Katrina, a lesson was learned. Most people directly affected did not need psychiatric treatment. What they needed was what came to be known as "doughnuts and information." Donuts refers obviously to just that: comfort food, but it implies more. Handing out donuts to people in emergency shelters was one way to simply provide human contact. The other ingredient was information: generally, the more people could be told factual information about the disaster, the better. Human beings do not fare well with intense stress accompanied by confusion or ambiguity. People were comforted by being told exactly what happened (9-11), and finding out about their home and family members.

Bet You Didn't Know

Getting groups of people to share their thoughts and feelings in the immediate aftermath of a large-scale trauma has actually been shown to make matters worse for some survivors. This form of crisis intervention, sometimes called Critical Incident Debriefing, made intuitive sense; it seemed to be the compassionate thing to do. However, strongly encouraging people to "open up" and share their feelings with others actually increased the degree of trauma for many.

Post 9-11, mental health crisis workers now know that it is helpful to intervene with people who *request* counseling or with those who previously have been suffering from a mental illness. For others, the intervention of choice is to provide information: information about what is happening, brief information about what to commonly expect in the weeks following exposure to traumas (such as anxiety, recurring memories, nightmares, etc.) , and finally to let people know whom to contact if they do later want to seek professional help.

How to Help

What most people exposed to trauma need are four things:

1. The opportunity to talk about what happened. However, not forced or too strongly pressured to talk. People must do this at their own pace.

2. Some traumatic events, unfortunately, are accompanied by significant shame or guilt. Even though rape victims are 100 percent not to blame, many feel ashamed, and worse, many others respond to them as if they had done something to provoke the rape. If there has been a car accident and a parent was driving the car in which their child was killed, the parent may feel intense guilt. Traumatized people must be comforted and never judged!

3. Create safety. Having recently been overwhelmingly frightened and powerless, people need to be in a place of safety, with family or friends and making sure their immediate environment is safe (sadly, many inner-city people are traumatized by violence, and yet they return to their homes and neighborhoods that are anything but safe. They experience the ongoing sense of pervasive danger). Survivors of domestic violence may need to move into a women's shelter.

4. Eventually, to overcome trauma, people must face their fears. This can be done by repeatedly processing the experience, by talking with friends, clergy, or therapists. And often, people must eventually go back to the scene of the trauma. For example, someone who was involved in a catastrophic automobile accident and is now afraid to drive, he needs to gradually get back on the road. This is all about facing fears, but done in a gradual way.

Shattered Assumptions

At the heart of psychological trauma is the shattering of many basic, human assumptions. Although we all know, at least intellectually, that bad things do happen to good people and the world is not fair, when tragedy and trauma strike, it can pull the rug out from beneath you. Many people may question their belief in God, or never again feel safe in the world. Nothing prepares us for these kinds of horrible life events.

Courage

Psychiatrist Scott Peck said, "The absence of fear is not courage … the absence of fear is some kind of brain damage." Traumatic events scare the daylights out of people, and often they shatter our world. And people suffering more severe outcomes (PTSD), unfortunately, cannot simply forget it or put it out of their minds. Yet, there are ways to come to terms with life in the aftermath of trauma. Again, I must quote poet Robert Frost, "The best way out is through."

The Least You Need to Know

◆ Most people are exposed to at least one highly traumatic event during their lives. Yet most people are resilient and do not develop severe psychiatric symptoms.

◆ A critical ingredient in facing and overcoming trauma is to understand the nature of human responses to trauma, and to see that you are not crazy: that is, to make sense of the events and your reactions.

◆ A second key factor in recovery from trauma is to understand that repeatedly thinking about and speaking about the trauma is a part of the mind's way to heal itself. But this must not be rushed. You must find ways to do this without feeling overwhelmed.

◆ Post-traumatic stress disorder responds very well to psychotherapy and psychiatric medication treatment, but it is best to get treatment sooner than later. More chronic cases of PTSD can be much more challenging to treat.

Chapter 23

To Thine Own Self Be True

In This Chapter

- ◆ Living a life shaped out of compliance
- ◆ Your true self strives for expression
- ◆ The realization of inner truths often is accompanied by significant anxiety
- ◆ Your best shot at feeling truly alive comes from discovering your true self

"To thine own self be true," is a saying we all have heard. The reality is that many people live their entire lives in ways that are fashioned largely out of compliance. This inauthentic way of living is a surprisingly common source of feelings of depression, emptiness, and meaninglessness. In this chapter, we will carefully consider this issue and explore ways to discover your true self.

Forgetting Who You Really Are

All of us come into the world simply and naturally being who we are. If infants could talk, they might say, "I yam what I yam." However, soon thereafter this free and completely uninhibited child starts to encounter the world of other human beings who begin a process of socialization. Rewarding some behaviors, such as smiling at grandma, and discouraging others, such as knocking over house plants. Bit by bit, as every human being encounters these social pressures to act in certain ways, parts of the natural self start to become inhibited. This is the process that gives shape to the child's emerging character.

Thankfully this shaping of character works; people become civilized. It would be unfortunate if adults continued to cry and fuss every time they get hungry or continued to poop in their pants. The problem is, however, in some if not many young children, the pressures to stifle self-expression and to "behave" are too strict and too pervasive. Some children grow up in homes in which kids are never allowed to get angry or to speak back to their parents. Or when they express their own thoughts and opinions, they encounter comments from their parents that belittle, humiliate, or shame them. "You're so stupid … you don't know what you're talking about." Sometimes pressure to be a certain way is enormous; the consequences of just being who you are, if not approved of by your parents, may include brutality, inappropriately intense shaming, or threats of abandonment. "I wish you were never born!"

Bet You Didn't Know

In or about 400 B.C.E., Socrates said, "The goal of life and education is to bring out the divine spark within people that had been covered up by false information from the world … truth was already there … a truth the world got you to forget." The truth of who you really are in your heart of hearts. This is not exactly a new-age concept.

The False Self

Noted child therapist D.W. Winnicott described the notion of a false self. Children subject to severe conditions, as previously mentioned, go into life developing a self that is fashioned out of compliance. Every waking moment is devoted to stifling inner needs, feelings, and thoughts in order to please others or to avoid abandonment. When this is carried to an extreme, it results in what Winnicott calls a false self. All the child knows of who she is, is this overly constricted, compliant self. Sometime she may notice inner feelings of anger, but bites her tongue and stifles the emotions. Sometimes she clearly disagrees with her parents, or teachers, or other people in power, yet she swallows her thoughts. In the most extreme cases, true inner longings, needs, beliefs, thoughts, and opinions become so hidden away that the child doesn't even know what she really thinks or feels. It is as if she took a part of herself, locked it in a closet, and then even forgot the closet existed.

Some people move through life never feeling angry or irritated, never voicing strong opinions, and always subjugating themselves to others.

Prices Paid for Living Out of a False Self

There are three common consequences of living only from a false self. The first is that many actual and necessary emotions are inhibited or even completely shut out of awareness. As we saw in Chapter 21, one essential ingredient for emotional healing following significant losses is mourning, and expressing that range of intensely felt painful emotions that accompany loss. A false self, so cut off from feelings, is a major liability. People who don't have access to these emotions are much more likely to not heal following losses. Depression and psychosomatic illnesses are a common consequence of unprocessed grief. Another result is that those who do not successfully mourn losses often become very uneasy about getting close to or attached to another person. This can result in long-lasting social isolation, withdrawal, and loneliness.

Think About It _____

The following are often disowned aspects of the self: vulnerability, intimacy, sexuality, neediness, anger, assertiveness, sadness, grief.

The second consequence is that feeling such a great need to be compliant, those with a false self may never be able to truly find their own voice. Thus, generally, others tell them what to do, how to think, and what to feel, and they are inclined to passively submit. This, in itself, can result in feelings of powerlessness and low self-esteem.

The final price paid by living from a false self is a lack of aliveness. People may live with this for many years, yet in midlife some begin to really notice how they feel. Usually the first awareness of this is experienced as a vaguely felt sense of emptiness, uneasiness, low-grade depression, and/or a lack of enthusiasm about life.

Discovering the False Self

Joann was perplexed. Why had she become so exhausted and blue during the past six months? She also felt a profound lack of enthusiasm for almost everything. As she took stock of her life, it seemed clear that nothing really bad had happened; no losses, no tragedies, absolutely nothing that might explain her low mood. She decided to see a therapist. She felt uncomfortable and somewhat confused as she went in for her first session with a therapist.

"I have a good life, good kids, good husband ... financially we are secure. I don't have any reason to feel so down." Her therapist listened carefully and then encouraged Joann to just talk a bit about herself, taking her time to look closely at her life.

During the first three sessions, as Joann shared her thoughts about her life with her therapist, a theme began to emerge. In so many ways, she had devoted her life to caring for the needs of others. For instance, as a dutiful daughter in high school, she was quick to put her own needs aside for the sake of her younger brother or to make life easier for her parents. Likewise, in her married life, she had settled into a role in which she was always there for everyone, to fix things, to listen, to rescue, to console. She also discovered that she rarely complained and generally just went along with whatever her husband said or did. It started to become increasingly clear that somewhere along the path of her life, she had set aside her inner self (her needs, her feelings, even her own beliefs) to take care of others. And this had been done to excess. She also came to see that she almost never voiced her own opinions. Joann had lost touch with her inner self.

Life roles that are totally devoted to caring for others, those based on excessive compliance, a strong desire to never make waves, or to live out the dreams of others (like making career choices favored by a parent) can and often do leave people estranged from their own inner self. And, often this can set the stage for distress, loss of vitality, or depression. Dr. Albert Schweitzer said, "Living superficially is a sign of soul sickness." I think this is what Joann was suffering from.

Most times, such reactions come on gradually. And like Joann, the source of a low mood is often, at first, an ill-defined mystery.

One of the most important sources of energy, enjoyment, and aliveness comes from living a life that is in synch with who you really are. A life burdened by over-compliance or excessive sacrifice of the self can choke off aliveness just as surely as moving a plant out of the light can cause it to wither.

Confiding in another (for example, a therapist or trusted friend) can often lead you to greater clarity about inner, but suppressed, needs, urges, and feelings. Therapeutic writing, as was discussed in Chapter 13, also may lead you to a greater awareness of a buried, inner self.

Am I Living Out of a False Self?

Some people go from cradle to grave living within the confines of a false self, never realizing that a more authentic self lies buried within their mind. How can you tell if you are living life from a true or false self? The following exercise can be helpful.

My role in life, as scripted by others:

1. What are/were my parents' dreams or goals for me in terms of lifestyle, career, and relationships? How did they really want me to "turn out"?

2. In what ways have I not fulfilled my parents' hopes or dreams?

3. What are two or three times during childhood or adolescence where I can recall having a significant difference of opinion with my parents? Then reflect: looking back on this now, what might this tell me about myself (my personal or unique beliefs, values, desires, or needs)?

4. If I recall voicing differences of opinion, how did my parents react? Did they listen, ignore, scold, or criticize?

5. In what ways have I inhibited myself (not followed my own desires, hunches, or instincts) in order to either please my parents (or others) or to avoid their criticism? (Pay particular attention to those times when you may have noticed swallowing feelings or stopping yourself from disagreeing with others.)

6. In present-day relationships (as a husband, wife, as an intimate partner, as a parent, as a friend, as an employee) what do others want or expect from me? What roles do they want me to play? Do I see a common theme here?

7. How am I currently inhibiting myself?

8. What roles or expectations, imposed on me by others, do I know, in my heart of hearts, are not my choosing? What roles or expectations do I privately resent or feel burdened by?

After considering these questions, it is likely that you may have a clearer notion of ways in which you have stifled your true self. Knowing this is the first important step in beginning to make changes and starting the journey to discover your truer self.

Collapse of the False Self

Winnicott also wrote of the collapse of the false self. It's as if those sealed closet doors closing off parts of the self begin to open on their own. They can be blown open by major life events. For example, a very painful loss may break through into that buried part of the self that naturally would feel grief. Or finding out that her husband has had an affair might crack open the door containing natural and normal feelings of anger in a woman who has always been very passive and compliant.

Here, "getting in touch with your true feelings" may be a very frightening thing to do, at least initially. Having lived only from a false self for 35 years, the emergence of these very unfamiliar feelings often cause enormous anxiety. These feelings are so alien that they result in people feeling overwhelmed, destabilized, or sometimes fearing that they are going crazy.

The first reaction, of course, is to do anything to seal the crack in the closet door; "Just get me back to what I'm accustomed to." A common way that people do this is to try and numb themselves with drugs or alcohol. And many people find all sorts of ways to emotionally grit their teeth.

Another way of responding to this is to understand that the emotional symptoms, such as anxiety, are like signals from one's deeper self saying, "Something is not right." Author and meditation teacher Pema Chodron says, "Anxiety is a messenger telling us we are about to go into unknown territory." That unknown territory is the experience of buried emotions and needs. Many people who choose to go into psychotherapy spend a fair amount of time navigating through this scary and sometimes overwhelmingly unknown territory. However, at some point they begin to see some rhyme and reason in what they are experiencing. As the authentic emotions come more and more to the surface, most people find that they can face and tolerate these emotions.

Furthermore, often they go beyond just tolerating. They begin to "own" the feelings, seeing them as understandable human responses to painful or difficult life circumstances.

Think About It

Author Vernon Howard says, "Our life transformation is in exact proportion to the amount of truth we can take without running away."

This pathway to greater awareness of one's inner, truer self is not easy. It clearly is the road less traveled, and requires a lot of courage to face these inner realities. But it can be life-changing.

Finding Your Self

Psychologist Sheldon Kopp said, "Too often as children, we were encouraged to try to be something other than ourselves. It was demanded that we assume a character and live out a life-story written by someone else. The plot line was given and improvisations were seriously discouraged or completely unacceptable, and the direction was an oppressive form of close-quarter tyranny. [The False Self] is, in part, the result of being miscast into a scenario plotted out in accord with somebody else's unfulfilled dreams and unfaced anxieties."

Try this exercise:

1. Set aside all pressures to conform or to meet others' needs, at least for a few minutes. In your mind, ask these questions: "What would I most like to do (social activities, recreation, career, education, daily schedules, living arrangements, household chores, living location, and so on)? And, what qualities would I like in my intimate relationships?" Explore this thoroughly—really get into this exercise! Using your wildest imagination, write a script (as if you were creating a character for a novel) for a life/lifestyle based entirely on your inner needs, desires, values, and talents.

2. After completing the script, sit with this a bit, reflect, and then honestly ask yourself, "To what degree am I living my life in accord with my unique inner self?" Such an exercise can often help you identify chronic sources of dissatisfaction or disappointment that may be spurring, and may also point out possible solutions.

It is common for most people to be only vaguely aware of such inner disappointments or the underlying loss of self. Self-discovery can be an important step in addressing problems that you may be having in relationships or in your current lifestyle. But be prepared, because this kind of examination can also result in a painful awakening. Honestly confronting inner truths is often the key. Buddha said, "Look into your own mind to find out what is true ... the truth is recognized and not taught or learned."

Often, what is equally important is to then take actions to change your life. This may involve more open discussions with intimate others requesting and negotiating for changes in the relationship, or deciding upon new directions in your educational or career pursuits. In the words of the author and poet Kahlil Gibran, "... to weave the cloth with threads drawn from your own heart ... to change all things you fashion with a breath of your own spirit."

The best shot we humans have at creating a life worth living may rest, in part, in being able to discover who we truly are, and then living life in accord with our own inner needs, desires, values, and beliefs.

The Least You Need to Know

◆ The false self may afford a sense of familiarity and safety, but it can be as confining as being in prison.

◆ Many symptoms of anxiety and depression can be seen as messengers from the unconscious mind saying, "Something is wrong" ... and what is wrong is that you are not feeling fully alive or authentic.

◆ It is understandable that when confronted with vague but very unpleasant feelings of anxiety or depression, you just want to brush it under the rug or run away back into your familiar life. But to do so can keep you locked in the prison of a false self.

◆ Finding yourself may be one of the most important discoveries in the journey of your life.

24

Helping Children Deal With Emotionally Painful Times

In This Chapter

◆ Truth-telling and validating a child's feelings

◆ Getting your children to share their feelings with you

◆ The impact of upsetting media on a child's sense of safety in the world

◆ Signs to help determine if your child needs professional help

Although most of this book has been devoted to coping with the demands of adult life, in this chapter I want to spend some time talking about how to help young people in your life.

Helping Your Children

Want to hear a crazy belief? It's okay to circumcise infant boys, because it only hurts for a while, and besides, they will never remember it. This is not a statement for or against circumcision, but an example of the distorted thinking some people in our society have about the experiences of suffering in young children, including emotional suffering.

Some kids are lucky. They are born into intact, loving families. They are held and cared for, and protected from dangers and emotional calamities. But many children come into the world only to find domestic violence, damaged parental relationships, huge family stresses, poverty, and sometimes trauma and tragedy. Many innocent children are neglected or abused. Many children must experience the fear and pain of medical procedures to correct birth defects or other accidents or illnesses. Some children are victims of horrible burns. And lots of kids lose a secure family. There are 2.5 million divorces each year in the United States, and many unfortunate children lose a parent, sibling, or other loved one to death.

How can we help our kids when they must face and live through these kinds of very difficult life experiences? In short, the keys are truth-telling, validating, holding, providing safety, sharing your feelings, and getting them to open up.

Truth-Telling

Children, to a greater or lesser degree, are exquisitely sensitive to what is happening in their world, for example, serious illness of a parent or grandparent or marked marital discord. Kids sense these kinds of things and have strong feelings about it. In order to protect children from being overwhelmed, many parents do not talk openly about what is happening and may create the pretense that things are "fine." Thus children are picking up on two messages, "Something is terribly wrong here" and "Things are just fine." This is crazy-making, it leaves kids feeling more insecure in their life, and it may influence their developing characters, e.g. the belief that people are deceitful.

Here is the key, and it involves a balancing act. It's important to tell children something about what is happening, but also temper this by having what you say fit their age and level of intellectual development (telling them something they'll be able to understand). And second, shield them from some unnecessary details that they simply don't need to hear. I wish there were some formula that could guide parents in finding this balance. There isn't, and each child and each particular circumstance are so different. But at the heart of this communication with your child is truth-telling, and underlying messages include, "I want to be honest with you," "I know that you probably sense something is distressing," and "You deserve to know (at least a bit) about what's happening."

Validating

When children are hurt, scared, sad, or worried, they need to know that those who love them notice their pain and care enough to validate it. Sometimes parents may be oblivious to their child's suffering; this is not uncommon in homes where there is significant alcohol or drug abuse. Sometimes overwhelming stress or depression in a parent may be so intense as to override their natural instincts to be attuned to their child's feelings.

However, maybe more commonly, children perceive some form of these parental messages, "Don't be such a sissy," "It's not that big a deal," "You are just too emotional," or a kind of cruel, "Don't worry—be happy" comment. In the extreme, very distressed children are actually told, "You are not upset."

To be acknowledged and validated (for the child to feel like a parent or other loved one really gets that he is suffering) not only provides comfort in the moment, but this kind of experience also delivers a powerful message to that child's emotional heart: "You matter to me … I believe you … and I am here to help you."

Holding

Especially for young child, holding and rocking them can provide enormous comfort and support. Often this act of love can do far more than any words spoken. We all know when children begin to grow up; there comes a time when it's not cool to hug your parents (especially in front of friends). I still occasionally accidentally call my 26-year-old son "Honey" in front of his friends. He looks at me like "Dad!! For gosh sakes, don't embarrass me." And many children are different, but a pat on the shoulder or a hug, for many kids and teenagers, continues to convey concern and love.

Bet You Didn't Know

Researcher Megan Gunnar contacted 150 Canadian parents who had adopted infants from Romanian orphanages. As you may know, these infants received almost no holding or physical comfort living in these emotionally barren orphanages. Dr. Gunnar followed these adopted babies for nine years to see how well they developed. Babies adopted by parents before the age of four months were healthy and emotionally well adjusted at age 9. Those adopted after they were in the orphanage for eight or more months were deeply emotionally disturbed, despite being cared for and loved by their healthy adopted parents. Other researchers have clearly demonstrated the importance of physical holding and rocking; it not only matters in terms of emotional health and bonding, but also makes a huge difference in terms of brain development (especially the development of the emotional brain).

Providing Safety

After a death in the family, or a marital separation, or a very frightening event (like your house burning down), beyond feelings of grief, all children feel terribly anxious. Something has dramatically shaken their sense of basic safety in their world. It is important to keep open to these feelings, long after the difficult events subside. Talk to children and give them permission to talk or cry. You don't want your child to get the message, "You need to just get over it," because it's rarely that simple.

It is also helpful to create a safe environment. If your home has been burglarized, have your kids help you put in extra locks or other security measures. Likewise, if you or your spouse have been assaulted, show the children concrete ways you are taking precautions to fortify your house or do other things to increase a sense of safety. During a divorce, one of the most loving things you can do is to agree to not draw the children into taking sides or to burden the children with too much of your own suffering.

If children are very frightened after a traumatic event, they may want to sleep with their parents. It's hard to know the right way to handle this and it will depend on the circumstances. If Mom was in a serious accident but is recovering in the hospital (i.e. there is likely to eventually be a good outcome), you may let your children sleep in your room for a night or two, but also tell them that it's just for a couple of nights, and you have confidence that they will be able to return to their own beds soon (again, the age of the child does matter here). If a child has a parent dying from a terminal illness, it certainly may be appropriate for them to sleep in the parent's room for a somewhat longer period of time.

Again, no formulas here. But you've gotta trust your heart and also give your child the clear message that you believe in her ability to make it through this very difficult time. And in fact, many, if not most, kids are surprisingly resilient.

Sharing Your Feelings

Another balancing act. Parents who hide their grief, for instance, and never shed a tear may have good intentions. However, it's generally very helpful if you do show children some of your real emotions. You are not only modeling such behavior for them (giving them permission to be emotional), but also, when they see your pain, it helps them feel more okay about sharing their own inner feelings.

It must, however, be stressed that children should not be pulled into the role of "rescuer." Parents may be going through their own anguish, but children should be told that they are not responsible for fixing their parent. It is not uncommon for some kids to immediately take on the role of mom or dad's comforter. This is more than children can be reasonably expected to do.

Getting Your Children to Open Up to You

Encourage them to talk. Don't give up if at first they withhold a lot. You can say, "As hard as this is, I believe that you do have a lot of hurt (grief, anger, whatever) inside of you, and I really believe it will help to talk about it with me." I have said to my own children, "Even if you don't wanna talk about it, I cannot and will not ignore the fact that you are upset …."

Once again, so much depends on their developmental level, and also on their own personality style. Some children temperamentally are just more introverted or inhibited. But it still never hurts to make an invitation to talk, and keep the door open if they have a change of heart and need to open up to you.

When children do talk about upsetting things, for example, a marital separation or a family illness, your ability and willingness to also be honest and open with them likely will help it be easier for them to share with you.

Other outlets for emotional expression, especially in younger children, are play and artwork, which should certainly be encouraged. Play and artwork are especially important mediums in which children can express and work out their feelings. Therefore, do encourage creative play with dolls, little soldiers, clay, building blocks, artwork (but not video games, which serve mainly to distract). And as seems appropriate, ask your children about what's happening in their play or artwork. For many children, play is a much more direct way to access and process their inner emotions than talking is.

Listen, Listen, Listen

Directly approaching children about emotionally upsetting things often is not successful, at least at first. What does, however, often work is to be with them doing something, like driving in the car or fishing. For me, my youngest son went through a very difficult time, and was mostly inclined to clam up about it. However, he and I took a three-hour rafting trip and a hike. Just the two of us. With no pressure, eventually he started opening up to me.

Dealing With Nightmares

Many children have nightmares. First let's distinguish between *nightmares* and *night terrors*. Nightmares are highly disturbing dreams. And it is appropriate to wake your child up, provide reassuring words, and ask him to talk about his dreams (a very ancient custom, not just something suggested by Sigmund Freud). Nightmares are often ways of processing difficult life experiences.

Night terrors, on the other hand, are incredibly intense outbursts of terror occurring during sleep that are not associated with disturbing dreams. They are also often associated with other kinds of sleep disturbances such as sleepwalking and sleep talking. These are considered to be neurologically based medical disorders and should be discussed with your physician if they seem to be a problem.

def•i•ni•tion

Nightmares are very frightening dreams that occur frequently when children are under significant stress. Night terrors may look like nightmares, however, they are generally not associated with scary dreams. The child is not truly awake, but is extremely terrified and may cry and scream. Night terrors are not due to emotional conflicts, but rather, are a type of biologically based sleep disorder.

Upsetting Media

The Columbine tragedy, 9-11, and other terrible events can be very upsetting to children. Even if you reduce exposure to or eliminate such TV news reports at home, you better count on your children hearing it from friends.

It is tempting to provide reassurance such as, "This will never happen to us/you." However, many mental-health professionals who help children have found it better to provide reassurance tempered with some truth and reality. For example, "This was a very, very terrible thing that happened. I know it scares you … it scares me, too. Please listen carefully to me … sometimes bad things like this do happen in the world. But it is also extremely unlikely to happen to you/us, and I will do everything I can to help protect you and keep you safe."

Signs That Your Child May Be Having More Serious Psychological Problems

Unfortunately, some serious psychological disorders begin in childhood or early adolescence. One third of cases of obsessive-compulsive disorder and of bipolar illness have their onset in this age group. Attention deficit hyperactivity disorder (ADHD), by definition, always begins in childhood and in 60 percent of cases lasts into adulthood. If a child or teenager is suffering from a significant psychological problem, it is crucial to get professional help as soon as possible.

The following behaviors or traits should alert parents that their child may be having more serious psychological problems and should be evaluated by a mental-health professional.

♦ Extreme social withdrawal

♦ Showing virtually no outward signs of vitality or enthusiasm

♦ Very intense and prolonged rages

♦ Cruelty toward other children or animals

♦ Fire-setting

♦ Bedwetting (especially if this has been overcome in the past but has re-emerged or continues beyond the age of 7)

♦ Soiling their pants

♦ Cutting or burning themselves

♦ Severe anxiety about going to school or being left with a babysitter

♦ Excessive preoccupation with rituals such as counting, hand-washing, peculiar eating habits

♦ Marked inability to get along with other children (either irritable or mean, or just extremely aloof and socially inappropriate)

♦ Severe sleep disturbances

♦ Inappropriate sex play or behavior, for example, sexualized drawings, sex play with dolls, touching their private parts in public, touching other children or adults in inappropriate sexualized ways, or the use of highly inappropriate language

Most kids go through some times when they may be more sensitive, more moody, or more anxious. However, if any of the previously mentioned problems become apparent, please take action. These behaviors may be signaling a more significant psychological problem and the sooner your child gets professional help, the better.

The Least You Need to Know

◆ There are a number of key ingredients in helping children cope with very distressing events. At the heart of these approaches is telling the truth and accepting the child's feelings.

◆ Children should not be pulled into the role of mediator between parents or rescuer for a distressed parent. Often this is more demanding than children can reasonably cope with.

◆ When talking to children about very upsetting things, a parent or grandparent must always do a balancing act … not saying too much (that might overwhelm a child), but also telling them the truth about what is happening. One must also carefully consider a child's age and level of intellectual development and talk to them in ways that they can understand.

◆ Some serious psychological problems can begin in childhood or adolescence, and parents need to know the signs that a child may be suffering from a more serious psychological condition.

Part 5

Professional Help in Dealing With Mood Problems

This final part of the book explores two primary forms of professional treatment for mood problems: psychotherapy and psychiatric medication treatments. If you are experiencing very significant problems with anxiety or depression, the good news is that treatments are generally very successful. It is important to be an informed "consumer" and to know the pros and cons of professional treatment. It is also important to know as much as you can about any psychiatric medication that might be recommended or prescribed.

Keep in mind that the focus of this part is on common depression and anxiety disorders and does not address the treatment of serious mental illnesses, which is beyond the scope of this book.

Psychotherapy and Counseling

In This Chapter

- Getting a glimpse at what usually happens in psychotherapy
- How talking can actually help
- Using therapy to get clear about how you really feel
- Targeting specific problems such as anxiety attacks or depression

Perhaps you are asking what psychotherapy is really like. It may not be what you think. You've had glimpses of psychotherapy in books, in the movies, and on television. Forget that. It's not likely that what you've seen has prepared you for what really goes on. If you're like most folks, you're thinking about therapy because you're experiencing significant distress or emotional pain—perhaps desperation—in your life. (Almost no one goes to therapy for the small stuff.) Under such times of great stress and personal uncertainty, everyone wants and needs to feel safe, and to feel some assurance that the decision to see a therapist was the right one.

Most people have lots of questions about this business of telling their troubles to a total stranger:

"What actually happens in therapy?" "What can I expect to get from therapy?"

"What are realistic and attainable benefits I might gain from therapy?"

"Is there a reasonable chance of getting the help I need?"

"Will it be worth the time, money, effort, and emotional investment to become involved in a course of brief therapy?"

Good questions! In this chapter, I'm going to offer you some straight talk about psychotherapy, and present how some people benefit from their experience of therapy. In this chapter, I focus on what's expected of you and what actually happens during therapy sessions.

What Can You Expect During the First Session?

You may be asked to fill out a background questionnaire to help the therapist determine if treatment with you is appropriate, and as a means of learning details of your history (educational history, number of people in your family, prior psychotherapy experiences, medical history …).

1. You will be asked to do your best at sharing openly your particular concerns, thoughts, and feelings.

2. You may be asked to complete assigned and agreed-upon tasks—homework assignments—outside the therapy hour. This occurs in some types of psychotherapy.

3. You will be expected to show up for sessions as scheduled and to pay agreed-upon professional fees. And to give advance notice in case of a cancellation (except in cases of last-minute emergencies).

4. You may be asked to fill out background questionnaires or complete one or more psychological tests to help your therapist access your personal situation and needs.

What Actually Happens During Therapy Sessions?

Therapy sessions vary, depending on who you are, what current problems you're experiencing, and the kind of therapist you hire. However, here is a summary glimpse of the "typical" course of therapy.

Phase 1: Getting Acquainted and Discussing What Concerns You Most

Effective therapists will help you get started during the first session. Most will help the therapy process get underway by asking their clients, "What are the main reasons you've decided to come to therapy?" or "I'd like to know what's most on your mind and what you'd like to accomplish in coming to therapy." The early sessions generally are designed to help you feel more at ease and begin discussing your main problems or concerns. At this beginning phase, many people entering therapy are unclear about what they are feeling, or they may be self-critical, for example, "I shouldn't be feeling this way." You and your therapist will be forming a "therapeutic alliance"—a working partnership that will help you get past your uncertainty and reach your goals in therapy.

Phase 2: Finding a Focus

As the discussion continues in further sessions, your therapist will do a lot of listening and ask questions to help you pinpoint a major focus—the major issues or problem you'll be dealing with in therapy. You and your therapist will identify specific problems, and find out in what ways these issues are especially important to you at this time in your life.

Psychotherapy doesn't provide a quick fix. In fact, people may find that they feel somewhat worse during the first couple of sessions—at least more keenly aware of distressing feelings. And the reality often is that once a person begins to take close look at difficult issues, emotional pain may be felt more intensely. If this happens to you, don't bail out! It's natural, normal, and fairly predictable—but it's an essential part of coming to terms with life issues that hurt. Fortunately for most, emotional distress at some point subsides as they begin to get a handle on life problems and cope more effectively.

Phase 3: Refocusing or Tuning Into the Problem

A common experience during the third phase of therapy is for clients to begin to understand their problems, and themselves, in a new light. Many times this involves a change of perspective and attitude. Such "problems" as being oversensitive to criticism, feeling taken advantage of by others, missing a loved one who has died, feeling overwhelmed and frustrated at work, start to seem more "understandable." The problems may seem just as painful, undesirable, or frustrating; however, many folks start to think, "My feelings make sense to me now" or "Of course I feel this way." The volume gets turned down on harsh self-criticism.

Here are some examples of such shifts in thinking:

From	To
This is crazy.	I don't like the way this feels.
I shouldn't be so upset.	I'm upset. What can I do about it?
This shouldn't be happening!	I don't want this to happen, but it is and it's upsetting.
I'm confused.	What the hell is the matter with me? Of course I feel this way!

Phase 4: Action-Oriented Skills ... Practice, Practice, Practice

"I am more aware of what I feel and I don't condemn myself so harshly. But I still feel bad. What do I do next?"

Often in psychotherapy, once the major problems or concerns have been clarified, the focus is shifted toward active problem-solving. Kimberly, for example, learned ways to reduce anxiety by providing inner support for herself prior to taking an exam at school. Robert developed assertive ways to communicate his feelings and needs to his wife. In one of his therapy sessions, Doug carefully planned out just how he was going to approach his shop foreman to share concerns he had about his work environment. Sherri began to write in her personal journal, discovered more about her own feelings, and learned to give herself permission to grieve the loss of her brother.

Psychotherapy became a place for these people to think things through, come to conclusions regarding actions they wanted to take, learn some new coping skills, and practice these skills during the session. As Robert said, "Having a therapist is kinda like having a coach. You can plan out what you want to do, practice it, get some feedback, refine it, and then get the extra push you need to do it for real in your life."

Phase 5: Fine Tuning

In the final stages of therapy, it is often helpful to summarize what's happened. It helps to be clear about several points:

1. This was my problem.

2. I came to see it as understandable ... not "crazy."

3. I felt okay about wanting to make a change.

4. I figured out which approaches work for me and which don't.

5. I felt supported by my therapist.

6. I put coping skills into action.

7. I got some results.

Getting better and feeling better usually aren't just due to fate, time healing all wounds, or good luck. You have to work at changing and discovering what helps.

Once you know how to cope more successfully, you're better prepared for the next time life becomes difficult.

Of course, it's not all this simple! Experiences vary. But the phases I've talked about here describe a common experience in therapy. Most people who succeed in psychotherapy typically don't feel ultimately "cured" or "fixed," but they do feel better. They leave therapy knowing that they've done some real work, and it was their effort that paid off. In particular, the most common outcome of successful therapy is feeling more okay about who you are!

How Can Talking Help?

Good question. You may be thinking, "I've already talked about this problem a lot ... What good will it do to go in and talk to a shrink about it?" or "I've talked this to death ... I don't see how talking about it again will help me."

Let's be clear: some types of talking aren't helpful and, in fact, some kinds of talking about emotionally difficult issues can increase your despair and may make matters worse! So to begin your understanding of how talk therapy works and how it can help, let's consider three types of talking: talk that hurts, talk that hides, and talk that heals.

Talk That Hurts

It's worth repeating: some kinds of talking, about emotionally difficult issues, can increase despair and just make matters worse! As we have seen in Chapters 13 and 14, three very common kinds of talking that often occur during stressful times virtually guarantee you'll suffer even more. Talk like this (whether it's actually spoken aloud or just "self-talk" in your head) works like a pain amplifier, turning up the volume on the intensity of emotional pain.

The first hurtful style is making extremely derogatory and crucial comments about yourself.

A second form of hurtful talk is jumping to inaccurate or unrealistic conclusions. Such conclusions may suggest extreme calamities ("I'm falling apart … I am completely out of control!") or all-or-none statements ("Absolutely nothing I do is right!"). This kind of talk just intensifies the idea that you are helpless and powerless—it's like throwing gasoline on your "distress fire."

The third common self-disturbing talk is making extremely negative predictions.

When these types of talking dominate, then in a real sense, talking does not help.

Talk That Hides

Many kinds of talk also take people far away from their honest inner emotions. Language can help people avoid or distort the truth. Let's look at several examples.

Quick Closure:

"Yes, I Know it's bad, but I'll get over it" … then changing the subject.

Minimizing:

"Oh, it's not that bad."

"Other people have gone through worse things, so I shouldn't complain."

"I feel sad, but I'm okay. I can handle it."

Injunctions:

"I need to be strong."

"I shouldn't cry."

"I shouldn't get so emotional … I've got to get myself under control."

Outright denial:

"I'm not upset. I'm … (sob) … okay."

In each of these statements, the words (or inner thoughts) direct your focus away from inner emotions or awareness of painful realities. This process can be temporarily help-ful, especially when you're feeling overwhelmed. These natural human maneuvers are designed to protect you from too much emotional distress. But this defensive stance can backfire and result in excessive blocking of honest emotions. As we saw in Chapter 13, healing is stopped in its tracks.

So how can talking help you heal?

Sometimes it seems we talk ourselves into emotional difficulty. Can we also talk ourselves out of it?

Only if we're oreally careful about how we talk …

Talk That Heals

Talking out loud about important thoughts, feelings, and experiences can be one of the most effective and rapid ways to get clear about your emotions. If talking is done in a safe and supportive relationship with a therapist, the chances are excellent that it can lead to healing.

An emotional crisis can bring on lots of vague, ill-defined, disturbing emotions and sensations. It's easy to feel confused and unclear during these times. You may notice an intense uneasiness or tension in your body, a lump in your throat, or tightness in your stomach. The confusing mix of emotions may only intensify anxiety, uncertainty, and helplessness.

If you're able to talk with an understanding person about your thoughts, feelings, and experiences, life often starts to make sense, bit by bit. You make connections between events and your feelings. It's as if you're shining a light into a dark cellar, gradually seeing clearly what's inside.

Most people don't like feeling uncertain and confused. As you gain clarity and understanding, you feel a greater sense of mastery and control. Talking—describing your emotions—often makes vague feelings concrete, and can help you understand them better.

Shawna's situation offers an example. She feels distant and alone in her marriage, as Tim has become increasingly preoccupied with work. The intimacy in their relationship has evaporated, causing her to feel sad and lonely. Here's a sample dialogue from one of her therapy sessions:

Shawna: Today at work, for no reason, I started crying. It was crazy. Nothing bad happened. What's wrong with me?

Therapist: Well, let's look at what was happening today. What went on in the office?

Shawna: Nothing, really.

Therapist: Well, maybe it will help if we go over it together. Tell me about today.

Shawna: I was at work. My girlfriend, Diane, was talking about her love relationship and how it wasn't working out. She's talked about it before, but all of a sudden, for no reason, I just started feeling terrible. I felt like I was going to cry. I'm not at all interested in her love life.

Therapist: You were starting to cry?

Shawna: Yeah. (She looks sad.)

Therapist: I wonder if there was something about your conversation with her that struck a chord within you. Tell me what comes to your mind.

Shawna: Well, I guess I thought, "Yeah, I know how you feel. Things never work out for me either. I'm married and I'm unhappy." (She starts to cry.)

Therapist: That hurts. Do your tears make sense?

Shawna: Yes.

In a brief interchange about the events of the day, the meaning and source of Shawna's pain became clear to her. This is not a fancy psychotherapeutic technique, and it is not magical. People help other people do this sort of thing all the time: one person listens and encourages another person to talk. Many therapists take this approach: "Let's see what's happened; I bet we can make sense of this." By asking questions, by listening, and encouraging discussion, the therapist helps the client become aware of the personal meaning of events and emotions.

If the therapist had said, "I'm sure it was nothing," or "Well, you're over it now," or "It was probably just PMS," the process would have been quickly ended. Shawna would be just as much in the dark as before the session.

Shawna had initially tried to close the door herself by answering, "Nothing really," to the therapist's inquiry, "Can you tell me what went on in the office?" The therapist nudged it open again, and she started to talk.

This is not just talking or "chit-chat." The goal is speaking out loud with another, moving toward understanding, discovering true feelings, and finding out what's really important. In this case, Shawna's sadness and confusion were replaced with greater understanding. As she became more aware of her own emotional turmoil, her feelings of sadness became an important issue for her to explore.

The talking helped Shawna open emotional doors, get in touch with her true feelings, understand herself better, and view reality clearly. Her choices and actions won't always turn out right, but they'll be more in sync with her genuine needs, beliefs, and values. This gives her the best shot at emotional health.

Getting Clear

One of the most important things that happen in psychotherapy is what I call getting clear. It is getting clear about certain truths: the truth of who you really are (how you feel, what matters to you) and getting clear about certain realities, such as the truth about who people are: what they really feel and how they really treat you.

You may recall Cindy and her husband David in Chapter 5. Despite David's comments, "You know I love you," Cindy was beginning to wonder if his words were entirely sincere. She so much wanted to believe him, but her gut was telling her something different.

Views of reality are strongly influenced by what others tell us, "You know your mother really does love you …. She's a good woman," "I really want to spend more time with you, honey, but I have a lot of work to do," "I am doing this for your own good." Views of reality are also shaped by injunctions, "Don't rock the boat," "Don't be so sensitive," "I shouldn't complain; others have it worse." These views that are in conscious awareness, I'll refer to as "Version One" of reality. Sometimes Version One may be accurate, sometimes not.

As we saw in Chapter 5, on another level, we may perceive, think about, and respond to the world in a very different way. This level is based more on direct personal experience, intuition, sensations, and feelings—a more immediate, gut-level response to what's happening in the moment. These perceptions and responses have little to do with what we have been told by others to think or believe. Rather, they come naturally from within the self—a type of inner truth. Let's refer to this internal view as "Version Two."

Versions One and Two may differ. Years ago, during her first menstrual period, Beth complained to her mother of painful cramping. Her mother responded, "You're too young to have a period!" The young girl was now confronted with conflicting views of reality: Mom's view ("You are not having a period") and her own view ("I hurt"). A self-confident child might say, "Mom you're wrong!" but many children will accept their mother's version of truth, and ignore the reality of their own experience.

The internal reality of physical pain, emotions, and needs can be ignored by thinking things like, "I'm making a big deal out of nothing," or "It's not that bad," or "Mom must know what's really happening." Or you can deny your feelings by blocking them from awareness—either partially or completely—leaving you out of touch with your inner reality.

Cindy started psychotherapy and began to explore her marriage to David. As Cindy began to look more closely into her heart and to trust her intuitive sense about David, she started to see more clearly her Version One and Version Two, and they weren't in agreement. For her, Version One meant, "David is a good man. He says he loves me. Things could be worse. I shouldn't complain" But gradually she saw her Version Two: "He's rarely at home. There is little intimacy. I feel empty, unhappy, and angry. He says 'I love you,' but his behavior tells a different story."

Discovering the truth about her relationship with David brought Cindy closer to objective reality. Though she knew Version One was fashioned on empty promises, words, and her own strong hopes, she wanted desperately to believe it. But it wasn't true. As she talked and explored her feelings since beginning therapy sessions, Version One faded and gave way to her real feelings. David may have had good intentions and sincerely believed that his words and promises of love were genuine. However, the bottom-line reality for Cindy was Version Two. She didn't like it, and it hurt, but it was real.

During psychotherapy Cindy learned to:

◆ Question her own personal Version-One views of important others (parents, spouses, relatives, friends), world views ("The world is fair," "Bad things don't happen to good people") and guidelines for living ("Don't be emotional," "Don't be so sensitive," "Don't get angry").

◆ Pay attention to her direct experience—inner reactions, sensation, longings, and emotions. Not to deny what she knows is true.

Facing the truth often means pain … but doing so enabled her to heal and grow!

"The Truth Shall Make You Free"

The Biblical saying is proven every day by clients in therapy. Your truth cannot be defined or dictated from without, but must be discovered from within.

Think About It

Therapist and author Bill O'Hanlon says, "The truth shall set you free, but first it'll probably tick you off or scare the hell out of you."

When you make time to really talk about your thoughts, feelings, and other inner experiences, one outcome is often an increased awareness of inner truths. "My childhood was not happy." "My father didn't truly show me love." "My job isn't gratifying." "My mother hurt me." "I feel a lack of closeness in my marriage." Such discoveries both hurt and help. You must face and grieve the loss of illusions (for example, the illusion of a happy childhood or a meaningful marriage).

Ultimately, Version Two may be okay. You may start to see your partner for who she really is. Maybe that's all right, or maybe not. Accurate awareness may ignite open conflict or promote problem-solving in a relationship; it can lead to marital counseling or even to divorce. But increased awareness of inner truths may result in less confusion and a stronger sense of self.

Within each person there are may "truths," so the approach is not aimed at finding "one truth," but the discovery of all your beliefs, needs, and emotions. It's a lifelong process. As you begin to clarify these aspects of yourself, you can sort out who you are, figure out what problems you want to tackle, and feel more solid about the actions you choose to take.

Specific Psychotherapies for Particular Psychological Problems

In the next chapter, we will take a brief look at some very common types of depression and anxiety disorders. What I've discussed thus far in this chapter are general issues regarding psychotherapy. For particular disorders, certain types of therapy can also be used successfully to reduce symptoms such as anxiety attacks or depression.

One of the most common versions of specialized psychological treatments is *cognitive therapy*. Cognitive therapy employs many of the techniques we discussed in Chapter 14. In addition, especially for the treatment of anxiety disorders, there are exposure components to the therapy (thus, such treatments are often referred to as exposure-based cognitive therapy). The exposure facet of the therapy involves gradually exposing yourself to the things that you most fear. For instance, if you have a dreaded fear of heights, a part of exposure therapy is to very gradually face the fears, perhaps by first stepping on only the first step of a ladder. Then, in a graded fashion, start stepping up higher. The key to exposure therapy is to overcome intense anxiety during each step of progressive exposure, and gradually feel a sense of mastery. Such treatments have been highly successful in treating many forms of anxiety and depression.

def•i•ni•tion

Cognitive Therapy is a specific approach to psychotherapy where the therapist uses various techniques (such as the thought record described in Chapter 14) to help the client improve his own ability to think clearly. A number of such techniques can help people develop a more realistic and balanced perspective on their lives and can improve their effectiveness in problem-solving. Cognitive therapists also often assign "homework" projects for clients to work on between sessions.

Understanding Your Therapist's Credentials

There are a number of professionals that are trained and licensed to provide psychotherapy:

◆ Psychologists (Ph.D., Psy.D.: doctor of psychology, or Ed.D: doctor of education with specialty in counseling psychology): psychologists have earned a doctoral degree in psychology and generally are required to do one or two years of supervised internship before being eligible for licensing. Some psychologists also are specialists in conducting psychological testing.

◆ Psychiatrists (M.D. or D.O., osteopathic doctors): have training in medical school as well as doing residency training in psychiatry. Many psychiatrists provide psychotherapy and most are trained in the medical treatment of psychiatric disorders (prescribing psychiatric medications).

◆ Clinical Social Workers (MSW: Master's in social work or DSW: doctor of social work): have training in conducting psychotherapy and have completed several years of post-degree internships. Some also specialize in medical social work and work in hospitals and other medical care settings to help medically ill patients cope with their illnesses.

◆ Marital and Family Counselors (Master's degree therapists; some have earned a Ph.D. or Psy.D.): provide family and marital counseling.

◆ Pastoral Counselors: Most ordained ministers, priests and rabbis provide what is referred to as "pastoral care" which is very brief counseling sessions that focus on spiritual issues. Some have additional training in counseling and may offer more in-depth counseling.

This should aid you in finding and selecting the appropriate professional.

The Least You Need to Know

◆ Psychotherapy is not just about talking or chit-chatting. It is a way to deeply explore what really matters to you in your life.

◆ Therapy is a place to make decisions about changing your life and getting support for doing so.

◆ Cognitive-behavioral approaches have a solid track record of effectiveness in treating very specific types of psychological problems.

Chapter 26

Professional Treatments for Anxiety and Depression

In This Chapter

- ◆ Serious depressions and anxiety disorders are very common

- ◆ Am I just "down" or is it really major depression?

- ◆ Biochemical imbalances in the brain or hormonal changes (especially in women)

- ◆ Bipolar (manic-depressive) illness is more common than you might think

- ◆ Psychological and medical treatments are very effective

Many people experience significant struggles with anxiety and depression. These common emotional problems affect people from all walks of life. Effective medical and psychological treatments have been developed, and yet most people in our country never seek treatment. In this final chapter, we will take a look at these common psychological problems and briefly discuss professional treatment options.

Normal Folks and Serious Disorders

It must be emphasized from the outset that many people who have had very difficult or tragic lives fall prey to depression and other types of serious mood disorders. At the same time, it is very often the case that entirely psychologically healthy, emotionally mature individuals can also develop certain types of depressions or bipolar illness. Many, many thousands of successful, competent people and those often considered to be the "worried well" get hit by serious depression. Most of the time these serious mood disorders have little to do with weaknesses of character; in part this is due to the fact that many depressions and anxiety disorders are due, at least in part, to biological changes in the brain.

Depression

Many people occasionally will say that they feel depressed. This can refer to a host of unpleasant emotions such as feeling "blue," moodiness, feelings of sadness, disappointment, discouragement, being unmotivated, or just feeling "out of sorts." For most of us, feeling down in the dumps occasionally or being saddened temporarily is a normal part of human life. These are understandable reactions to a myriad of difficult life experiences.

In the United States, however, every year 10 percent of the population experiences a much more devastating mood disorder, referred to these days as either major depression or clinical depression. Over the life span of the average American, the prevalence of major depression is even higher, affecting 17 percent—one out of six Americans will at some point in their lives suffer with this form of severe emotional disorder. With such a high incidence, it is hard to imagine that anyone has not either experienced depression personally or known close friends or relatives who have had episodes of clinical depression. The bottom line—major depression is an extremely common experience.

Some people may be at greater risk for developing depression. Depression is, to some degree, influenced by genetics and can run in families. But it is important to state that depression can happen to anyone, under certain circumstances. It occurs in people from all cultures around the world. Depression is, however, about twice as likely to occur in females than in males.

Major Depression Versus the "Blues"

Major depression differs from minor bouts of sadness in a number of ways that are discussed in detail later in this chapter. However, its main characteristics are as follows:

1. It is extremely severe.

2. If not treated, it generally lasts for months or even years.

3. It often results in significant disability. (In addition to tremendous personal suffering, during episodes of major depression, otherwise capable people often cannot function well at work or in school, marriages may fall apart, and loving parents may find it nearly impossible to really interact with, love, and guide their children.)

4. Rates of alcohol and other types of substance abuse are higher during episodes of depression.

5. For untreated or inappropriately treated people, there is a risk of suicide (the lifetime mortality risk from suicide is 10 percent).

6. Chronic depression contributes to poor physical health, especially to increased risks of heart disease, osteoporosis, infectious diseases, and, possibly, an increased risk for Alzheimer's disease.

Clinical depression is obviously much more than a mere case of the blues. It is a common and often devastating emotional illness. The real tragedy is that only one third of those experiencing a major depression ever receive treatment. Most of these people somehow grit their teeth and suffer for months and months (the average length of an episode of depression is from 9 to 15 months, unless treated). Yet, according to the National Institute of Mental Health, 80 percent or more of those experiencing major depression can be successfully treated, and in many cases, symptom relief can occur in a matter of weeks. Dr. David Burns, author of the popular book *Feeling Good* says, "Depression feels hopeless even though the prognosis is excellent."

This high rate of treatment success is due to the development of several effective types of therapy, including some types of psychotherapy, medication treatment (antidepressant medications), and exercise, which have a remarkably good impact on reducing depression.

A Recurring Illness

For half of people experiencing a major depression, the current episode will be a once-in-a-lifetime event. However, for the other 50 percent of people experiencing serious depression, unfortunately, the disorder will recur. In this group, many will experience ongoing, chronic depression, while most will be plagued with recurring episodes of the illness. Although this may sound bleak, the good news is that psychological and medical treatments for depression also have been shown to be very effective in preventing relapse. Thus, when considering treatment for depression, it is important to focus not only on resolving the current episode but also on taking steps to prevent recurrence of the disorder.

Not Everyone Will Understand

It is a very common experience for those going through a depression to hear comments from concerned friends or family revealing that the concerned person does not truly understand the nature of clinical depression. For example, people make statements like these: "You just need to look on the bright side." "Just try to snap yourself out of it." "You need to try harder—you need to pull yourself up by your bootstraps." They may even say, "Don't worry—be happy." Their intentions may be good, but they simply do not understand. An old saying is "Good advice is free and it's worth the price."

True clinical depression drags people into a kind of emotional paralysis from which it is difficult to escape, despite considerable effort.

Signs and Symptoms of Depression

A brief list of symptoms was presented in Chapter 7. Here we'll look at depressive symptoms in more detail. It is useful to consider two main sets of depressive symptoms. The first set is referred to as Core Symptoms, which are symptoms that are seen in nearly all types of depression.

The following are core symptoms common to all depressions:

◆ Mood of sadness, despair, emptiness

◆ Loss of interest in most normal life activities and an inability to feel a sense of vitality, pleasure, or aliveness (the psychiatric term for this is *anhedonia*)

◆ Low self-esteem, lack of self-confidence

- Apathy, low motivation, and social withdrawal

- Excessive emotional sensitivity

- Negative, pessimistic thinking

- A tendency to take things personally

- Irritability

- Indecisiveness

- Suicidal ideas

def•i•ni•tion

Anhedonia is a common symptom of serious depression. It is a loss of a sense of aliveness and vitality. Regardless of what happens in a person's life, nothing evokes happiness, interest, or enthusiasm. When anhedonia is present, life loses all meaning—people can no longer experience the beauty of a sunset, a funny movie, the laughter of their grandchildren, the inspiration of a favorite hymn, or the pleasure of good food or physical intimacy. And when nothing matters, then people invariably withdraw from life. The sadness and discouragement of depression is enough suffering, but add anhedonia to this and depression feels even worse. Fortunately, anhedonia is a symptom of serious depression that typically responds well to professional treatment.

A second group of symptoms are the biological or physical symptoms of depression. These symptoms are associated with chemical malfunctions in the brain that can occur in many types of depression.

The following are biological symptoms of depression:

- Appetite disturbance—decreased or increased, with accompanying weight loss or weight gain

- Fatigue

- Decreased sex drive

- Restlessness, agitation, or conversely, a loss of energy

- Impaired concentration and forgetfulness

- Pronounced anhedonia—total loss of the ability to experience pleasure

- Sleep disturbance—early-morning awakening, frequent awakenings throughout the night, and occasional hypersomnia (excessive sleeping)

When a person is being evaluated for possible depression, the mental-health professional (or primary-care physician) should ask specifically about the presence or absence of these symptoms (both core symptoms and biological symptoms). Not all depressed people will have all of these symptoms, but they usually will have several. In general, for a diagnosis of depression to be made, such symptoms must be present for a period lasting at least two weeks.

Biochemical Imbalance

Some types of depression appear to be associated with an underlying biological cause (a neurochemical disorder). The presence of one or more of the physical symptoms of depression strongly suggests that at least a part of the problem can be traced to a biochemical disturbance. The biological changes in brain functioning can seem to come out of the blue (i.e. may occur in the absence of major, difficult life events). Such depressions are called endogenous depressions, meaning to "arise from within." They also can be set in motion by the medical illnesses or drugs mentioned in Chapter 8 and outlined in detail in Appendix B. However, most commonly depressions are caused by stress. Here life stressors provoke not only emotional responses, but also begin to significantly derail brain chemical functioning.

There are also genetic factors that influence the emergence of biological depressions. Some depressions tend to run in families. Consequently, obtaining a family history (to see if there are blood relatives who have had mood disorders) may provide important clues to the diagnosis.

The reason it is important to determine if there is some form of underlying chemical imbalance is that for those individuals, antidepressant medications may be quite effective.

Dysthymia

Dysthymia is a very long-lasting type of low-grade depression. It is not as severe as major depression, but can be experienced almost every day for a period of at least two years, and often longer. It is believed that this disorder affects about 6 percent of the population. Those suffering from dysthymia are burdened by an almost-constant low-grade depression. This usually manifests in the following symptoms:

◆ Moodiness

◆ Low self-esteem

- Persistent lack of enthusiasm

- Fatigue

- No zest for life

- Irritability

- A strong tendency for negative, pessimistic thinking

- Often seen by other people is being boring, pessimistic, cranky, or just miserable people

People with dysthymia can be treated by psychotherapy, and some recent studies have shown that a number of people with dysthymia also respond well to antidepressant medications. The response rate to medication treatments is about 66 percent.

When medication treatments are successful for people with dysthymia, these patients often make comments like, "I have never felt this good in my entire life." This kind of very positive result has led many investigators to conclude that probably some forms of dysthymia are caused by a chronic neurochemical malfunction.

def•i•ni•tion

Dysthymia is a low-grade, chronically depressed mood that is experienced almost every day over a long period of time. People suffering from dysthymia tend to see the world in a pervasively negative way.

Hormone-Driven Depressions

About 75 percent of all women notice some changes in their emotions when they are premenstrual. For most, the changes are very slight. However, as previously discussed in Chapter 8, it has been estimated that about 5 percent of women experience intense mood symptoms during this part of their menstrual cycle. This is technically referred to as premenstrual dysphoria. The emotional changes can include depression, anxiety, and/or irritability. In recent years many psychiatric specialists have noted that the serotonin-specific antidepressants medications (referred to as SSRIs: Prozac, Paxil, Zoloft, Celexa, and Lexapro) appear to be effective in reducing these mood symptoms (and are more effective in accomplishing this than other classes of antidepressants). The emotional brain is packed with estrogen-sensitive receptors, and it makes sense that significant fluctuations in female hormones (especially estrogen) may destabilize the chemical functioning in the emotional brain.

It should be noted that exercise, exposure to bright light (sunlight), and some dietary changes (e.g., reducing caffeine) also may play an important role in the treatment of premenstrual dysphoria.

Other Hormone-Related Depressions

In approximately 10–14 percent of women giving birth to a baby, within four to eight weeks, a severe depression can occur: post-partum depression. Hormonal changes associated with childbirth play a role, but it is also very important to note that sleep deprivation during the weeks following delivery is another key factor increasing the risk of post-partum depression.

Some women also develop severe depressions in the peri-menopausal period of life (in the years leading up to and including entry into menopause). Most of the time these depressions occur in women who have had previous depressions associated with various changes in female hormones. It is that same group of women who have had pre-menstrual depression and/or post-partum depression who are most at risk.

Atypical Depression

It has been estimated that between 15 and 20 percent of people experiencing clinical depression suffer from a particular subtype of major depression called Atypical Depression (atypical meaning not typical). The symptoms of atypical depression include the following:

♦ Severe fatigue

♦ Appetite increase and weight gain

♦ Excessive sleeping (technically referred to as hyper-somnia)

One reason for listing this disorder separately is that the presence of atypical depressive symptoms is a warning sign for possible bipolar (manic-depressive) disorder. Three fourths of people who suffer with atypical depression have a form of bipolar disorder. The medical treatments for major depression and for depression seen as a part of bipolar disorder are very different, and that is why this distinction is so important. Also, if a person actually has bipolar disorder, over a period of time the use of antidepressant medications may actually make the disorder more severe.

Treatments for Depression

Most depressions can be successfully treated. Anyone with significant depressive symptoms should seriously consider getting professional treatment ... and do not delay. The longer depression goes untreated, the harder it is to treat. A comprehensive discussion of treatments for depression is beyond the scope of this book. However, I'd like to briefly summarize those treatments that have documented success in the treatment of depression:

♦ Psychotherapy (including a version of psychotherapy called cognitive-behavioral therapy).

♦ Antidepressant medications are effective in many types of depression (as noted previously, this is especially so if the depression is severe and if it is accompanied by the physical symptoms of depression). One significant problem, however, is that most people treated with antidepressants are prescribed medications by primary-care doctors, and often there is a lack of follow-up. The results are that the majority of times the outcomes are inadequate. Antidepressants are discussed in Appendix D.

♦ Exercise has been shown to be quite effective in treating depression. The trick is getting a depressed person to exercise. (Let's face it, it's hard to get most people to exercise.) However, the research on exercise therapy for depression is very promising.

♦ High-intensity light therapy can be a successful treatment for some forms of depression (especially those that are seasonal depression, i.e. winter depression).

♦ For very severe depression, ECT (electro-convulsive therapy, often called "shock therapy") continues to be a highly effective treatment. This is generally only offered if the depression is extraordinarily severe and/or if antidepressant medication treatment has not been successful.

Possible Meltdown _____

Seventy-five percent of prescriptions for antidepressants and 90 percent of prescriptions for antianxiety drugs are written by primary-care doctors. Due to a lack of close follow-up in primary care, as little as 15 percent of those who are treated actually experience a good response to medications. Treatments with these medications warrant close follow-up to ensure adequate dosing and to monitor for side effects.

Bipolar Disorders

Bipolar disorder, which is also known as manic-depressive illness, is characterized by wide swings in mood that alternate between *mania* and depression. These two emotional states can be viewed as opposite ends, or "poles," of a continuum, hence the term bipolar ("bi" is the Latin term for two). During an episode of mania, a person's mood is abnormally elevated, euphoric, or accompanied by pronounced irritability. The depressions associated with bipolar disorder can be equal in severity to those seen in major depression.

The following are core symptoms of mania:

- Excessive euphoric or high feelings

- Irritability

- Distractibility

- Unrealistic and inflated beliefs in one's abilities—called grandiosity

- Dramatic mannerisms

- Racing thoughts, technically referred to as flight of ideas

- Loud, pressured, and rapid speech—difficult to interrupt and subject to changing topics, often unrelated

- Increased energy, activity, restlessness

- Decreased need for sleep; requiring only four to five hours of sleep a night without daytime fatigue the next day

- Increased sex drive—provocative behavior, can be promiscuous

- Poor judgment

- Abuse of substances, particularly stimulants and alcohol

- Spending sprees or excessive gambling

def·i·ni·tion

Mania is a severe mood episode associated with bipolar disorder. It is most noticeable by the presence of an upbeat mood, elation and/or extreme irritability, and impulsive behavior. Hypomania is a less severe form of mania.

Some people experience what is called *dysphoric mania*. This is an especially severe form of mania where there is agitation, marked insomnia, extreme irritability, and depression (not euphoria).

On average, 5 percent of the U.S. adult population is afflicted with bipolar disorder. It often first appears in adolescence or early adulthood (usually before the age of 30) and is considered a long-term illness, characterized by patterns of multiple episodes (recently it has been discovered that up to one third of cases of bipolar disorder begin in late childhood).

def•i•ni•tion

Dysphoric mania is an especially severe form of mania where there are classic manic symptoms accompanied by extreme irritability and depression.

Bipolar disorder can strike even very competent and emotionally mature people. It has nothing to do with one's ego strength, level of intelligence, or track record of effective coping. Stress can play a role in provoking episodes, however, bipolar disorder is considered primarily to be a medical/neurological illness.

For the majority of people with the disorder, the symptoms of bipolar disorder can be treated effectively with psychiatric medications (mood stabilizers). However, up to one third of people suffering from bipolar disorder go for years misdiagnosed. Treatment with psychiatric medications is often very challenging owing to numerous side effects associated with mood stabilizers. If bipolar disorder is suspected, please consult with a psychiatrist. This is not a disorder that should be treated by primary-care doctors.

A comprehensive discussion of medical treatments for bipolar disorders is beyond the scope of this book. It is, however, important to state emphatically that medical treatment is absolutely essential. Untreated bipolar disorder always gets worse and failure to treat can often have disastrous consequences. Aside from the enormous personal suffering, the divorce rates are about twice the national average, careers are ruined, health problems abound, and the suicide rate can be as high as 15 percent.

Anxiety Disorders

Anxiety is a part of life. Indeed, it is hardwired into our brains. As we've seen when people feel anxious or threatened, they are likely to respond with an increase in tension and physiological arousal, called the "fight-or-flight response."

For all people, distressing life events can provoke anxiety. However, people with anxiety disorders can experience the full set of these biological reactions without an actual threat being present. Or they may experience severe anxiety reactions to relatively minor stressors.

There are several types of anxiety disorders, including situational anxiety, social phobia, panic disorder, generalized anxiety disorder, and obsessive-compulsive disorder. Of these, panic disorder and obsessive-compulsive disorder (OCD) are at least somewhat influenced by genetic transmission. Also both have the notable abnormalities in brain functioning that account for a good deal of the symptoms. The distinctions between these various types of anxiety depend on whether the anxiety is brief or constant, and whether it is generalized (i.e. experienced in all situations) or specific to a particular situation.

1. Situational anxiety refers to what is often simply called "stress." It is an overly anxious reaction to a distressing situation.

2. Panic disorder is distinguished as sudden attacks of very severe anxiety that last for only a few minutes. Often, after several such attacks, people may also begin to develop phobias (e.g. if they have had a panic attack while driving, they may become very afraid to drive).

3. Generalized anxiety disorder manifests as a near-constant anxiety primarily characterized by constant tension and worry.

4. Obsessive-compulsive disorder (OCD) is distinguished by compulsive, ritualistic behaviors such as repeated hand-washing or checking and rechecking to make sure the oven has been turned off or the doors have been locked, and/or frightening thoughts (e.g. fears regarding dirt, germs, disease, and contamination).

5. Social anxiety disorder is characterized by very intense anxiety felt only in social situations, such as dating, applying for a job, or interactions with strangers, such as while standing in line at the grocery store, and public speaking.

6. Post-traumatic stress disorder (was discussed in detail in Chapter 22).

Altogether, these disorders affect between 10 and 20 percent of the population at any given time, and some 20–25 percent of people over their lifespan. In their more severe forms, anxiety disorders cause tremendous suffering, are very disabling, and are sometimes associated with increased risks of health problems. Often some of the symptoms begin in childhood, so that the person has a life-long struggle with anxiety. In this chapter, we will take a separate look at panic disorder, generalized anxiety, OCD, and social anxiety disorder.

Medical Causes of Anxiety

As we saw in Chapter 8, sometimes anxiety can be caused by an underlying medical illness (also see Appendix B).

In addition, as we have seen, many drugs can cause anxiety. Among them are amphetamines, asthma medications, caffeine, central nervous system depressants (such as withdrawal from alcohol), cocaine, nasal decongestants, steroids, and appetite suppressants.

In the initial evaluation of an anxiety disorder, it is always a good idea to have a physical examination, including appropriate laboratory tests, and to give a thorough drug history, including prescription, over-the-counter, and recreational drugs. If a medical condition or drug usage is found, it is important to first treat the underlying disorder that may be causing the anxiety or to address the drug use. Then, if necessary, treatment targeted specifically at anxiety can begin.

Panic Disorder

Panic disorder is characterized by acute attacks of anxiety, which are so severe that sufferers often fear they will go crazy or die (many people are afraid that they are having a heart attack). These episodes come on very suddenly, are very intense, generally lasting last from a 1 to 15 minutes. The attacks are accompanied by any or all of the symptoms of a fight-or-flight reaction (see Chapter 3).

Typically, panic disorder will begin with a single, isolated panic attack. This attack is often so frightening that the person often becomes anxious and fearful about having another attack. She develops significant anticipatory anxiety about having another attack and may begin, therefore, to experience at least some degree of anxiety most of the time, re-experiencing full panic attacks periodically.

People suffering from panic disorder often come to feel more secure at home and develop phobias about traveling any distance away from home. They are uncomfortable especially when they feel trapped and are unable to go home immediately, as when caught in heavy traffic or in a crowd. Thus, people with panic disorder go from having discrete, severe anxiety attacks, to having near-constant anxiety and phobias of specific activities, punctuated by periodic full-blown panic attacks. This can progress to *agoraphobia*, a condition where the fears are so pervasive and intense that people essentially becomes housebound.

def•i•ni•tion

> **Agoraphobia** is a fear of being in public places such as the grocery store or shopping mall.

Panic disorder can be aggravated by stress, but there is rather convincing evidence to suggest that it is largely a biochemical problem in the brain.

Also, it must be noted that certain cardiac and respiratory diseases can produce what appear to be panic symptoms, thus it is vital to be checked out medically if you experience panic attacks.

Two types of treatment for panic disorder have been developed; both are generally very effective in reducing or eliminating panic symptoms. Exposure-based cognitive therapy for panic disorder is the psychological treatment of choice. Medical treatments for panic include the use of either tranquilizers, (e.g. Xanax, Ativan, Klonopin) or antidepressants. The advantage of tranquilizers is their fast action. Assuming that the dose is adequate, tranquilizers can reduce panic symptoms generally within a few days. The down side of tranquilizers is that they are habit-forming. Antidepressants (all antidepressants with the exception of Wellbutrin) can successfully treat panic disorder. However, you must take medications daily for three to four weeks before symptoms begin to subside. Unlike tranquilizers, antidepressants are not habit-forming.

Think About It

Exposure-based cognitive therapy is a specific type of psychotherapy that has been found to be highly effective in treating most anxiety disorders. It generally includes three features. The first is teaching the therapy client effective anxiety management techniques that enable him to have greater control over the intensity of anxiety symptoms. Second, the cognitive aspect is helping the client to use particular thinking that reduces the perception of impending catastrophe; for instance, during a panic attack, to say to oneself, "This is a panic attack. It is unpleasant, but is not dangerous … these attacks usually only last five minutes … just hang on, it will be over very soon."

The final piece is exposure. Once a person has mastered various anxiety-reduction techniques, then he is instructed to gradually face things he fears. For instance, if he has a fear of driving, he would begin by just sitting in the car in his driveway … and gradually progress, over a period of weeks, to doing things that are more challenging, such as actually driving the car. This gradual approach is monitored so as to result in experiences of mastery at each step of the way.

Generalized Anxiety Disorder

Generalized anxiety disorder (GAD) is seen in individuals who feel quite anxious and tense most of the time. It is not associated with exposure to specific stressful events. Normal, everyday life events cause excessive anxiety, especially worry. It has sometimes been called "what ifing" disease. People are constantly worried about "What if ... something bad happens?" Many of us worry, but with GAD it can become so severe as to dominate a person's life. GAD responds well to typical "talk therapy" (as described in Chapter 25), to exposure-based cognitive therapy, to exercise (actually a very good treatment for GAD), and to three classes of psychiatric medications: BuSpar (a non-habit-forming tranquilizer), standard tranquilizers (e.g. Xanax, Ativan, Valium, and Klonopin—but remember, these are habit-forming), and to antidepressants (all except Wellbutrin).

Obsessive-Compulsive Disorder

Obsessive-Compulsive Disorder (OCD) is characterized by obsessional thoughts and/or compulsive behaviors. Obsessional thoughts are intrusive thoughts that are very distressing to the person thinking them. They evoke a great deal of fearful anxiety, such as fears about oneself or loved ones becoming ill, infected with deadly viruses, or dying.

Compulsive behaviors are ritualistic behaviors that the person feels compelled to perform to ward off some impending calamity, or to reduce the feeling of intense anxiety. Examples include repeatedly checking locks, compulsive counting, tapping a certain number of times, positioning objects in specific ways, or excessive hand-washing.

When the disorder is severe, much of the OCD person's time is occupied by the symptoms, so that performing even a simple task can become very time-consuming.

Obsessive-Compulsive Disorder may be aggravated by stress, but it is considered to be a biological illness due to abnormalities in the brain chemical serotonin. Interestingly, these abnormalities tend to normalize during treatment, whether treatment is exposure-based cognitive-behavioral therapy or medication treatment. The drugs used to treat OCD are antidepressants that increase brain levels of serotonin: Prozac, Zoloft, Paxil, Lexapro, Celexa, and Anafranil.

Social Anxiety Disorder

Lots of us feel at least somewhat uneasy in some social situations. However, in those plagued with social anxiety disorder, the anxiety can be overwhelming. One of the main results of social anxiety disorder is that people are so inhibited about interacting with others that they are very likely to find it difficult to meet people and develop intimate relationships. Many such people often suffer from significant loneliness and may become quite depressed. The best treatments for social anxiety include exposure-based cognitive therapy, group therapy, and some medications, primarily antidepressants (again, with the exception of Wellbutrin).

Why Treat Anxiety Disorders?

Except for situational stress, most anxiety disorders we have addressed in this chapter can become very chronic if not treated. Not only does this result in prolonged suffering, but many people thus affected will also turn to alcohol to quell some of their anxiety, and may eventually become addicted to alcohol. In addition, very chronic anxiety has been associated with an increased risk of heart disease. Treatments for anxiety disorder are often very successful. If medications are used, they should always be accompanied by psychotherapy. And keep in mind that exercise is very effective in the treatment of anxiety. Generally, for it to be helpful, you'll need to be involved in regular exercise (e.g. three times a week for 20 minutes) for at least three months to reap the positive benefits.

The Least You Need to Know

◆ Significant anxiety and depressive disorders affect a very large number of people.

◆ Professional treatment for depression and anxiety is often very successful.

◆ Most prescriptions for antidepressants and antianxiety medications are written by primary-care physicians. Successful treatment outcomes in these settings are disappointingly low due to two factors: lack of close follow-up and neglecting psychotherapy.

◆ Specific types of psychotherapy have been developed for treating anxiety and depression. If you are considering professional therapy, be sure to ask your potential therapist if she offers these particular forms of psychotherapy.

Glossary

aggression   Not truly taking other people's feelings into consideration. Often, aggressive remarks contain comments that attack the other person, or are belittling, humiliating, intimidating, or threatening.

agoraphobia   A fear of being in public places such as the grocery store or shopping mall.

anhedonia   A common symptom of serious depression. It is a loss of a sense of aliveness and vitality. Regardless of what happens in a person's life, nothing evokes happiness, interest, or enthusiasm. When anhedonia is presents, life loses all meaning, for example, people can no longer experience the beauty of a sunset, a funny movie, the laughter of their grandchildren, the inspiration of a favorite hymn, or the pleasure of good food or physical intimacy. And when nothing matters, people invariably withdraw from life.

assertion   Communicating in an honest and direct way, telling someone how you feel and/or asking for a change in her behavior. It is tempered by a respect for her feelings.

behavioral inhibition   The capacity of the mind and the brain to hold back outward emotional reactions when inwardly strong emotions are being activated. This is commonly referred to as "emotional control."

bereavement   The state of having lost someone close to you.

blood-brain barrier   A complex arrangement of tightly packet cells in the brain that operate to keep certain potentially dangerous chemicals out of the brain. The blood-brain barrier also, to some degree, can make it difficult for certain large molecules to enter brain tissue.

brain-derived neurotropic factor (BDNF)   A protein that is considered to be "neuro-protective." It helps facilitate the repair and maintenance of nerve cells in the brain. It also can activate neurogenesis, which is the birth of new nerve cells.

circadian rhythm   The term circadian comes from the root words circa (meaning about or approximately) and dies (meaning a day) … thus about a day. The circadian rhythm is controlled in the brain by what is known as the "endogenous circadian pacemaker." This is the internal biological clock that regulates the release of many hormones, influences sleep and awake times, and controls body temperature. All of these fluctuations in the body occur at approximately the same time each day. And the rhythm repeats itself every 24 hours.

cognitive therapy   A specific approach to psychotherapy where the therapist uses various techniques to help the client improve his own ability to think clearly. A number of such techniques can help people develop a more realistic and balanced perspective on their lives and can improve their effectiveness in problem solving.

coping   Adaptation and survival. It includes taking direct action in your life to solve problems. And it also involves internal, psychological experiences, such as thinking, planning, and feeling.

decompensation   A term used to describe a marked breakdown in emotional controls.

deep sleep   This is considered to be restorative sleep. Deep sleep is especially important for reducing daytime fatigue and maintaining good emotional control. This is also referred to as slow wave sleep or restorative sleep.

defense mechanisms   Automatic and unconscious ways that the mind blocks awareness of inner painful or frightening emotions.

dissociation   A psychological defensive reaction to being emotionally overwhelmed. It results in a feeling of numbness and lack of strong emotions. Dissociation is often accompanied by two other psychological defenses: derealization, a peculiar feeling that the world seems unreal, and depersonalization, the sense that you are not real (feeling odd and estranged from your normal experience of self). Many experts believe that these symptoms are attributable to changes in brain chemistry that often follow emotional trauma.

dysphoric mania   An especially severe form of mania where there are classic manic symptoms accompanied by extreme irritability and depression.

dysthymia A low-grade, chronic depressed mood that is experienced almost every day over a long period of time. People suffering from dysthymia tend to see the world in a pervasively negative way.

ego This is a term that has been used in a number of ways. The ego, in psychological literature, often is synonymous with the concept of "self"; having a well-developed ego might mean having a solid sense of self. The ego is also considered to be those aspects of the human personality that are devoted to coping and survival.

ego strength The degree of emotional sturdiness in the face of strong emotional challenges.

emotional recovery The amount of time it takes a person to calm down after a stressful event. The calming generally refers to decreased physical activation, but also includes feeling emotionally relaxed and in control.

essential amino acids The human body makes a number of amino acids. However, essential amino acids are not produced in your body and must be derived from your diet. Several of these are the key ingredients in the manufacturing of brain neurotransmitters that regulate mood. Two that you may have heard of are tryptophan and tyrosine.

exposure-based cognitive therapy This is a specific type of psychotherapy that has been found to be highly effective in treating most anxiety disorders. Central to this treatment is first teaching anxiety management techniques and then helping the client to face their fears in a gradual, one-step-at-a-time fashion.

fight-or-flight response An automatic biological reaction to the perception of danger in the environment. It is characterized by some or all of the following symptoms: intense physical arousal (heart pounding, sweating, trembling, shortness of breath), emotional changes (feelings of panic, dread, or fear of going crazy or dying), and the impulse to escape.

generalized anxiety disorder This manifests as a near-constant anxiety primarily characterized by constant tension and worry.

grief This represents a large array of feelings that often accompany bereavement, such as sadness and loneliness.

healing Regaining emotional stability and reducing emotional suffering in the aftermath of difficult life experiences.

hypersomnia Sleeping too much. Despite this, most people with hypersomnia also experience significant daytime fatigue. Although hypersomnia can occur in typical, garden-variety depressions, it is frequently associated with bipolar depression (a depressive episode seen in the context of bipolar illness).

hypomania   A less severe form of mania.

injunctions   Rules for behaving that initially are spoken to children, but with time become a part of the child's own internal self-talk. Injunctions do not encourage or support. They scold and criticize.

intra-psychic   This refers to all privately experienced feelings, needs, thoughts, perceptions, and memories.

intrusive symptoms   Highly emotionally charged and vivid memories, images, thoughts, and feelings that come into a person's mind following exposure to traumatic events; often seen in post traumatic stress disorder. The symptoms are a replay of the traumatic event or elements of that experience. They are considered to be intrusive because they occur without conscious choice. Intrusive symptoms also include nightmares.

koyaanisqatsi   This is a Hopi (Native American) word meaning "life out of balance."

light sleep   Twilight sleep, halfway between asleep and awake. Also referred to as stage one sleep.

mania   A severe mood episode associated with bipolar disorder. It is most noticeable by the presence of an upbeat mood, elation, and/or extreme irritability, agitation, and impulsive behavior.

mourning   Refers to various aspects of emotional healing that take place following a painful loss.

neurogenesis   The birth of new nerve cells.

neuropsychiatric disorders   Psychiatric syndromes that are presumed to be either caused by changes in brain chemistry or in which, once the disorder begins, noticeable changes in brain functioning begin to develop. Owing to the fact that they involve some degree of chemical malfunction in the brain, treatments that directly target and normalize brain biochemistry are important to consider (such as the use of antidepressant medications).

night terrors   This may look like nightmares, however, they are generally not associated with scary dreams. The child is not truly awake, but is extremely terrified and may cry and scream. Night terrors are not due to emotional conflicts, but rather are a type of biologically based sleep disorder. They can be treated with certain types of prescription medications.

nightmares   Very frightening dreams that occur frequently when people are under significant stress.

nonassertion   Being passive or timid. When acting in a nonassertive way, people do not speak out and may allow someone to repeatedly use or abuse them.

normative   A term that simply reflects whether or not something is common, i.e. whether it happens to most everyone. It doesn't necessarily imply good or bad. Death is normative; enjoying a vacation is normative.

obsessive-compulsive disorder (OCD)   This is distinguished by compulsive, ritualistic behaviors such as repeated hand washing or checking and rechecking to make sure the over has been turned off or the doors have been locked, and/or freighting thoughts (e.g. fears regarding dirt, germs, disease, and contamination).

panic disorder   This is distinguished by the sufferer experiencing sudden attacks of very severe anxiety that last for only a few minutes. Often after several such attacks, people may also begin to develop phobias (e.g. if they have had a panic attack while driving, they may become very afraid to drive).

parasympathetic nervous system   The parasympathetic nervous system sends nerves throughout the body, and when it is activated, it rapidly produces a calming effect.

post-traumatic stress disorder (PTSD)   A severe reaction to exposure to highly frightening and traumatic life events. Symptoms include intense anxiety, insomnia, intrusive memories, nightmares, and emotional numbing.

premenstrual dysphoria   Changes in estrogen levels that often have an impact on mood. Five percent of women suffer from premenstrual dysphoria. Dysphoria is a term meaning unpleasant mood and this can include irritability, anxiety, and/or depression. Premenstrual dysphoria is a marked mood change that occurs on a very regular basis in the days prior to menstruation. Symptoms can be so severe as to be incapacitating. Premenstrual dysphoria is considered to be a biologically based mood disorder.

psychoactive   When a particular drug has a noticeable effect on brain functioning. Some psychoactive drugs have a negative impact on the brain, while others have a positive effect. For example, anti-convulsant drugs affect many types of nerve cells in the brain and successfully reduce seizures in people suffering from epilepsy. Antidepressants are often very effective in reducing the symptoms of severe depression.

psychological growth   This is about transformation, fundamentally changing something about yourself. This typically includes discovering who you truly are: what you feel, think, value, and believe in, and then beginning to live your life in accord with these truths.

reality testing   This is a psychological term that refers to the ability of the brain and mind to carefully consider and reconsider perceptions. Rather than jumping to abrupt conclusions, reality testing involves a more careful and thoughtful consideration of information coming into the brain.

REM sleep   REM is short for "rapid eye movement" sleep. Here the brain is very active; it is during REM sleep that most dreaming occurs.

rumination   This is the tendency to have troublesome thoughts going through your mind again and again. It is also a kind of worrying that never leads to any real solutions. In common vernacular, rumination is sometimes called "stewing in your own juices."

seasonal affective disorder   A type of depression that is caused primarily by reduced photic stimulation (decreased amounts of light entering the eye). This type of depression is most frequently accompanied by increased appetite, weight gain, lethargy, fatigue, low motivation, and hypersomnia (sleeping too much).

self-regulation   Refers to a number of actions people take to reduce tension. Most of the time these are done without conscious awareness. They include benign actions like stretching and yawning, and extend to more problematic behaviors such as excessive consumption of alcohol.

situational anxiety   Refers to what is often simply called "stress." It is an overly anxious reaction to a distressing situation.

sleep hygiene   Refers to a number of specific steps that one can take to improve the quality of sleep.

social anxiety disorder   Characterized by very intense anxiety felt only in social situations, such as dating, applying for a job, or interactions with strangers (e.g. standing in line at the grocery store, public speaking).

temperament   Refers to those rather enduring personality characteristics that are influenced by genetic factors.

validation   A term often used in psychology to describe the experience of sharing a thought or a feeling with another and seeing that what you have said has been accepted, understood, and not judged.

working through   The process of carefully thinking about, feeling emotions, and finding personal meaning in particular difficult life events. Over a period of time, as people go through this process, generally two things result: first, some of the intensity of painful emotions diminishes, and second, people come to a greater understanding about what has happened and how it has affected them.

Medical Disorders, Conditions, and Medications That May Cause Mood Symptoms

When people experience noticeable negative moods or extreme emotional reactions, it is important to first make sure the mood changes are not caused by biological factors. Such factors include the effects of prescription and over-the-counter medications, recreational drugs, and medical illnesses or conditions. Many people know if they have been diagnosed with a particular medical illness. However, sometimes people do not know that they have a particular medical condition and the primary symptoms of an underlying disorder can be mood changes. Thus, it is advised to check with your doctor to rule out medical causes for emotional symptoms.

Medical Disorders or Conditions That May Cause Mood Changes

Medical disorders or conditions that may cause depression:

1. Addison's disease

2. AIDS

3. Anemia

4. Asthma

5. Chronic fatigue syndrome

6. Chronic infection (mononucleosis, tuberculosis)

7. Chronic pain

8. Congestive heart failure

9. Cushing's disease

10. Diabetes

11. Hypothyroidism (note: hyperthyroid may cause depression, but if so, it usually is accompanied by significant anxiety. After hyperthyroid is treated, people become hypothyroid, and this may lead to depression, especially if their replacement thyroid hormones are not carefully regulated.)

12. Infectious hepatitis

13. Influenza

14. Malignancies (cancer)

15. Malnutrition

16. Menopause

17. Multiple sclerosis

18. Parkinson's disease

19. Porphyria

20. Premenstrual dysphoria

21. Post-partum depression

22. Rheumatoid arthritis

23. Strokes (especially in the left hemisphere)

24. Syphilis (especially in late stages)

25. Systemic lupus erythematosus

25. Ulcerative colitis

26. Uremia

Medical disorders or conditions that may cause anxiety:

1. Adrenal gland tumors (pheochromocytoma)

2. Alcoholism

3. Angina pectoris

4. Cardiac arrhythmia

5. Central nervous system degenerative diseases (e.g. Alzheimer's)

6. Cushing's disease

7. Coronary insufficiency

8. Delirium

9. Hyperthyroidism

10. Meniere's disease (in the early stages)

11. Parathyroid disease

12. Partial-complex seizures

13. Post-concussion syndrome

14. Premenstrual dysphoria

15. Pulmonary embolism

16. Mitral valve prolapse (may not cause anxiety, but often people with mitral valve prolapse also suffer from anxiety)

Medical disorders or conditions that may cause mania (in those individuals with bipolar disorder):

1. Injury or trauma to the brain (e.g. stroke)

2. Hyperthyroidism

3. Infections such as encephalitis

4. Seizure disorders

5. Brain tumors

Medications That May Cause Mood Changes

Medications that may cause depression or moodiness:

1. Interferon

2. Antianxiety drugs: tranquilizers (Valium, Librium, Xanax, Ativan, Klonopin)

3. Antihypertensives (for high blood pressure); (Reserpine, Inderal, Methyldopa, Aldomet, Guanethidine sulfate, Ismelin sulfate, Catapres, Hydralazine hydrochloride, Aspresoline hydrochloride)

4. Antiparkinsonian drugs (Levodopa, carbidopa, Sinemet, Levodopa Dupar, Larodopa, Amantadine hydrochloride, Symmetrel)

5. Birth control pills (Progestin-estrogen combination; various brands)

6. Corticosteroids and other hormones (Cortisone acetate, Prednisone, Cortone, Estrogen, Premarin, Ogen, Estrace, Estraderm, Progesterone and derivatives, Provera, Depro-Provera, Norlutate, Norplant, Progestasert)

Medications that may cause nervousness, irritability, or anxiety:

1. Appetite suppressants

2. Asthma medications

3. Decongestants (pills and nasal sprays)

4. Steroids (e.g. prednisone)

5. Tranquilizers (withdrawal from)

Medications that may cause mania (in those individuals with bipolar disorder):

1. Stimulants (e.g. cocaine or amphetamines)

2. Certain antidepressants, notably tricyclics

3. Some medications used to lower blood pressure

4. Steroidal anti-inflammatory medications in higher doses, such as prednisone

5. Thyroid hormones, such as levothyroxine

Pleasant Activities

The goal of this appendix is to help you increase the number of pleasant or meaningful activities in your life. This can help bring on more balance, something especially important to do during difficult times. The best activities to choose are those you have enjoyed in the past. However, when people are feeling significantly overwhelmed or depressed, it's often hard to think of even one potentially pleasant activity. Listed here are some suggestions to get you started.

Step one is to come up with your own list of several activities that you choose to pursue. It is also a good idea to sit down with a close friend or family member and brainstorm. Come up with a list of activities you've done in the past and others that you have never considered. In addition to enjoyable activities, also list some things you can do that would be interesting or meaningful.

Step two is to get out your calendar and schedule two or three of these activities per week. It may also be helpful to make a commitment to your spouse or a close friend that you will indeed do these activities (or invite them to join you). The reason for this is that people often have good intentions in planning to do these activities, but when the time comes to actually take the time to take care of themselves, it may just seem more important to attend to problematic life issues.

You must carve out time and make sure you actually follow through with pleasant activities. Also keep in mind, this is not just about having fun (although, there's nothing wrong with that), but it is also about making sure your life maintains some balance. This, in itself, is a potent stress management strategy.

1. Reading novels or magazines

2. Watching TV

3. Renting and watching a video

4. Learn a new craft or hobby (many craft stores offer classes)

5. Camping

6. Working in politics or for a political or social cause

7. Having lunch with friends

8. Taking a shower

9. Being with animals

10. Singing in a group

11. Going to church socials

12. Playing a musical instrument

13. Going to the beach

14. Rearranging your furniture

15. Reading the Bible or other spiritual works

16. Going to a sports event

17. Playing sports

18. Going to the movies

19. Cooking meals

20. Having a good cry

21. Going to a restaurant

22. Looking at beautiful flowers or plants

23. Saying prayers

24. Canning, making preserves, etc.

25. Taking a bath

26. Making food or crafts to sell or give away

27. Painting or drawing

28. Visiting people who are sick or shut in

29. Bowling

30. Gardening or doing yard work

31. Shopping

32. Sitting in the sun

33. Going to a zoo or amusement park

34. Playing board games

35. Doing outdoor work

36. Reading the newspaper

37. Swimming

38. Running, jogging, or walking

39. While taking a walk, trying to see new things you have never noticed before

40. Playing Frisbee

41. Listening to music

42. Knitting, crocheting, or needlework

43. Starting a new project

44. Having sex

45. Bird watching

46. Repairing things

47. Bicycling

48. Giving gifts

49. Going on outings (to the park or a picnic)

50. Playing basketball

51. Helping someone

52. Seeing beautiful scenery

53. Hiking

54. Going to a museum

55. Fishing

56. Going to a health club

57. Writing letters, cards, or notes

58. Going to luncheons, potlucks, etc.

59. Being with your husband or wife

60. Going on field trips, nature walks, etc.

61. Expressing your love to someone

62. Caring for houseplants

63. Collecting things

64. Sewing

65. Going to auctions, garage sales, etc.

66. Doing volunteer work

67. Seeing old friends

68. Writing to or emailing old friends

69. Calling old friends

70. Going to the library

Quick Reference Guide to Antidepressant and Antianxiety Medications

Antidepressant and antianxiety medications are among the most widely prescribed medications in our country. When properly prescribed, they can provide considerable help for those who suffer from more severe forms of anxiety and depression. As I have noted in several of the chapters of this book, most prescriptions for these classes of medications are written by primary-care doctors.

While many primary-care physicians are knowledgeable in the treatment of anxiety and depression, two significant problems exist. The first is that often there is grossly inadequate follow-up and not enough time for appropriate patient education. The majority of people treated for anxiety and depression in primary-care settings never take these medications for long enough or at adequate-enough doses for them to be effective. Second, it is always important to combine medication treatment with psychotherapy. Again, in primary-care settings, often there is not a referral made to a psychotherapist.

This appendix addresses many basic questions people have regarding antidepressants and antianxiety medications. The discussion of other classes of psychiatric drugs (e.g. mood stabilizers and antipsychotic medications) is beyond the scope of this book.

Note: To the best of my knowledge, doses and side effects listed below are accurate. However, this is meant as a general reference only and should not serve as a guideline for prescribing medications. Brand names are registered trademarks.

Antidepressant Medications

In the 1950s and 1960s, tricyclic and MAOI antidepressants were discovered. These drugs were found to be effective, but had noticeable side effects and were quite dangerous if taken in an overdose. The antidepressants listed here are often called "new-generation antidepressants," and have considerably safer side-effect profiles.

Generic Names	Brand Names	Typical Adult Daily Doses
trazodone	Desyrel	50–400 mg
fluoxetine	Prozac, Sarafem	20–80 mg
bupropion	Wellbutrin	150–400 mg
sertraline	Zoloft	50–200 mg
paroxetine	Paxil	20–50 mg
venlafaxine	Effexor	75–350 mg
nefazadone	Serzone	100–500 mg
fluvoxamine	Luvox	50–300 mg
mirtazapine	Remeron	15–45 mg
citalopram	Celexa	10–60 mg
escitalopram	Lexapro	5–20 mg
duloxetine	Cymbalta	20–80 mg
atomoxetine	Strattera	60–120 mg

Uses: to treat major depression, dysthymia. In addition, the following disorders can be treated by all antidepressants except Wellbutrin, which may increase anxiety: panic disorder, generalized anxiety disorder, social anxiety, and obsessive-compulsive disorder (OCD). Additionally, the following antidepressants may be used to treat premenstrual dysphoric disorder: Prozac, Sarafem, Zoloft, Paxil, Celexa, Luvox, and Lexapro. Antidepressants should be used with caution in treating bipolar disorder. They may aggravate that condition.

Onset of positive effects: generally two to six weeks. Must be taken every day as prescribed. It is often very difficult for people to wait the required several weeks before experiencing noticeable signs of recovery. Unfortunately these drugs do not work quickly, thus patience is required. During the first few weeks of treatment, exercise will generally help to relieve some depressive symptoms until the medication effects begin to emerge.

Note: when antidepressants are used to treat premenstrual dysphoric disorder (PMDD), the positive results are often experienced several hours after taking the first dose. This very rapid onset of actions is only seen in PMDD and not in any other types of depression.

How long must they be taken: generally if there is a positive response to antidepressants, it is advised to keep taking the medications for a minimum of an additional six months to prevent acute relapse. For many people this does not make sense, because they have recovered from the depression, but this additional six months of treatment greatly reduces the likelihood of relapse. For the treatment of PMDD, generally the medications are only taken for the duration of premenstrual symptoms (this varies from one woman to another, but generally are taken only for a few days each month).

Caution if discontinued: all antidepressants, except Prozac, if taken for more than a few weeks must be discontinued gradually. Otherwise, withdrawal effects can be experienced, including nausea, general body aches, occasionally a peculiar electrical shock sensation going through the arms or head (not dangerous, but unpleasant and odd), and anxiety. The symptoms feel like you have the flu. Gradual discontinuation over a period of four to six weeks can prevent such withdrawal symptoms.

Laboratory tests: not required

Common side effects:

- ◆ Nausea

- ◆ Heartburn

- ◆ Energized or anxious feelings; i.e. "activation" (typically subsides within one to two weeks)

- ◆ Headaches

- ◆ Sedation (primarily with Remeron and Desyrel)

- Difficulty falling asleep (often subsides in a few weeks)

- Sexual dysfunction: primarily inorgasmia (difficulty achieving an orgasm despite adequate arousal); can occur in 14 to 30 percent of people treated with antidepressants. One exception: very rare with Wellbutrin

- Weight gain (primarily with Remeron; with other antidepressants, weight gain can occur in up to 10 percent of people, however, the weight gain typically does not occur until the person has been taking the drug for a period of time longer than six months)

- Muscle tremor

- Rash

Rare side effects (if these occur, patient should immediately contact the treating doctor):

- Soreness of mouth, throat, or gums

- Severe rash

- Seizures

- Unusual bruising or bleeding

- Severe nausea, vomiting, and flu-like symptoms

- Severe agitation or restlessness

- Yellow tinge to skin or eyes; dark-colored urine

- Rapid shift into mania or hypomania; racing thoughts

Habit-forming/addiction potential: none

Interactions with other medications: (varies depending on the drug). Do not take with St. John's Wort, 5-HTP (dietary supplement), MAOIs, cimetidine (Tagamet).

Safety during pregnancy: most experts agree that some new-generation antidepressants are safe for use during pregnancy (e.g. Prozac, Zoloft, Effexor, Wellbutrin and Luvox); however, recently concerns have been raised regarding the drug Paxil during pregnancy. (Note: the following antidepressants have only recently come to the market and there is inadequate data to evaluate safety during pregnancy: Cymbalta, Strattera, Lexapro, Celexa, Serzone, and Remeron). High doses of Desyrel should not be used during pregnancy.

Breast-feeding: antidepressants are secreted in breast milk, but the amounts are extremely low. Most experts agree that it is safe to breast-feed while taking new-generation antidepressants.

Recent concern regarding antidepressants and increased suicide: there has been a good deal of media attention regarding potential risks of antidepressants and increased suicidality (especially in children and adolescents). The initial concern came from studies in England that raised concerns about increased suicidality in young patients treated with the antidepressant Paxil. In this study, which included 1,300 patients, Paxil was compared to placebo and reports of increased suicidality were seen in 1.2 percent of placebo and 3.4 percent of Paxil-treated subjects. This difference is statistically significant. It is important to note that there were no actual suicides in this group of youngsters and a number of so-called suicidal "events" occurred in the Paxil group when the children stopped taking the medication.

In trying to understand and address this issue, one significant problem is that the concept of "suicidality" has been very loosely defined in this and other studies. Most times it includes reports of increased thoughts about suicide, suicide gestures, nonlethal-intent self-mutilation (as is often seen in borderline personality disorders), and, in one instance, even a report of a child slapping herself qualified as a suicide attempt. Of course, actual suicides and lethal attempts are also included under this umbrella of suicidality.

Concerns regarding increased suicidality have had a significant impact. Currently the United Kingdom Committee on Safety of Medications has banned the use of all antidepressants for use in patients under the age of 18, with the exception of fluoxetine (Prozac). In the United States, the FDA has also responded to concerns about increased suicidality by requiring drug companies to issue warnings about the use of these drugs with younger clients. They also initiated a study to investigate the data: they are currently evaluating a database of 4,400 teenagers treated with antidepressants and final conclusions are pending. It is interesting to note that in this large group of adolescents treated with SSRIs, there have been no suicides. A recent large study conducted by the National Institute of Mental Health evaluating the effect of antidepressants in the treatment of teenagers with serious depression found a significant decrease in suicidality among those treated with antidepressants. It has also been documented that in geographic areas where antidepressants are in widespread use, suicide rates have dropped among adolescents. This has been reported by the Center for Disease Control and Prevention.

Despite these findings, it must be kept in mind that suicidal thoughts and feelings are common among people with serious depression, and that antidepressants, in some instances, may contribute to an increased risk especially during the first two weeks of treatment. (Note that most of these medications take three to four weeks to become effective in reducing depressive symptoms.) When there is an increase in suicidality during the first few weeks of treatment, any of the following may be contributing factors:

◆ Activation and increased restlessness (an occasional side effect of starting these medications that typically last from a few days up to 10 days after starting treatment) may add to a general sense of emotional discomfort.

◆ Antidepressants can provoke dysphoric mania in some people who, in fact, have bipolar disorder.

◆ Increased energy may occur before a decrease in depressed mood (the person then has the energy to carry out a suicide attempt).

◆ Noncompliance: most suicide victims who have been prescribed antidepressants are found on autopsy to have little or no traces of antidepressants in their blood, suggesting that they were not, in fact, actually taking the medication at the time of the suicide.

◆ Patient-initiated discontinuation: there are two common, problematic results that might account for increased suicidality: antidepressant-withdrawal symptoms (mentioned previously) and/or the loss of what had been a positive antidepressant effect, plunging the patient back into depression.

It is also worth noting that the vast majority of people who do, in fact, commit suicide are not receiving any form of psychiatric treatment.

What is clear is that untreated major depression carries significant risks of potential suicide; antidepressants take several weeks of treatment before the first signs of clinical improvement, and depression can worsen during this start-up period of treatment. In evaluating these kinds of concerns, it is always important to differentiate between media hype and scientific data.

Antianxiety Medications

As mentioned, many anxiety disorders are treated with antidepressants. In this section, we'll discuss other options for treating anxiety. Benzodiazepines are commonly referred to as minor tranquilizers or antianxiety medications.

Generic Names	Brand Names	Typical Adult Daily Doses
Benzodiazepines used to reduce anxiety:		
diazepam	Valium	4–30 mg
chlordiazepoxide	Librium	15–75 mg
clorazepate	Tranxene	15–67.5 mg
clonazepam	Klonopin	0.5–2.0 mg
lorazepam	Ativan	2–6 mg
oxazepam	Serax	30–60 mg
alprazolam	Xanax	1–4 mg
Non-benzodiazepine used to reduce anxiety (nonhabit forming):		
Buspirone	BuSpar	5–40 mg
Benzodiazepines used for sleep:		
temazepam	Restoril	15–30 mg
triazolam	Halcion	0.25–0.5 mg
estazolam	ProSom	1–2 mg
zolpidem	Ambien	5–10 mg
zaleplon	Sonata	5–10 mg
Non-benzodiazepine prescription sleeping medication (nonhabit forming):		
eszopiclone	Lunesta	1–3 mg
ramelteon	Rozerem	8 mg

Uses: to treat anxiety disorders (such as panic disorder, generalized anxiety disorder, social anxiety disorder, and severe situational stress; not generally helpful for OCD or PTSD: these two disorders are more effectively treated with antidepressants) and insomnia.

Onset of positive effects: 30 to 60 minutes. Tranquilizers only stay in the body for a few hours (4 to 12 hours depending on which medication is prescribed). Thus generally they must be taken several times a day.

How long must they be taken? Situational stress, by definition, is time limited, thus medication use may be for only a few days or a few weeks. However, most other anxiety disorders tend to be quite chronic. For this reason, if medications alone are used, people often take the drugs for a period of many years. However, a common and effective approach is to begin with the use of medications but also become involved in psychotherapy. Psychotherapy (as described in Chapters 25 and 26) can afford more long-lasting benefits. Once psychotherapy is effective, often medications can be gradually phased out or the dosage can be reduced.

Laboratory tests: none required

Common side effects:

♦ Drowsiness

♦ Dizziness

♦ Forgetfulness

♦ Slurred speech

Less common side effects:

♦ Confusion

♦ Nervousness

♦ Rash

♦ Loss of balance; falling

Habit-forming/addiction potential: significant risk for people with a prior personal or family history of alcoholism or other forms of serious drug abuse. As noted in the preceding table, Lunesta, Rozerem, and BuSpar are nonhabit forming. Also as noted previously, if antidepressants are used, these drugs are not habit-forming.

Interactions with other medications: when taking benzodiazepines, any other type of medication that causes drowsiness or impaired alertness and reaction time can be potentially dangerous, especially if driving an automobile. In addition, alcohol should not be consumed when taking benzodiazepines.

Safety during pregnancy: benzodiazepines typically are not to be used during pregnancy.

Breast-feeding: benzodiazepines are secreted in breast milk and should not be used when breast-feeding.

Special concerns about discontinuation: if benzodiazepines are being taken on a regular basis, the body develops a tolerance for the medication. When this happens, typically the drugs continue to work to reduce anxiety, but the problem is that when tolerance has developed and the drug is discontinued abruptly, withdrawal symptoms result. Withdrawal symptoms usually include nervousness, agitation, difficulty falling asleep, and, on occasion, seizures. This needs to be taken very seriously. If patients have been taking a benzodiazepine on a daily basis for more than six weeks, and especially if the dose is moderate to high, withdrawal reactions are a very real risk. One should never abruptly stop taking the medication without first consulting with their treating physician. It is also a good idea for patients to monitor their supply of the medications so that they can request refills in a timely fashion. Many people find it helpful to keep at least a two-day supply on hand in the event that it takes longer than usual for a prescription to be refilled.

A Final Word About Medications

Despite advances in drug safety and clear benefits for many individuals suffering from more severe depressions or anxiety, all medications have side effects and limitations. Any treatment with psychiatric drugs must be accompanied by psychotherapy. In the words of noted psychiatrist Roy Menninger, "There will never be a pill that can mend broken hearts, fill empty lives, or teach people how to love one another."

Self-Help Resources

Mental Health Advocacy Groups

National Mental Health Association
1021 Prince Street
Alexandria, VA 22314-2971
www.nmha.org.index/cfm

National Alliance for the Mentally Ill
www.nami.org

National Mental Health Consumer's Self-Help Clearinghouse
www.libertynet.org/mha/cl_house.html

General Online Psychology Resources

American Psychological Association
www.apa.org

Self-Help and Psychology Magazine
www.shpm.com

Internet Mental Health
www.mentalhealth.com

At Health
www.athealth.com

Health Touch
www.healthtouch.com

Mental Health Net
www.cmhc.com

Mental Health Infosource
www.mhsource.com

Alcohol Resources

Alcoholics Anonymous
www.alcoholics-anonymous.org

Depression Resources

Depressive and Bipolar Support Alliance (formerly National Depressive and Manic
Depressive Association)
730 North Franklin Street, Suite 501
Chicago, IL 60610-3526
www.dbsalliance.org

Depression After Delivery
PO Box 1282
Morrisville, PA 19067
1-800-944-4773
www.beharenet.com/dadinc

Postpartum Support International
927 North Kellog Avenue
Santa Barbara, CA 93111
805-967-7376
Online contact: THONIKMAN@compuserve.com

Dr. Ivan's Depression Central
www.pstcom.net/depression.central.html

Bipolar Resources

www.moodswing.org

www.bipolarhappens.com

Anxiety Resources

Anxiety Disorders Association of America
11900 Parklawn Drive, Suite 1200
Rockville, MD 20852
www.adaa.org

Anxiety Disorders Education Program
www.nimh.nih.gov/anxiety

Obsessive-Compulsive Foundation, Inc.
PO Box 70
Milford, CT 06460-0070
203-878-5669
Online contact: JPHS28A@prodigy.com
http://pages.prodigy.com/alwillen.ocf.html

Therapy Resources

Psychology Today magazine's Free Find-a-Therapist database
www.PsychologyToday.com

Questions About Psychiatric Medicine

Medication—Health Center's Pharmacy Page
www.health-center.com/english/pharmacy/meds/default/html

Recommended Readings

Anger Management

Eifert, G. H., McKay, M., and Forsyth (2006) *Act on Life, Not on Anger*. Oakland, CA:
    New Harbinger Publications

Anxiety

Bourne, E. J. (2005) *The Anxiety and Phobia Workbook*. Oakland, CA: New Harbinger Publications

Assertion

Alberti, R., and Emmons, M. (2001) *Your Perfect Right (eighth edition)*. Atascadero, CA: Impact Publishers, Inc.

Bipolar Disorder

Fast, J., and Preston, J. (2004) *Loving Someone with Bipolar Disorder*. Oakland, CA: New Harbinger Publications

———— (2006) *Taking Charge of Bipolar Disorder*. New York: Warner Books

Depression

Preston, J. (2005) *You Can Beat Depression (fourth edition)*. Atascadero, CA: Impact Publishers, Inc.

Divorce

Fisher, B., and Alberti, R. (1999) *Rebuilding When Your Relationship Ends (third edition)*. Atascadero, CA: Impact Publishers, Inc.

Grief and Loss

Rando, T. A. (1991) *How to Go On Living When Someone You Love Dies*. Champaign, Ill.: Research Press.

Psychiatric Medications

Preston, J., and Johnson, J. (2006) *Clinical Psychopharmacology Made Ridiculously Simple (fifth edition)*. Ft. Lauderdale, Florida: MedMaster, Inc.

Preston, J. O'Neal, J. and Talaga, M. (2006) *Child and Adolescent Clinical Psychopharmacology Made Simple*. Oakland, CA: New Harbinger Publications

Spirituality and Existential Issues

Peck, M.S. (2003) *The Road Less Traveled: 25th Anniversary Edition*. New York: Touchstone

Kushner, H. S. (2001) *When Bad Things Happen to Good People (twentieth anniversary edition)*. New York, NY: Schocken Books

Stress

Davis, M., Eshelman, E., and McKay, M. (2006) *The Relaxation and Stress Workbook*. Oakland, CA: New Harbinger Publications

Index

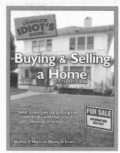

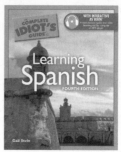

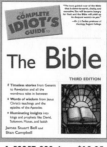
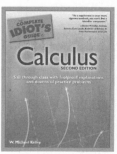